Many books have been written about the Hatfield-McCoy feud, but no one before has taken the time to dig deep into the records, to uncover and compare confessions, interviews, and letters forgotten for half a century.

Here, finally, is the true story: a look at the people and the times in a revelation that will make you wonder how it could ever have really happened.

"Vivid account of a famous feud . . . Truth is stranger, and indeed more thrilling, than fiction."

—Louisville *Courier-Journal*

"A great contribution to Americana . . ."

—Chicago *Sunday Times*

"Jones' story has all the blood-curdling suspense of a mystery and the bullet-peppered action of a Western."

—*Rocky Mountain News*

A MOCKINGBIRD BOOK

The Hatfields and The McCoys

Virgil Carrington Jones

MOCKINGBIRD BOOKS • ATLANTA

COVER PHOTO: DEVIL ANSE HATFIELD SEATED IN THE CENTER OF A GROUP OF HATFIELDS AND OTHER CLANSMEN. Standing from left to right are O. C. Damron, Elias Hatfield, Troy Hatfield, Joe Hatfield, Tom Chaffin and W. E. Borden. The two children are unidentified. Devil Anse's wife, Levicy, and another child are visible in the doorway at the back.

SBN 89176-014-8

This edition published by arrangement with The University of North Carolina Press.

First Printing: October, 1974
Second Printing: September, 1976

Printed in the United States of America

MOCKINGBIRD BOOKS, INC.
P.O. Box 110, Covington, GA. 30209

To My Wife
A staunch West Virginian, by God or by chance

Preface

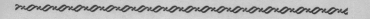

MY DECISION TO WRITE THE STORY OF THE HATFIELD-McCoy feud was not something that came to me easily. I am not one of those who customarily like feuding, fisticuffs or fracases, and the thought of such a bloody vendetta, legendarily carried on by desperate brigands back in the mountainous wilds well away from protection of the law, brought up the chill bumps. It made me settle down in a corner and talk to myself when people were not around. I had visions of starting the feud all over again, with me as the No. 1 target in a no-man's-land between the two factions.

Months went by during which I rolled the feud over in my mind as a possible subject. At last, strictly on a trial basis, I got up enough nerve to start research. I began to thumb through the records, feeling my way, gradually becoming more interested, and constantly building up the conviction that the actual story of the Hatfield-McCoy feud needed to be written. Here was a violent chapter out of American history that was not just a tragic quarrel between two backwoods families, but a strife that eventually developed into a dispute involving two states, which was carried to the United States Supreme Court for settlement. In a short while, I was completely sold on the idea and hard at work.

For a full year I labored in the files at the Library of Congress before I went out into the field. Often during this period I thought of myself as an interloper, trespassing into the affairs of others and snooping into the private lives of people with whom I had no connection or acquaintance.

But shortly after I went into the field, things changed. I sat one day on the front porch of a modest home high in the mountains of Kentucky, talking with an old lady who as a child had been a neighbor of the feud people and had a clear recollection of them and their actions. While she stared off along the forested slopes that once had echoed with the gunfire of angry feudists, I prodded her memory and primed her conversation with appropriate bits from my own knowledge of the subject. I led her on, from episodes to personalities. We talked of the romance of Rose Anne McCoy and Johnse Hatfield. "What did Johnse look like?" I asked. She turned her head and stared at me for a moment. "Just like you," she said. From that moment on, I knew I had been taken into the clan.

I began actual writing of the book late in 1945, dividing my time between the manuscript and my regular work with The Curtis Publishing Company. Just as I was getting well into the story, I was given leave of absence to serve as executive secretary to William M. Tuck, who was just taking office as Governor of Virginia. While this was an opportunity to gain valuable experience and friendships, it was not an ideal setup for writing a book.

The Governor took me in as a personal friend and, because living quarters were impossible to find, assigned me to a room in the Mansion. Busy days lay ahead. From early morning until late at night, I was at his side, during a time when he was fighting some of the toughest battles of his administration. Through it all, there was little time for me to get down on paper the story of the Hatfields and the McCoys. But I wanted to go on with it; so I cut down on my sleep. From four to six o'clock in the morning, sometimes earlier, sometimes later, I kept the typewriter in my bedroom rattling.

Often the Governor joined me in the early dawn to read over some of the manuscript I had written or, as a lawyer by profession, to discuss some legal point involved in the court battles that grew out of the feud. He was a constant source of encouragement and did much toward speeding the work on the book, both then and after I left him at the end of my leave of absence.

I also am much indebted to Mr. H.W. Straley, III, of

Washington, a connection of both of the feud families, for his invaluable aid in assembling details and in editing the manuscript. I owe much, too, to Miss Virginia Salton and her mother, Mrs. Ella Salton, and to Mr. Emmett Keadle and his sisters, the Misses Lucy C. and Virginia M. Keadle, all of Williamson, West Virginia, who helped me establish contact with the feud country. My thanks go in addition to Mr. Amos Runyan, member of the Kentucky House of Delegates, who made this way into spots I would never have found to check details for me, and to many others who helped me one way or another, including officials at the Library of Congress, the U.S. Supreme Court, and the Kentucky and West Virginia capitals.

Now that the manuscript is out of the way, my greatest satisfaction lies in the fact that it represents, I believe, the first factual account of this most famous of American feuds. It is based as nearly as possible on actual records, including heretofore uncovered confessions of the feud leaders themselves, rather than on legend and hearsay.

I hope the book provides enough information to set aright the public conception of the feud. The names Hatfield and McCoy are household terms the world over, but many people, especially those of the younger generation, look upon the feud as a myth rather than a bloody and brutal vendetta that took many lives within the recollection of people still living. I should like also to have it answer the request often made of American G.I.'s when they first put foot on foreign soil in the recent war: "Tell us about the Hatfields and McCoys."

V. C. JONES

Washington, D. C.
October, 1947

1

Men Who Match The Mountains

ALONG THE BORDER OF KENTUCKY AND WEST VIRGINIA, where Tug Fork flows down to become a part of the Big Sandy, an amazing epic of mountain love and hatred boiled up in the closing half of the last century to leave behind it a trail of graves and burned homes. Oldtimers who remember the bloody vendetta of the Hatfields and McCoys speak of it as the most famous feud in history, and sometimes they lower their voices and glance over their shoulders to make sure no one is within hearing distance who might take offense, for the feeling never has died out that the war some day will start anew.

It was during the period of reconstruction, midway between the Confederate War and the war with Spain, that guns barked in the brutal conflict between the two families. At the start, shooting was confined to a small, isolated area, so far back in the mountains that newspapers completely ignored the rumors of violence that come down out of the hills. Then, just before the hostilities subside, the press and the nation at large awakened suddenly to the fact that neighbors of long standing had for many years been shooting at each other with murderous intent and, not infrequently, with murderous result. The law promptly stepped in, and the feeling between Kentucky and West Virginia became so bitter that they prepared to send troops against each other.

Meantime, what the public was able to learn about

the backwoods killings sounded absurd. The families involved lived on opposite sides of a narrow stream, the Hatfields in West Virginia, the McCoys in Kentucky. Their troubles had been brewing for years, stirred by a combination of things, not the least of which was the discovery that a Hatfield youth, slipping across the Tug to lie with a McCoy girl, finally had got her pregnant.

Most of the witnesses to this spell of internecine slaughter have their details in order, except when it comes to these two young lovers. There the temptation is too great and they allow their imaginations to wander.

It was a great romance, they all agree, and a pity the Hatfield leader never would allow his son, Johnse, to marry the McCoy leader's daughter, Rose Anne. But they have never been able to get together on the outcome of the girl's pregnancy. As they tell it, the baby born of this love affair ranges all the way from a miscarriage to a strapping boy who took up arms to protect his mother.

There is general disagreement, too, over the factors that led to the feud. Even the feudists themselves have never agreed on this point. All sorts of stories have arisen, and perhaps in a combination of these lies the answer. It is difficult to fasten the blame on any two or three persons. Those who remember the leaders of the opposing clans, William Anderson (Devil Anse) Hatfield and Randolph (Rand'l) McCoy, recall them as simple, hospitable mountaineers, affectionate and home-loving. Because of their rustic natures, no injury would have seemed grave enough to induce them to declare war on each other.

At the time their trouble reached the open-warfare stage, Devil Anse Hatfield was in his middle forties, an ex-captain of the Confederate army, long recognized for his ability to handle a gun. He was a bearded six-footer, a Stonewall Jackson type, whose height was somewhat diminished by rounded shoulders and a slight stoop. His hair was thick, his eyes gray and deep-set below bushy eyebrows, and his nose was hooked like a scimitar. He wore a dark brown beard that swelled in size as it swung downward from a big mustache, but it got little farther than his collar before it rounded off, leaving bare the bosom of his shirt. His customary footwear was knee-length boots, with trousers stuffed in top, mountain fashion. This outfit he occasionally varied with long trousers and heavy brogan shoes. People liked Devil Anse because he loved pranks, was jovial, even clownish by nature, and was an excellent storyteller who doted on unfolding tales of adventure before a blazing log in the huge fireplace of his cabin. He was noticeably illiterate, but behind this illiteracy was native intelligence that made up in large degree for his lack of book learning.

Randolph McCoy, on the other hand, was twenty years the senior of his enemy. Except for the stoop to Hatfield, they were much alike in appearance. McCoy had broad shoulders, sullen gray eyes, and a full mustache and beard; he too was tall. White hairs were plentiful in the thatch hanging below the black slouch hat he usually tilted back on his wrinkled head. His shirt collar at most times was open and his sleeves were turned back at the wrist. The greatest difference between the two men was in their temperament. McCoy was a kindly old man, unable to throw off his troubles with jest and jovial raconteuring and, because of advanced age, burdened at times by his sorrows. Foremost in his mind, always, was the villainy of the Hatfields and the sadness they had brought upon him. The fight that came from his side of the Tug was carried on by persons other than himself. His own preference, often spoken, was that the law be allowed to take its course.

By far the greatest blame for continuation of the vendetta lay with the sons of the leaders and with their confederates. And foremost in sharing this blame was Devil Anse Hatfield's second eldest, named for the parent, but more commonly called Cap. This young mountaineer, just breaking into his twenties, was heavily built, even bulky in body. He prided himself on his marksmanship and he had a reputation for handling a rifle that caused some men to fear the sight of him. Somewhere back in his childhood, an injury had caused one eye to turn watery blue, and then a percussion cap had disfigured the other in such a manner that he appeared wall-eyed. His hair was dark and long, and he combed it down in a wavy line across his forehead, just above the eyes. Occasionally he wore a stubby beard, but as a rule the hirsuteness of his face was confined to heavy eyebrows and a full, shaggy mustache that drooped like the arch of a horseshoe. Cap Hatfield could be congenial and friendly, but he could be cruel and vindictive, too, a fitting match for another leading figure in the feud, his active and ever-threatening great-uncle, Jim Vance, a tall, heavyset veteran, typically mountaineer, whose major identification was a long dark beard that hung almost to his waist. They liked each other, these two killers, and they paired off willingly to fight side by side in keeping up the Hatfield end of the feud.

Cap's elder brother, Johnson, shortened to Johnse by mountain vernacular, was just the opposite in temperament. About him was virtually no belligerence. Rather, he was the dandy of the neighborhood, only a year or two older than Cap, of medium stature, slim, dark. At the height of his young manhood, he wore a neat mustache, not bushy like Cap's, and dressed a little too fancy for the average mountain youth. The girls raved over his looks in gushing and immodest tones, but about his love-making they giggled and whispered. Johnse Hatfield's reputation as a Romeo was widespread.

Because of its earlier start, the McCoy family had more sons of fighting age than the Hatfields. The eldest of these, Floyd, was considered chicken-hearted by his enemies and was allowed in most instances to go unmolested. Jim, a slim man in his early thirties, was the most likeable of the group, even to the opposing clan. He was married, cool-headed, a hard worker, and steady in his actions, and he did more to placate than to antagonize. But down the line the stock was different. Tolbert would fight at the slightest provocation, especially after downing a few drinks, and Calvin, Phamer, sometimes called Dick, and Randolph, Jr., were willing understudies.

Supporting each clan were numerous confederates. Marriage and other family ties were all the excuse needed to induce a mountaineer to pick up his gun and go to the defense of the neighbor with whom he sided. For that reason, many of those who took part in this bloody feud bore the name of neither Hatfield nor McCoy.

It was a strange state of affairs that prevailed in the forest-clad hills around these men. There was virtually no police authority. Courts were few, and those convened were dominated by factions. The mountaineer of that day, keen-eyed, hard-bitten, courageous, felt that he was a law unto himself. His life was primitive and so were his passions. Inflamed with hatred, he could be cruel and remorseless against a private enemy. Little wonder then that his retaliation left behind it a wide assortment of violences.

Perhaps the one factor that contributed most to the prolonged trouble beween the Hatfield and McCoy families was the terrain in which they fought. It is considered the roughest in the eastern United States, for in ages past nature frolicked with unsteady hand along the borders of West Virginia and Kentucky, where they come together between the Ohio River on the north and Virginia on the south. Horizontal beds of limestone lay next to sandstone and shales and important seams of coal, and somewhere in the great upheaval of bygone years these beds were thrown into folds, leaving alternate belts of hard and soft rock exposed. Sometime during the geological turmoil, uplift permitted renewed erosion to wear away the soft belts, so that mountain ridges of hard rock were separated by parallel valleys. Springs bubbled up and, with the rains, ran together into streams that dissected the area into a maze of narrow gorges and steep-sided hills. Between parallel ridges some of these streams flowed for long distances before turning suddenly through transverse passes formed by erosive cutting of gaps. Up along the ridges to the crests, hundreds of feet above in some instances, trees grew thick and tall. The winds blew hard, trying to shake them off, and as the breezes became stronger, so the trees became stronger, full in the low country and hardy and tough in the high country.

For well over a hundred miles along the border of the two states, rivers have served as the dividing line. From the east, Tug Fork picks up out of springs and branches and goes down to join with Levisa Fork and becomes the Big Sandy River, flowing into the Ohio at Catlettsburg, wild and rambunctious timber market of the 1880's. At points along its course before it reaches the Big Sandy, the Tug is swelled in size by smaller streams —creeks bearing such names as Peter, Grapevine, Thacker, Blackberry, Sulphur, Mate, Sycamore, Pond, Turkey, and Buffalo.

In years gone by, the terrain through which flowed the streams—the feud country—constituted a region unto itself, a wilderness shut off from the progress of the world and touched but lightly by civilization. Only a few miles away were main-traveled highways, once buffalo trails, winding along the easiest paths to the Trans-Appalachian basin of the Ohio—from Virginia by way of the James River Valley, across the mountains and down the Great Kanawha. Along this route often moved frontiersmen and their families, but it was rarely they turned their faces toward the Tug. In that direction the country was wild and dangerous, best left to Indians and bears.

As the crow flies, the feud site is sixty miles westward from Charleston, the capital of West Virginia, over a road that climbs steadily at first and then sharply later, winding incessantly as the distance increases. Coming eastward from Frankfort, Kentucky's capital, in the opposite direction, it is a much longer drive, over rolling country to the edge of the mountains at Mount Sterling and then steadily upward. At Pikeville on the Kentucky side and at Williamson, Matewan, and other key towns on the West Virginia side, the country is the same—rugged, rocky, and difficult for motorist or pedestrian. Mountains run up like walls, with little flat land between, and the people who live there like it that way. They have mortal fear, some of them, of country where there are no hills to protect them from the winds.

Visitors strange to the area find that climbing a hill is like climbing a ladder and that the trek up a mountain side without shrubbery is almost like the ascent of a tree without limbs. Roads wind round and round, and the traveler has a feeling that he is above the rest of the world and nearing heaven; then he tops a rise and goes down and down, still winding, along what seems a corkscrew from the sky. Sometimes the road has to be shared with a trickling mountain stream, and now and then this goes on for long stretches. But all travel is slow, retarded by beautiful scenery, as well as by the rough terrain. Coal chutes rise out of nowhere, high overhead, and coal cars, misfits in pastoral surroundings, come shuttling out of mysterious tunnels, heaped high with shiny black wealth, and groan their way slowly through the mountain passes toward a more advanced society. These last developments came in as the feud was dying out and had much to do with putting a stop to the killings.

First attempts to settle along the valleys in this precipitous region met with little success. Savages lurked in the mountain forests in sufficient numbers to drive away the whites, and occasionally they struck with a fresh outbreak of scalping. This condition continued until the last decade of the eighteenth century; then blockhouses were thrown up to afford protection from hostile arrows, and the emigrants, mostly Scotch-Irish, gained a permanent foothold.

By the turn of the century, several families had chosen home sites. More came with the years, and prominent among these later arrivals were branches of the Hatfields, McCoys, Vances, Chafins, Smiths, Weddingtons, Varneys, Evanses, Clines, and Trents. There were still others, all prolific families, in the way of their generation, but none more so than the Hatfields and McCoys. Devil Anse Hatfield sired twelve children; his neighbor and enemy, Randolph McCoy, thirteen. Marriages were kept close home, within the circle of friends, with the result that the greatest procreators rose to dominance.

The life they began after moving into the mountains was a new life—their own, shut off from the rest of the world. These pioneers were our true early Americans, of pure strain, strong with customs and idioms. They laughed with a quiet chuckle, and they were observant and retiring people. Their language was, and continues to be, flavored by the vigorous English of Shakespeare. Their odd speech they explained to outlanders in this fashion: "The words o' you'uns don't fit our mouths, so we don't use 'em." No visitor ever went through a land where they needed less. Doors were left unlocked, and board and lodging to the wayfarer were free.

Before they received this hospitality, visitors first had to pass through the backwoods gauntlet of approach. As they moved up the mountain trails, a faint and bloodcurdling "ee-o-ee" could be heard at intervals in the distance. This strange call preceded them and went from ridge to ridge, signal of the hill country that strangers were approaching. And at their destination the outlanders found people perfectly composed to their visit, ready to welcome with quiet reserve or to shun with cold silence, depending upon suspicions stimulated.

Settlers along the Tug came chiefly from Russell, Washington, and Wise counties, a short distance east in Virginia. Behind them they left assorted chronicles of success and sorrow, and sometimes a family skeleton or two.

The name of Vance, for instance, was amply recorded in ballad. This came about through the unerring aim of one Elder Abner Vance, staunch Hardshell Baptist of the Clinch River Valley near Abingdon, Virginia, and the erring behavior of his favorite daughter. In simple frontier verse it is told that Abner was a kindly man, a lover of home and peace and religion. So well was he ensconced in the affections of his neighbors that many of them swore he was acting in the ways of the Lord the day he took down his trusty shooting piece and blazed away with everlasting result at one Dr. Horton. This ill-fated medic, more attuned to debauchery than to caution, had just brought the transgressive daughter, wiser in the ways of seduction, back to the elder's doorstep. Vance's bullet caught up with Horton in the middle of Clinch River, knocking him from his horse. While the physician sank to a watery grave, the Primitive Baptist fled to the wilderness, there to remain in hiding for years. When he finally came out, confident that time had restored his innocence if not his daughter's virture, it was to find the law waiting for him without mercy. He was tried and sentenced to hang. And hang he did, leaving behind the echo of a funeral sermon, delivered in his own words, and the theme for a ballad that legend says he himself wrote between the glances at the gallows just outside his prison window.

Building sites blazed off along the Tug were miles apart, in narrow, isolated valleys or clinging to the mountain slopes. Travel was by way of wide detours along the streams, or by sharp and difficult climbs up the steep divides. Streams of clear water came out of the mountain hollows with breakneck speed, at some points descending on an average twenty-five feet to the mile. Trees grew with precarious footing—poplar, oak, cherry, locust, walnut, ash, hickory, linden, beech, sycamore.

The timber hidden beneath their spreading branches created little attention in the early days, but later, when lumber took on a premium, men looked at it with ardent speculation.

By the early 1820's, enough settlers had come into the feud country for counties to be laid off. Kentucky designated the land next the river on her side Pike County, in honor of the distinguished General Zebulon M. Pike of 1812 war fame. Pikeville was its seat of government. West Virginia named her border county at the point Logan, after the Indian chief of the Mingo tribe, and laid off Logan Court House as the seat. Through the years these communities grew slowly. Mountain villages they started and mountain villages they remained. It took three days of hard riding over the roughest trails, often for miles along creek beds, to reach the nearest railroad. It was just as difficult to make the trek to centers of trade. Mail came in by horsback over post-roads, rough and terrible.

Devil Anse Hatfield and Randolph McCoy built their cabins within a few miles of each other. Hatfield raised his in West Virginia, at the mouth of Peter Creek, where it flows into the Tug. From his doorstep to McCoy's was a short walk in that day; at best, seven or eight miles. After crossing the Tug into Kentucky, the trail led up Blackberry Creek to Hatfield Branch, then to the right up steep mountain slopes, to the ridge at Turkeyfoot, and down a few yards on the other side, in the high country. From their respective county seats—Logan in West Virginia and Pikeville in Kentucky—both cabins were equally distant, roughly twenty miles on a direct line.

Neither abode was large or anywhere nearly approached the needs of the family that lived beneath its roof. There were two big rooms, one for eating and one for sleeping. In the latter, beds were placed in rows and assigned to members regardless of sex. Larders were always well filled, when not with the few vegetables which could be grown from the hilly soil, with the wild game which abounded in the forests. No stranger ever visited either home that he did not find plenty to eat and a place to sleep, always the best in the house. The feather bed, not the tick stuffed with corn shucks, was his.

Men spent their days largely at hunting and fishing, at moonshining, and at logging and the other heavy chores of the woods. Back at their cabins meanwhile, the women turned their hands to a number of things. Between them they chopped in the garden, made clothing, rugs, and chair bottoms, or puttered over ginseng, feathers, beeswax, dried fruits, beans, and sorghum. Corn was the main crop, even though domestic animals were scarce and usually limited to horses and cows. Cooking was done over the open fireplace, and there the family customarily gathered after eating. Their faces and their clothes they washed in a near-by stream, in summer; in winter, in water from stream or spring.

The Hatfields and McCoys were high-strung, honest, proud, perhaps a little too proud for the wilderness in which they eked out their meager frontier living. Students who in later years have tried to discover the cause of the feud have placed a major share of the blame on family pride; that and a tendency on the part of some of the male members to sow their seed wherever lustful desire happened to strike.

The families were of strong stock. From them in later years have come men of leading professions—doctors, lawyers, and even a governor and United States senator. Some of them were students while the vendetta was in progress, and this doubtless accounted largely for the willingness of the leaders, in a sudden bid for peace, to move their homes away from the Tug.

Mountaineers are recognized traditionally as moonshiners. The Hatfields and McCoys were no exception. The only time that one of them came in to answer to the law was on a charge of selling whiskey of their own making without first paying the federal tax. This to them seemed no crime. They felt that not even Uncle Sam could tell a mountain man what he could do with his corn. Liquor flowed freely in the feud country and no doubt had a lot to do with the years of trouble. Certainly Johnse Hatfield, Devil Anse's chief agent for disposing of his mountain dew, caused no end of temptation and bother to the McCoys and Kentucky police with his frequent trips to Pikeville to sell moonshine.

Making liquor was a major occupation with mountain families. Their gatherings, especially at election time, were little better than drunken brawls. But rare was the mountaineer, especially in the feud country, who became so full of whiskey that he could not steady the barrel of his gun.

Fiction has given the West a reputation for marksmanship. This may be justifiable if not phrased in the superlative, for perhaps no area in the world had as deadly gunmen during the last century as that along the Tug and Big Sandy. There babies were born with guns resting beside their cribs. They grew up with their fingers bent to the pull of the trigger, not so much in protection against wild animals and Indians as against the anger and vengeance of each other. Two members of the United States Geological Survey, traveling through this section, once got a native to demonstrate has shooting ability. He stood empty-handed and instructed them to toss a half-dollar into the air. One of the visitors complied, and two shots rang out. When the coin was recovered, there was evidence two bull's-eyes had been scored. The first bullet had sent the fifty-cent piece spinning, and the geologists could not understand how it had been hit a second time. But more amazing was the fact that they had not seen the man draw his gun or return it to its holster.

This handiness with a gun marked members of both factions, as well as their descendants. They were recognized as men who could take care of themselves, no matter where they went. The stranger who met them thought first of his own safety, confident that the hand he had just shaken would flash a gun in a moment. Sometimes it did. That happened the time a salesman for a leading shoe company was traveling through West Virginia by train one night and went back to the smoker for a cigarette. He was alone for a while, until a slim mountaineer walked in and took the seat opposite him. They nodded to each other, but at first there was no conversation. Presently they got to talking, and the salesman suddenly realized he was conversing with the notorious Sid Hatfield, of a later generation than the feudists, but with an equally wide reputation for notches on his gun. After a few minutes, Sid pulled a flask from his pocket and suggested they have a drink. "No, thanks," said the salesman. "I don't believe I care for any." Sid reached back in his pocket and this time pulled out a long revolver which he laid on the seat beside him. Then he tendered the bottle again, this time with the gruff invitation: "I said have a drink." In telling of this experience later, the salesman always wound up with the remark: "I never got so drunk in my life."

2

1861-1865
The First Man Falls

THE WAR OF '61 MADE A PRIZE OF THE PART OF VIRGINIA lying along the western slope of the Alleghenies, that section where the Hatfields and McCoys had settled. It made a prize of its forests and mineral wealth and put especial value on the Great Kanawha basin, where the wealth was richest. Both North and South became aware that here might lie the balance of power for victory. Natural advantages favored the North, for it was a simple matter to load troops on river packets and send them down the Ohio to within a few miles of any scene of action. The South, meanwhile, would have to move its soldiers by land, in a long trek over one of the greatest mountain barriers on the North American continent. Both combatants centered their attention early on this rich source of supply.

The most marked division of sentiment was noticed along the Kentucky-Virginia border. Emissaries sent there by the Confederate States to learn the exact condition of things reported that there was much disaffection in Kentucky, that President Lincoln already had distributed arms to men in the mountain regions, and that the distribution was still in progress. Across the border, feelings were just the opposite. The Virginia counties, even to within thirty miles of the Ohio River, were solidly with the South. It was announced officially that the people there "would no doubt capture any arms that might find their way over the borders."

Nowhere was the line more sharply drawn than along the Tug. At Pikeville, Kentucky, military enthusiasts were clamoring for recruits to assist the North, while at Logan, in southwest Virginia, sentiment was just as strongly for the South. Troops went out from both areas. As they went, an aged Virginian of the region, who was almost blinded by amaurosis, wrote a bit of advice to Virginia's Secretary of the Commonwealth, G. W. Munford. The western part of the Old Dominion was about to break away and form a new state. The amaurosis victim, Henry J. Fisher, as if he saw the Hatfield-McCoy feud in the making, advised against the division. "Border quarrels will always occur and reprisals will be made," he warned. "That will lead to hostile incursions, and that to a border warfare, so that war in fact will exist, though no war be declared."

By late '63, the border warfare foreseen by the aged writer was in full swing, and the hottest part of it was along the Tug and Big Sandy rivers. There renegade bands of guerrillas were ranging the respective shores in behalf of the North or the South. The most prevalent name among adherents of the Union in the Kentucky border counties was McCoy. Just as predominant among the Confederate independents on the West Virginia side were the Hatfields. It was not then, or ever, the time for a Hatfield to draw on a McCoy, or vice versa, merely through hatred of the name, for there were backsliders in both families, and intermarriage was common.

These opposing guerrilla bands of mountaineers made it dangerous during the last two years of the war for unidentified Northerner or Southerner to make his way up the Big Sandy or the Tug. The bands were organized presumably for home defense, but their activities were not always confined to legitimate undertakings. The spoils they claimed often failed to be in keeping with the rules of warfare. Likewise, bullets from their guns occasionally made their way into places where they should not have been, and more rarely into victims for whom they were not intended. The reputation of these fighters was not good, even among their own adherents. But their warfare went on with irregular intensity. They fought when the occasion arose and, whenever the fighting waned, often as not spent their idle moments raising unadulterated hell around some mountain moonshine still.

One of the most feared bands on the West Virginia side toted guns under the leadership of Devil Anse Hatfield. He had fought at the beginning of the war with the militia. In 1862, he enlisted in the regular Confederate army and became a first lieutenant of Company A, Forty-fifth Virginia Infantry. The following year, as a captain, he left the regular service to take up the warfare of an independent in Logan, Pike, Wayne, Cabell, and other border counties.

Hatfield married less than a week after the war started, taking as his bride a neighborhood girl, Levicy Chafin. Then he shouldered his rifle and went off to battle. His knowledge of the military was insignificant, but his ability with a gun was amazing. It took only the slightest pretext to induce him to display his marksmanship, and he usually sent his bullets wherever spectators wanted them to go.

One day Confederate partisans, drawn by firing in the mountain wilds of Logan County, were surprised at what they found. The noise came from the depths of a ravine in which lay a large body of Union soldiers, spread out in attack formation. They were shooting from the shelter of rocks and aiming at a knob that towered above everything around it. Somebody back in history had dubbed this high point Devil's Backbone. It was an isolated crag reached by a single path up through the rocks. At the top, a bit of barren tableland, stretched like a floor between protecting ridges, offered the best in natural forts.

Up toward this point the Union invaders spasmodically sent their bullets. Hour after hour the firing went on. Guns sang out down in the bottom and their slugs whined upward to strike harmlessly against the face of rock.

Pitted against this fusillade was a single rifle, its shiny black barrel pointing ominously from above. At first one crevice and then another it appeared, steadied, and belched its lead down into the ravine.

As the exchange went on and on, spasmodic puffs of smoke broke with frenzied persistence from the guns in the bottom, and were answered with more measured delay by a single puff from above. At times a sudden fury speeded up the firing, and the partisans hiding in the trees knew it represented another casualty for the Union, another bull's-eye for the sharpshooter on the ridge.

The sun sank and darkness began to blot out the crag; then the firing slackened and finally died away. For a while there was silence; then the Federals gave up and withdrew, laboriously lugging their wounded over the rocks.

Later, in the black of night, the lone gunman came down. Once clear of the crag, he made his way along intricate trails and across impossible terrain with the ease of a forest animal. In the military legend, the wisest think twice before fighting an enemy on his own ground, and the one-man army of the Devil's Backbone, the lanky Captain Devil Anse Hatfield, had proved the maxim true.

End of the war left behind only one important death among the Hatfields and McCoys. The lone victim was Harmon McCoy, brother of Randolph. Death so soon saved him a world of grief. He had been wounded once in an exchange with Devil Anse, and from then on there was bad blood between them. The day Harmon's body was found in a cave near the Hatfield home, the fast-running waters of Tug Fork took on new meaning as the line of demarcation between West Verginia and Kentucky. Blame for the death was placed then, and occasionally in later years, on the leader of the Hatfields, but there were people along the Tug who told a different story. They claimed Hatfield at the time was sick in bed with a fever, too sick even to think of killing Harmon McCoy or to pay any attention to a rumor that Harmon was coming to settle a score. But at his bedside was an ally who was fully capable of defending the ill man. Some folks said it was this ally, Anse's uncle, old bearded Jim Vance, who stole away into the mountains with a deadly bullet in his rifle and murder in his eye.

3

1873
A Hog Goes to Court

THE YEARS IMMEDIATELY FOLLOWING THE WAR WERE peaceful along the Tug. Lapse of time served more to increase the Hatfield-McCoy families than to boom their animosity toward each other. Devil Anse's first two sons, Johnse and Cap, had been born during the war, and now, almost as regularly as the years rolled around, came other children. Across the river, Randolph McCoy's family already was well advanced, but even he recorded an increase or two during the period.

If the feud was under way at this time, there was no open evidence of it. It is true that division in war sentiment and some bitterness over the mysterious death of Harmon McCoy generated ill feeling between the closely allied families, but, other than this, their relationship was normal. Excitement of the war had passed, and back in the hollows of the mountains nothing gave warning that trouble was brewing. For that matter, never was there any marked beginning to the hatred which gradually built up between the clans.

Time and cause underlying the feud somehow have been lost in the past. Succeeding generations have advanced several theories, but none appears to have clear and definite support. One of these is that the trouble dated back to the Civil War; others that it was the result of influences which developed later. A statement given the press by Devil Anse Hatfield in 1889 substantiates these latter conjectures. *The Wheeling Intelligencer,* which had arranged the interview, drew from the feud leader's words this conclusion: "Contrary to the general impression, which is that the feud dates back to the Civil War, the first troubles occurred in 1873, when a difficulty arose between Floyd Hatfield, a cousin of Anse, and Randolph McCoy, who had married sisters, over a sow and pigs." But it seems more logical to conclude that the feud was the outgrowth of a combination of developments, each aggravating the bad feeling between the two families and each hastening the date of the actual outbreak.

At any rate, the pigs definitely contributed toward the growing ill feeling. They were of the long, lean, razorback variety, and their ugly snouts constantly hedgehopped the ground for bits of food. They were self-sustainers, roaming the fields and forests as wild animals, living largely on mast, seasoning well into tasty meat. Only the curious-shaped notches carved in their ears identified them as property. By these brands, strangers and neighbors were to know that the pork thus developing would in time grace the table of the family whose particular cipher disfigured the ear.

The pigs' part in the feud came through that cousin of Devil Anse, Floyd Hatfield, a man who took little part in the trouble in later years. There was no notice of the animals the day he drove them down out of the mountains and fastened them up at his home near Stringtown, Kentucky, on the McCoy side of Tug Fork. But they promptly drew attention a day or two later when Randolph McCoy, a mile or two from him own cabin, drew up to talk beside the pigsty. The common bond that existed between him and Hatfield because of their marriage to sisters was shattered suddenly by a roar out of Randolph.

"Floyd, that thar ain't yo' hog!"

Hatfield leaned over the pigsty to identify the particular pig at which his brother-in-law pointed.

"Why ain't it?"

" 'Causen, hit's mine."

The crude expletives that followed have not been preserved for posterity. McCoy rode away from Hatfield with sharp words burning on his tongue and searing in his ears. The burning was still in his ears when he drew up a short while later at the cabin of the Reverend Anderson (Parson Anse) Hatfield, pioneer Baptist minister and another of Devil Anse's cousins, down in Racoon Hollow. Preacher Anse was the nearest thing to a judge they had in that part of the mountains.

It was an exciting day when Floyd Hatfield came to trial. Word had spread, and the mountaineers deserted their farm patches and their moonshine stills to witness the administration of justice. Family after family trekked down into the Hollow, Hatfields and McCoys predominant. With the Hatfields came their followers, most of them related by blood—Chafins, Mahons, Vances, Ferrells, Statons. Similarly backing the McCoys were the Sowards, Normans, Stuarts, Colemans, Gateses, Rutherfords, and others. In the crooks of their arms they carried long-barreled rifles and in their hearts they carried the will to use them. Most of the weapons had been carefully cleaned that morning, and the supply of cartridges brought along was remarkably heavy. There was no promise of open warfare, but when a man considers it necessary to hale into court the husband of his wife's sister, it is time, in the language of the mountains, to be prepared.

Preacher Anse's cabin teemed with people. They sat on his furniture and his bed and his doorstep, their guns stacked along the outside wall, and they stared with curious intentness at Exibit I, a long, lean hog, feet bound, blinking from the floor. This hog was the quietest of all. It had done most of its squealing when it was taken from its litter at Floyd Hatfield's pigsty and it had exhausted its energy on the way from Stringtown.

Evidence is of little value when witnesses are ruled by influences stronger than conscience. Man is hard to turn when he is harboring something he is convinced in his own mind is right. So Preacher Anse found it that day.

Witness after witness took a seat in the cane-bottomed chair that had been placed directly in front of the judge. They talked as their clan adherence dictated, and on this basis their testimony was equally divided. Preacher Anse, clever mountaineer on occasion, recognized his helplessness and turned to the old maxim that a plurality of heads is better than one. He empaneled a jury, six from each side, and called for a fresh review of the evidence. Under the unwritten rule that possession is nine points of law, Floyd Hatfield had the advantage. But there were just as many people who might say that the hog belonged to McCoy.

By far the most important witness from the defense angle was Bill Staton, banded to the Hatfields by marriage. His was no second-hand information. He swore on oath that he himself had been present and had seen Floyd Hatfield carve the ear of Exhibit I, all other testimony to the contrary notwithstanding. There was no eyewitness who could say the same for McCoy.

Staton's testimony almost set off the shooting. Coarse mumbling came from the background as the crowd bristled and shuffled heavy boots on the floor. The judge was thoroughly acquainted with the temper of his informal court. He promptly declared the testimony at an end and turned the case over to the jury.

No charge to the jurors emphasized the importance of the decision so entrusted. No guarded and closed jury room aided in the deliberation. The jurors remainded where they stood or sat, puffed up with the gravity of their responsibility and waiting to be polled.

One by one Preacher Anse took individual judgments. As answers were given, the worries of this untouted, unsung, and unrewarded mountain judicator increased, for down the line the results were true to form. Hatfield clansman nodded toward Hatfield and McCoy clansmen toward McCoy. More than half the votes were taken before there was a break in this staunch factionalism, and even then the judge breathed no sigh of relief

But the balance had been tilted. Selkirk McCoy had broken the deadlock. Selkirk McCoy, husband of a Hatfield, had saved the day. Selkirk McCoy, savior and traitor combined, had added fuel to a fire already blazing. Selkirk had said, in effect, that both men had their rights, that there was no evidence to contradict any of the witnesses and that the testimony, to him, indicated that the hog was Hatfield's.

There have been bigger trials, bigger courts, bigger crimes, but rarely a verdict so ponderous In this outcome a die was cast. Years would pass before the hatred thus engendered would fade; generations would follow in which the family names of Hatfield and McCoy could never be mentioned without thought of feuds and dangerous mountaineers. The razorback, driven down from the mountain side with her litter, hurried the day of a famous vendetta, for the ownership had not long been settled before Randolph McCoy accused Staton of swearing to a lie and hurled a rock at him.

The trial was followed by years of accumulating hatred. Occasional outbreaks upset the factions, stirred individual tempers to fever heat, yet without goading them to mob spirit or aftermath of prolonged hostility. But constantly inside the mountain cabins during this period there was growing bitterness. Talk continued to pit clan against clan, to revive issues better left to the past, to align individuals according to their names, their sympathies, and their family ties. Of these spats and clashes, only two of consequence took place before 1880, both within a short time of each other and both involving Bill Staton.

The first of these occurred one day as Staton and his brother John laboriously poled a flat-bottom boat up the Tug Fork. It was a tough pull against a stout current, and they struggled hard at their task. Suddenly around a curve ahead appeared another boat, drifting rapidly downstream. In this second scow stood two men who caused the Statons to bristle. One was Floyd McCoy; the other, his brother Calvin.

For a few moments the boats whirled, prey to the current, before the men recovered from their temporary paralysis and bent again to their poles. As the flat-bottoms moved slowly to shore in opposite directions, firing began. This was kept up from cover along the banks. For hours, bullets whined at intervals from side to side or sank their ill-pointed noses harmlessly into the fast-coursing waters.

Darkness brought stillness. Later a moon climbed over the tall trees and carved black shadows out of the wilderness. Moonbeams glistened on the ripples along the stream, throwing out showers of silvery light around derelict logs stranded on sand bars and on the water slapping against the muddy scows deserted along the bank.

There was no more shooting. Both sets of brothers had given up the fight and departed.

Bill Staton was furious over this outbreak, which rightly could not be considered a victory for either side. But his anger was no more than that of the McCoy boys. They had vengeance in their eyes, too, as they retreated from the river that night. It brought action a short time later when they waylaid Staton at an opportune moment, struck him down with a club, and administered a brutal beating.

Staton was a powerful man, a man of revenge, and the punishment he took from the McCoys made clear the goal of his fast-ebbing life. He turned all the personal force at his command against these enemies. One by one, whenever he met them, he loosed his wrath with a vengeance that brought strong conviction to the opposing faction: McCoys would never be safe in the mountains as long as Staton was alive.

Staton had been missing from his home for days before residents along Tug Fork became aware of it and sent searching parties to comb the mountain trails. Attention of one of these groups was drawn to a flock of vultures circling in the distance. Footsteps were turned in that direction and soon the mystery of the missing man was solved.

Staton's body, almost decapitated by a close gunshot, sprawled near his rifle. On all sides was mute evidence of what his life had been in its closing moments. The leafy earth had been torn by the boots of angry men, and foliage next the ground in a small area hung withered and dead. There were scars left by a tussle of extreme violence. The top of one bush had been broken off, and this created special interest. Men who made their way to the scene stared at the broken bush from all angles and noted that its top branches were just the height for leveling a rifle.

The body of Staton was brought back to his home and buried. Then a new search was started, this time to find who had done the killing.

The noose tightened rapidly. Most obvious of clues was the sudden disappearance of two of the Kentucky clan leader's nephews, the brothers, Paris and Sam McCoy. They could not be found and their relatives refused to discuss where they might be. Search for them was spurred by Devil Anse's brother, big, powerful Ellison Hatfield, who had married Staton's sister. He swore out a warrant for their arrest and asked Devil Anse to serve it, but Anse refused on the grounds that he and the McCoys had always been good friends.

In a few days, Paris McCoy was brought in, limping from a wound in the hip. He had been found out in the mountains lurking in a cave. His story turned the heat on his brother.

He and Sam, he related, had been walking through the woods and had come upon Staton. Before they were aware of his presence, Staton without warning broke off the top of a bush, rested his gun on this tripod from nature and blazed away, striking Paris in the hip. He fell, raised to one elbow and shot Staton in the breast. They came together in a wrestling, kicking, biting scramble. Then, when Staton bit him in the cheek, his screams brought his brother into action. Sam ran in close to the fighters, put his gun against Staton's head and pulled the trigger.

The Hatfields now beat the trails to find Sam, and in a few weeks they had him. But their efforts to make him pay the penalty for murder went for naught. Trial brought a verdict of justified killing in self-defense.

Now there were new angers—those brought on the Hatfields by their failure through legal procedure to avenge the death of a clansman and, just as unadulterated, those nurtured by the McCoys because of the rising resentment of their neighbors across the river. Each faction awaited its chance.

Opportunity came first to the McCoys. For months the grand jury of Pike County had held an indictment against Devil Anse's son, Johnse, for selling whiskey in Kentucky. It was well known that the young mountaineer, enjoying the thrill of youth, was peddling moonshine in the adjoining state to supply himself with money. But no one ever had done much to stop him. Tolbert McCoy, ingenious son of Randolph, saw his chance. He got himself deputized to arrest the Hatfield youth and kept a sharp eye along the Tug. At last he succeeded. With the aid of his brothers, Jim and Phamer, he captured Johnse and headed him for the jail at Pikeville.

This was a journey never finished. Along the way, Devil Anse, apprised of his son's arrest and supported by others of his clansmen, caught up with the McCoys and took the prisoner away from them.

4

1875
An Outlaw Meets a Feudist

ONE DAY WHILE THE ANIMOSITIES WERE THUS BUILDING up between the Hatfields and McCoys, Devil Anse squinted down the long barrel of his Winchester from one of the ridges overlooking the Tug. Yards below, a horseman came into his gun sights. This rider sat oblivious of the vicious weapon of death trained on him from above. His interest appeared to be altogether in the mad, scapering whirl of water in the stream ahead of him.

Except for the noise of the fork, dead silence lay along the forested mountains rising up from the banks on each side. It was calm after a storm, the aftermath of an early Setpember gully-washer that had swept furiously through the Big Sandy region, leaving the skies blue, the trees dripping, and the Tug full to overflowing. Water piled up fast in the steep gorges of the Alleghenies, in maelstroms of increasing violence.

Hatfield bent back a branch, the better to level his sights at the horseman. Near the end of the gun barrel, a tiny speck no larger than a pin head caught his eye. He lowered the weapon and scratched at the speck with his fingernail. It came off easily, and he grunted with disgust. Uncle Jim Vance had been annoyingly wild with his ambeer the night before.

Again the gun was rested on the bush and the barrel pointed downward. It came plain to Devil Anse, as the sights played about the figure of the rider, that this man waiting beside the stream was no McCoy, nor any other enemy of the Hatfield clan. As much of the rider's face and figure as he could see was strange, and there were other things that marked him an outlander. His overcoat was too new and bright, his guns too pearly, his horse, a shiny black mare, too nervous and high-strung. This fellow had ridden along the mountain trail with every air of wanting to put distance behind him. He rode well, but with the vigilance of the hunted.

Satisfied with what he saw, the mountaineer turned to his own horse waiting patiently behind him, looped the reins around a tree, and started down the steep slope toward the stream. He traveled easily, in the gait of an experienced hunter. Scarcely a leaf rustled beneath his feet.

As he stalked into the clearing next the river, the man on horseback saw him coming and spoke first. "Hello."

Hatfield surveyed him carefully. The stranger was a man in his early thirties, with broad forehead and alert, active eyes. On his head was a black slouch hat, with just enough mystery about it to arouse suspicion, and on his chin was a goatee-like patch of sandy whiskers that brought a false air of jauntiness against the tiny knot of a black string tie. His coat, a reversible, was checkered, in squares nearly two inches across, and it was so long it almost concealed his brown, half-length boots.

"Howdy," said Hatfield.

"I was thinking about crossing here," the stranger said, "but I guess the water's too deep and treacherous."

"'Tis fer a truth," agreed Hatfield, standing, spraddle-legged, his gun in the crook of his arm. "Yuh better turn back."

The stranger looked over his shoulder, upward, along the steep side of the mountain. "Thanks," he said.

He pulled his black mare around and started up the trail. Devil Anse watched him go until he disappeared in the heavy growth of trees; then stood listening to the clatter of hoofs until they got well up toward the ridge. As their echo died away, he climbed with long, rhythmical strides to his horse, untied the reins, and went on his way toward Catlettsburg, the rip-roaring little mountain town on the banks of the Ohio.

This meeting along the Tug, on the border of Logan and Pike counties, was between two of the most dangerous men in American history—one a leader in a bitter and tragic vendetta, the other Frank James, brother of the famous Jesse. While they talked that day, Huntington, expanding town of 3,000 population, almost due north beside the Ohio, was recovering from its greatest bit of excitement to date. A few weeks earlier, four men had come into the neighborhood separately. One had stopped at a hotel and had registered as J. C. Johnson of Tennessee. During ensuing days, this man made himself conspicuous by a show of prosperity, depositing money at the town's bank and going there frequently to discuss business. A second fellow boarded at a near-by farm, dealt a little in stock, and purchased four fine horses—two bays, a gray, and a brown. The remaining members of the quartet kept in touch, but out of sight.

On Saturday, September 4, 1875, the four men met without creating suspicion and rode to a farm near Huntington, where they sought lodging for the week-end. Their host noticed that they took particular care of their horses—two bays, a gray, and a brown—grooming them often and frequently bathing their backs with arnica.

At 2:00 P.M. Monday, four men in long linen dusters trotted leisurely into town and tied their horses across the street from the bank of Huntington. One was the recent depositior, J. C. Johnson of Tennessee.

It was a beautiful autumn day, and along the sidewalks people were keeping up a constant parade to and from the twenty-odd stores in plain view. From the windows of homes scattered about the area, women with their knitting looked out upon the four newcomers and thought nothing of it. Neither were they alarmed when one man remained beside the horses, another entered the store before which they were tied, and the other two strolled slowly across to the bank.

What happened during the next few minutes was hidden from the view of the knitters. Not once was there a show of nervousness in the streets. Activity seemed as casual as a courthouse sale. There were no masked robbers, no show of guns, nothing to indicate that the capital of the bank of Huntington suddenly had been reduced by more than $10,000.

The man who had gone alone into the store had asked for a cigar. Three loiterers watched him inquisitively as he made his purchase. When his change was returned to him, he bit the tip off the cigar, spat it out upon the floor and asked quietly, "Any of you men got shooting irons?" The trio stared at him blankly. A smile played around his mouth and they were sure he was making fun until he slowly drew a .45 from his pocket.

"A couple of my friends are having trouble making change across the street and they don't want to be disturbed," he said.

Next morning the *Wheeling Intelligencer,* one of West Virginia's more enterprising newspapers, carried this news story, partially erroneous, on Page One:

"BANK ROBBERY IN HUNTINGTON, WEST VA."

"Cincinnati, Sept. 6–A gazette special from Huntington, W. Va., says:

" 'While Mr. Oney, cashier of the bank, was alone at noon today, three men entered, and, placing pistols at his head, compelled him to open the safe. A colored man happened in at this moment, and was also covered with a revolver and commanded to keep still, which he did. The robbers succeeded in getting possession of $15,000, with which they decamped. A confederate had horses waiting. The alarm was instantly given and the citizens and police started in pursuit, but failed to overtake the robbers, who escaped.' "

Pursuers soon came upon $30 in nickels and a draft for $5,000 thrown away by the bandits. The day after the chase began, this announcement appeared in one paper:

"Of those who went after the daring bank robbers, two have returned. The rest of the party, composed of about fifteen of the best men in the county, continued the pursuit. When last heard from, they had crossed the Big Sandy at Bear's Creek, with the robbers about half an hour in advance. It is now very certain that the robbers have been perfecting their plans for six months or more. They were more thoroughly acquainted with the country over which they traveled than those who had lived all their lives among the mountains, passing over the mountains and through cuts and creeks that were supposed by the inhabitants to be utterly impassable.

They captured a man about ten miles out, and compelled him to continue with them for an hour. They expressed their determination to die fighting, and left messages of defiance all along the route to those following."

The most amazing thing about the entire pursuit was the uncanny endurance of the robbers' horses. They raced for miles and miles over the mountains without becoming winded.

News of the robbery spread rapidly wherever there were wires to carry it, and not many hours passed before police were laying the blame on the James boys. As the pursuit lengthened, word went out that the bandits had separated and were traveling singly or in pairs. One town to which the warning came was Princeton, high in the mountains in the southern part of the state.

So Princeton was prepared for developments when a man in a reversible coat of checkered design rode into town one day and stopped at its one and only bank. More recent rumors had tipped off the populace that at least a part of the James gang was heading that way, and might try another holdup. All over town there was concealed evidence that things were ready for a showdown if a showdown were necessary, but the women folks were praying a pitched battle would not come. The male population, meanwhile, was poised for action. Men could be seen sitting about porches and yards, oiling their guns, a very regular and unexciting pastime except for the odd circumstance that most of the weapons were loaded to the last cartridge chamber even while they were being oiled.

It was fortunate at such a time, the town later learned, that it had in its midst a savior. This handy and welcome individual was David E. Johnston, bank vice-president and, when court day rolled around, judge of the Circuit Court. In the make-up of the worthy townsman was a strong power of speech, so dominant a power that one day it would take him to Congress.

"Let the James boys come," he invited confidently. "I'll handle them."

The banker-judge's words were uttered in the presence of the bank's cashier, Captain Hercules Scott, veteran of Gettysburg and other major battles of the late war. So when the stranger in checkered coat tied his horse and walked in to the teller's window, it was Scott who directed him to a door behind which sat Judge Johnston.

The door was closed on the tail of the checkered coat only a minute. Then it swung open—wide—as the judge walked out arm in arm with the visitor and let it be known they were going to his home for dinner—to talk business.

While the two broke bread, the town held its breath. A shot from anywhere, pulpit or work bench, would have brought armed Princetonians by the score.

But there was no shooting. The dinner went off quietly. If Frank James suspected that anyone was aware of his identity, he never allowed it to be known. Throughout the meal he ate heartily and listened to the words of his host.

Johnston gave full release to his power of speech. There was much to tell the guest, chiefly about the bank. Why, he said, here was an institution that was as safe as the American dollar. Only a robber who cared little for his life would attempt a holdup. The odds were too great. Take himself, for instance. Like the bank's president, H. W. Straley, he had served with Bowen's cavalry—for the South, mind you, suh—and he could shoot straight. At least 100 rounds a week he fired just to keep his hand steady and his sight keen. A better shot was Captain Scott, and he maintained his unerring aim, too. When business was not too rushing and the weather not too cold, it was his custom to take out his well-oiled Gettysburg pistols and get in a little practice from a window of the bank. Tiring of this, he frequently took down his trusty rifle, the one he had used while a sharpshooter in the early stages of the war. With that it was his custom to blaze away at whatever target came into his view, no matter how distant. Still another marksman usually was on hand during business hours, and even slept in the bank at night. This was Major Charles D. Straley, member of the Board of Directors and a veteran from Witcher's cavalry. A mighty potent man with a gun, too. Could bark a squirrel at ninety yards. The talk went on and on, with James showing less and less interest in the chief topic of conversation.

At last the meal was finished, and the two strolled back to the street, Johnston convoying his guest with the cordiality of a Kentucky colonel, the guest quiet and thoughtful.

Beside the tie-rack in front of the bank, James stopped and loosened the bridle reins of his horse. He shook the vice-president's hand, thanked him for the repast of which he had partaken so bountifully, and rode away north toward Beckley. Rumor came back days later that his men had been waiting for him in that direction, that he had met them and dashed on toward Logan County and the Tug and his uneventful meeting with the leader of the Hatfield clan. He gave two reasons for not returning to Princeton—the bank was too shoddy to have much money and it was manned by Rebel soldiers.

5

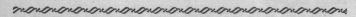

1880-1882
Mountain Romeo and Juliet

BY 1880 THE MCCOYS FOUND THEIR CHIEF WORRY THE frequent jaunts of the Hatfields across Tug Fork into Kentucky. The West Virginians came and went at will, always in bands, always heavily armed. They knew everyone by name, and even the McCoys were "uncle" and "aunt" and "cousin" to them. Except for their show of armed strength, they acted as if they came with good intention, although there was no effort to avoid making the impression that they would be peaceful citizens only if left alone. One observer said of them: "They are a high-spirited family, but they are kind, neighborly, and just to all who treat them justly. An enemy, however, might as well kick over a bee gum in warm weather and expect to escape the sting of the insects as to tramp on the toes of one of these spirited, tall sons of the mountains and not expect to be knocked down."

It made slight difference to them that they were unwanted. They came and they stayed and, worst of all, it was their nature to dominate. For instance, at elections the women customarily set out baskets of gingerbread in a way that indicated their choice of candidates. This bread was free to the electorate, and it was understood that the voter who partook of it agreed, by so doing, to support the political views of the particular woman by whom it was baked. The Hatfields completely flaunted this approach to female suffrage. They ate from all baskets, regardless of party alignment and despite the fact that a majority of them reside in an adjoining state and could not vote.

Not only that, they completely controlled elections in the Blackberry and Peter Creek precincts. Political contests were strictly local to them, confined to the narrow valleys and hollows bordering on the Tug, and that was the area in which they laid down the law, whether its people called themselves West Virginians or Kentuckians.

The intrusion from across the border caused strong resentment among the McCoys. Court records in Pikeville were dotted with cases brought by McCoys against Hatfields. Most of these efforts to gain revenge through legal procedure were continued or filed away. Law officers were well aware that, without tragic results, summons could not be served or arrests made among members of an armed band.

So warrants, without embarrassment or excuse, went unexecuted. Entries in the Pike County order book for one term of court alone include these futile charges against the West Virginians: October 13, Anderson Hatfield, carrying concealed and deadly weapon; October 14, Johnson Hatfield, carrying concealed and deadly weapon; October 15, Floyd Hatfield, giving spirituous liquor to a minor; October 16, Johnson Hatfield, carrying concealed and deadly weapon; October 22, Anderson Hatfield, Elias Hatfield, Sr., Thomas Chafins, John Chafins, Moses Chafins, John Staton, Elias Hatfeld, Jr., Floyd Hatfeld and Frank Elum, confederating and banding themselves together for the purpose of annoying and disturbing other persons and for the purpose of doing a felonious act.

The judge of the Pike County court was Basil Hatfield, brother of Preacher Anse. This gave a strange twist to the charge, often made, that no McCoy could be convicted in Kentucky, no Hatfield in West Virginia. The twist is not nearly so odd, however, when it is realized Basil was of a different branch of the family from Devil Anse, although the kinship was close. The Hatfields of Kentucky and the Hatfields of West Virginia sprang from two brothers, Valentine, who settled in West Virginia and sired nine sons and three daughters, and Joseph, who became a resident of Kentucky and had ten sons and one daughter.

One unheralded visit of the Hatfields that served as a red flag to the already angered McCoys occurred in the spring of 1880. The section of Pike County along Blackberry Creek was having an election and the polls were opened in a hollow of the mountains three miles from the Tug, where Hatfield Branch flows into the creek. The only house in the vicinity was that of Jeremiah (Jerry) Hatfield, of the Kentucky Hatfields.

Mountain elections were occasions flavored not alone by gingerbread. Many persons gathered at the polls who had neither the right nor the will to vote. They came—men and women—to escape from their loneliness, to mingle with the crowd, to listen to neighborhood gossip, and to take advantage of an opportunity to see people whom otherwise they would meet but rarely, and then, usually, by chance. There was no exaggeration in classifying such an assembly as an event. The men brought with them their jugs, as well as their guns, and long before the polls were closed and the ballots counted, many were too intoxicated to know or care whether their favorite won or lost. Such a day seldom passed without fist fights, and occasionally there was gunfire.

The 1880 spring election was no exception. By horseback and by foot, people came down out of the hills or followed the winding, rocky stream beds to Jerry Hatfield's humble cabin. He was no special host. It was just that his home was centrally located, on level ground, and surrounded by sufficient shade trees to enable the men to quaff their liquor and spin their yarns outside the rays of the sun.

This day saw the West Virginia Hatfields come in early, because a relative was among the candidates for election. Riding with them on this trip was Johnse, the dandy of the neighborhood.

During the morning, a horse walked into sight from the direction of the path that wound sharply up through the hollows for two and a half miles to the cabin of Randolph McCoy, squatting on the far side of the ridge. Astride the animal was a young man in his middle twenties and behind him a girl not yet past her first score of years. From the edge of the crowd, Johnse Hatfield watched Tolbert McCoy and his sister, Rose Anne, as they tied their horse among the others a short distance away from the gathering. In his mind as he looked on was hatched a plot as old as Eve. He saw the girl merge into the assembly, her black hair glistening in the rays of the rising sun, and he stared with lustful anticipation at the bounteous curve of her bosom.

The day advanced rapidly and excitement over the election increased. In the shade of the trees, there was much arguing, shouting, electioneering. Issues long settled in the minds of the voters were reopened, and the shortcomings of the candidates were reviewed in detail between heavy and frequent helpings of mountain dew. When lunch baskets were spread and hungry men set aside the jug to gorge themselves with something more solid, only a few had voted at the little table behind which sat the election officials.

The day had been remarkably free of angry spats and fist fights. Some of those in attendance noted that Johnse Hatfield and Rose Anne McCoy were conversing in a manner unrelated to the long-standing animosity between their immediate families.

Lunch was followed by a lull in political activity. Men heavy with alcohol and food stretched in the shade to sleep off their stupor. Others sat about swapping yarns, planning the future, and worrying about the cares of their own particular world.

Johnse and Rose Anne had disappeared. Far back in the bushes, well out of hearing of the noise at the election, they sat close together with their backs to a tree.

In the middle of the afternoon, balloting was renewed. Jugs again were raised and political fervor rose to fever heat. Voices had got beyond the picnic stage and shouts rang at intervals through the forest.

Johnse and Rose Anne still were missing.

The sun goes down early in the mountainous section of East Kentucky. It went down on this day with all the air of someone who knows something he is not supposed to tell, leaving an election satisfactory only to the majority, many of the voters too drunk to wander home in safety, and a boy and a girl locked in each other's arms. Rose Anne was a year the senior of Johnse Hatfield, but there were things he knew and did that more than made up for the difference one year can mean.

As dusk drew on, Johnse and Rose Anne returned to the trees around Jerry Hatfield's house. Most of the crowd had gone, including Tolbert McCoy. Rose Anne looked at Johnse and he saw the fear in her eyes. The secret they nursed seemed all at once to turn into a burden. No such trick of fate had they anticipated in their sudden romance. It would be hard to explain to Randolph McCoy. His daughter, he would say, should have come home with her brother. That was the understanding with which she had been permitted to attend the election. Where had she been? What had she been doing? There are some things a girl dares not tell, especially to her father.

The gossip that whipped through the mountains a few days later was vicious and frightening. People listened to it and held their breaths. At any moment the ridges might echo with the gunfire that neighbors of the Hatfields and McCoys knew was bound to come sooner or later. Johnse had taken Rose Anne home with him to live, and Devil Anse refused to permit them to marry, because Devil Anse did not want the blood of his arch enemy, Randolph McCoy, mixed with that of his own. Reactions varied and sympathies were divided, although Anse, behind his back, received most of the criticism from the public. Rose Anne had many champions. Even in the mountains, when a maiden loves a man, there is sympathy and tolerance toward her when she takes him into her bed. A facetious writer has described the romance in this manner: "Rose Anne was old enough to know better, but she allowed Johnse to persuade her that a marriage tie was in no way necessary to the consummation of love. Under cover of night, he snatched his Sabine bride away to Logan County, and busied himself in the equally illegitimate operations of becoming a moonshiner and a father."

But the anticipated firing was delayed. Instead of attempting a violent revenge, the McCoys sulked, swelled with hate, and got madder and madder. This Montague—Capulet romance further opened the way for the furious reprisals which were to take place between the two clans.

Several times during ensuing months, Randolph McCoy sent his younger daughters, Allifair, Josephine, and Adelaide, to persuade Rose Anne to return home. More than a year passed before she heeded their appeal, and then she remained with her family only a short time. Her father's reprimands were too frequent and too severe, and the threatening rifles of her brothers barred the approach of her lover. At the first opportunity, she slipped away.

The family later learned that she was staying with her aunt, Betty McCoy, at Stringtown, where she had found the freedom she desired. Stringtown was on the banks of the Tug, closer to Johnse's home. It was much easier and safer for him to slip across under cover of night from the West Virginia side. He came often. There, on the slopes skirting the stream, they pursued their lovemaking as never before. And, while they lay stretched, staring at the moonbeams dancing on the waters all the way to the distant shore, they occasionally talked over their troubles. Devil Anse still objected to their marriage and the McCoys still threatened violence if they caught Johnse with her. Rose Anne shuddered at some of the things the youth said. She knew this could not go on, that sooner or later her brothers would catch him.

Weeks stretched into months. Then one night it happened: her brothers surrounded Betty McCoy's home and surprised them in each other's arms. No violence occurred and no resistance was made to stimulate it. Johnse went along peacefully in the face of superior strength and superior guns. Before they left, the McCoys let it be known that they planned to take their prisoner to Pikeville and to turn him over to the law to answer there the many indictments held against him.

As soon as they disappeared, Rose Anne did a thing that endeared her to the Hatfields, and in later years caused Devil Anse to express regret over the heartache he had caused her. In the night, hatless and coatless, she ran across to the farm of Tom Stafford, borrowed a horse and, without waiting to saddle it, rode to tell the Hatfields of what was happening.

Devil Anse acted with the dispatch of his war days. At his home that night sat his brother Elias and wife. When Devil Anse asked him to come along, Elias held back. Peace between the clans was the desire of this swarthy and more serious-minded member of the family, and at his elbow sat a mate who championed him in his reluctance to do anything that would cause more trouble. But Devil Anse had no sympathy for such an attitude at a time when one of his sons was in the hands of the enemy. "Come with me or you are no Hatfield!" he roared, and Elias picked up his rifle and followed.

Before starting out, Devil Anse also rounded up his other sons and some of his neighbors. Along the way, still others were added to the party until it had stretched into a formidable group by the time the Tug was reached.

The Hatfields knew a short cut. On a mountain top between Stringtown and the road to Pikeville, they overtook the McCoys. Again the side with the most guns triumphed.

Not a shot was fired. So easily and so quickly was Johnse released that Devil Anse gave vent to some of his prankish nature. He insisted, with furious motion of his gun, that the McCoys get down on their knees and pray. They dropped down, all but one, and that one was admired and feared by the Hatfields more than any other member of his clan. Jim McCoy stood straight and dared them to shoot.

After the tense scene on the mountain, long hours lay ahead for Rose Anne McCoy, hours in which she listened for the footsteps of her lover, hoping and fearing he would come, knowing if he did it would mean his death. Resigned to what fate held in store for her, she went unwillingly back to her father's cabin. There she brooded and waited impatiently for the birth of her child. But fate had been against the love of Johnse and Rose Anne from the beginning. In the midst of her pregnancy, she went down with the measles and succumbed to miscarriage.

6

1882
A Trio in Death

KENTUCKY ELECTION DAY IN AUGUST, 1882, THE FIRST Monday of the month, came on the 7th. It was a very special occasion. In addition to the usual run of county and state offices to be filled, the electorate had to decide whether it wanted an increase in school tax. Such matters seldom appeared on the ballots; so voters on this occasion took their responsibilities to heart and tipped the jug an extra time or two, with the result that by night reports like these, published in the Louisville *Courier-Journal* of August 8, 1882, were coming from many parts of the state:

Lexington—"Today in this city, King Whiskey held high carnival in these ancient streets, and the temperance adherents are completely paralyzed by the result. . . . Fights were frequent all over the city, as many bruised faces and damaged optics can testify to, although nothing of a serious nature is chronicled. The circus being in town, many yaps and Negroes whooped up things and made it lively."

Garrand County—"Everything passed off quietly, but E. Best of Paint Lick was waylaid and shot, but not much hurt. The fire was returned by one of Best's friends and a Negro named Harry Yeaky was mortally wounded."

Lyon County—"Several fights took place in Eddyville today. Marshal Dogget, in attempting to arrest Tom

Jenkins, was cut severely by the latter in three places. Dogget knocked Jenkins down after the cutting, but did not hurt him scarcely. Jenkins is in jail."

Nelson County—"About 3 o'clock this evening, a difficulty arose between Ralph Livers and Dave Gravat of this place. Livers and Gravat were both under the influence of whiskey. Livers cut Gravat several times—once in the left side, directly under the heart. He is thought to be dangerously wounded."

Pike County was no exception. Its list of county offices open to election was long, and there also was the matter of picking an appellate judge. Fights were numerous all through the mountainous area, and off along the Tug a feud that one day would attract world attention advanced toward its worst stage of bloodiness.

Polls along Blackberry Creek were opened in the little hollow near the home of Jerry Hatfield. Beneath a tree stood a small table, and around it sat the election officials, cloaked for the day with sufficient authority to make them the hub of activity and attention. When a voter made up his mind, he approached the table and announced his choice of candidates for the officials to record. There was no secrecy. Voting was by word of mouth, a circumstance that put spirit and venom into political contests.

Preacher Anse Hatfield was one of the election officials on hand that day. He was now forty-seven years old, and more than ever was looked on as the father of his flock. Other Hatfields, including two by the name of Elias, were present, either officially or unofficially. One of these was the brother of Devil Anse. This Hatfield had come over from West Virginia with still another brother, the large and powerful Ellison, to watch political developments. The other Elias, more commonly known as "Bad 'Lias," was a brother of Preacher Anse, a hard drinker living two miles up Blackberry Creek from the polling place.

Early in the day it was evident some of the men gathered for the election were carrying grudges. Whiskey jugs scarcely had begun to circulate before Tolbert McCoy, Randolph's thirty-one-year-old son, picked a quarrel with Bad 'Lias over a small sum of money still owed by Hatfield for a fiddle he had bought from

McCoy. The argument took place back in the trees, some distance from the election table. Tolbert was backed up by his younger brothers, nineteen-year-old Phamer and fifteen-year-old Randolph, Jr., and argument had become vociferous when someone ran and told the minister about it.

Appearance of the Primitive Baptist Preacher Anse at the scene of the quarrel had its effect. Though Bad 'Lias, irrational with liquor, showed no respect for his brother's cloth and tried to continue the argument, the McCoys were persuaded to come closer to the election table. With this adjustment, the minister was satisfied that the trouble was over and went back to his official duties, cheered by the parting assurance of one of the boys who yelled after him, "All right, Uncle Anse, we'll do what you say."

But the excitement of battle had permeated the gathering. Tolbert McCoy still seethed inside, and the sympathetic words of friends, many of whom spoke in the interest of stimulating a good fight, served only to fan a temper ready to flare beyond control.

The day advanced and, with it, the tension. In the early afternoon, when voting activity was resumed, Tolbert's wife, Mary Butcher, approached him with a suggestion that they go home. He waved her away gruffly, and she left, knowing argument was futile while he was drinking.

A short while later, Ellison Hatfield approached the election officials and stopped beneath a huge beech tree. He had been asleep in an orchard near by and was just arousing from the heavy slumber brought on by too much liquor and food. Covering his face while he slept, and now the top of his head, was a large straw hat, of much wider brim than customarily seen in the neighborhood. It attracted the attention of some of the bystanders.

In acknowledgment of their taunts, Ellison waved the straw above his head.

"Boys, I just brought you some roughness for your cattle!" he shouted.

This encouraged laughter, which a moment later froze on the bystanders' lips. Tolbert McCoy separated himself from the small group in which he stood with his brothers and advanced toward Ellison Hatfield, his face distorted by anger and whiskey.

He walked to within a few feet of Ellison and stopped, staring belligerently.

"I'm hell on earth!" he screamed.

Hatfield, much the larger of the two, looked at him uncertainly. "What?"

McCoy repeated: "I'm hell on earth!"

"You're damn shit hog," replied Ellison.*

McCoy walked nearer, his fists clenched. He struck at Hatfield, at his stomach, swiping him across the front. Behind that blow was left an open gash from a knife blade, a wound out of which blood gushed and spread rapidly over the victim's shirt. Hatfield fell on McCoy and held him, trying frantically to grab the knife.

In the few seconds that followed, all the hatred and anger and revenge stored up in the McCoys broke loose. Foremost in their minds were the many things, justified or unjustified, the Hatfields had done to them—the murder of Harmon McCoy, the hog trial, the efforts of Ellison to convict Paris and Sam McCoy for the death of Bill Staton, and, more recently, the torture and shame brought on Rose Anne. Here was an occasion to obtain long-sought vengeance, to subdue and humiliate one of the leaders of the opposing clan.

While the crowd stood paralyzed, Phamer and young Randolph rushed in to help their brother. The fight became a melee, and eyewitnesses could see that the McCoys were stabbing Ellison over and over.

Preacher Anse, peacemaker and religionist, rushed over to separate the fighters. Ellison grabbed a rock. But before he could strike with it, a shot rang out and he slumped to the ground, drilled in the back.

Explosion of the revolver in the hands of Phamer McCoy was like a thunderclap. It was followed by dead silence except for the heavy breathing of the fighters, and then a low murmur stirred in the outskirts of the crowd and swelled as it worked inward. Preacher Anse knelt over Ellison. The shirt of the wounded man now

* These words stuck firmly in the memory of the Reverend Anderson Hatfield.

was almost solidly crimson. He lay face downward in the dirt, gasping, his quick breath shaking the leaves and grass where they had been scuffed up near his mouth.

Suddenly there was loud shouting as the Hatfields realized the outcome of the fight. Angry clansmen pushed in toward the circle forming around the wounded Ellison, guns out. At one side, the McCoy boys, realizing the damage they had done, struggled through the throng and attempted to escape. Ellison's brother, Elias, overcome with fury, ran out of the crowd and futilely emptied his gun after the fleeing figures. Elias meant to kill.

The next two hours were free of politics. Excitement was far too general for the crowd to be bothered with such a conventional matter as an election. The McCoys had been overtaken down in the woods and had been brought back to the custody of civil officers at hand, two justices of the peace, Tolbert and Joseph Hatfield, and a special constable. Matthew Hatfield. Four other men were deputized as guards. After the brothers had been taken into custody, they were seated together on the grounds until those in charge could decide what disposition should be made of them.

In the meantime, plans had been made to carry Ellison Hatfield back across the river to West Virginia. He had lost a lot of blood and was growing weaker rapidly. Someone brought a blanket from Jerry Hatfield's, and this, with two saplings, was fashioned into a stretcher. On the crude bier the wounded man lay and moaned while six of his friends toted him down the rough path toward the Tug. Their destination was the home of Anderson Ferrell, in Warm Hollow, a little below the mouth of Blackberry Creek.

At 4:00 P.M. (the time fixed by Randolph McCoy in his subsequent testimony), the civil officers prepared to move their prisoners toward Pikeville. Just before they left, Preacher Anse approached the McCoys. Their father was seated near, and the minister addressed his words to all four. He told them he had been listening to some of the talk on the grounds following the fight and was afraid. A part of this fear, he explained, was generated by the examination he had made of Ellison's wounds. There were twenty-six gashes, in addition to the hole left by the bullet. Some of the cuts were deep and it seemed to him death was near. He urged the McCoys to go on to the county seat that night so that they would be safe in case the Hatfields came across the river and tried to take them away from the officers. The father snorted in contempt, and so did his youngest son.

"We're fighters ourselves," said the boy. "An' we got plenty old axes 'n things to fight with."

It was dark when word of Ellison's plight reached Valentine Hatfield. This eldest of Devil Anse's brothers, known throughout the hills as "Wall," was the most dependable and conservative member of the clan, possessing characteristics of stability which induced his relatives to refer to him on occasions as "The Old Man." He was tall, powerful, well proportioned, with iron-gray hair, a full mustache, and rough, shaggy eyebrows, the last a screen from behind which eyes peeped rebelliously and made it difficult for him to maintain the proper degree of decorum as a justice of the peace. No one had ever paid attention to the fact that Wall had more than one wife and a sprinkling of children.

When news of the fight reached him via a young son, he was at the mouth of Beech Creek, four miles from home and ten miles upstream from the election site. He sent home for his horse, which was delivered to him by the Mahon brothers, Dock, Plyant, and Sam. These boys were closely connected with the Hatfields. Two of them were sons-in-law of Wall and all were nephews by marriage of the wounded man. Wall took them along with him, crossed the river and struck up Pounding Mill Branch, on a direct line for Blackberry Creek. Soon after they forded Blackberry, they met Wall's brother, Elias, who told them developments up to the moment. After some deliberation, the Hatfields decided to go after the prisoners and directed the Mahons to return to West Virginia.

Back in the Ferrell cabin in Warm Hollow, a small group of mountaineers hovered over the bed of a dying man. One of the watchers was Devil Anse Hatfield, for the moment serious, silent, with no thought of prank or practical joke. For hours he waited while his brother grew worse. At last, as if torn by the moans of the victim, he turned about and motioned for the other men in the room to follow him. Outside he stopped and made a brief announcement:

"We'll hang them McCoys."

The seven-man law force guarding the McCoy boys was slow getting started next day. They had stopped for food the night before at the home of Floyd McCoy, and then had gone on to John Hatfield's, farther up Blackberry Creek, to spend the night.

The departure from McCoy's had been somewhat tearful. News of the trouble her sons were in had traveled across the mountains to Sarah McCoy and she had hurried with all the haste of a panicky mother to overtake them. She caught up while they were eating, but she may as well have stayed at home. Even her own sons made light of her fears and her tears. Sarah left them reluctantly. She knew the tragedy which usually followed when mountaineers got together in armed bands.

It was eight o'clock in the morning before the officers steered the prisoners away from John Hatfield's and up along the winding trail toward Pikeville. They had gone only a mile and a half before they heard hoofs on the path behind them. Turning their horses about, they got their guns ready, expecting force, but only two men, Wall and Elias Hatfield, rode into view.

The Hatfields approached with peaceful air. They had been on the move all night, from the time they first had met downstream, and they were tired from picking their way in the dark along the mountain. Wall did the talking. He asked the officers in charge if the law did not specify that, in such a case as that of the McCoys, an accused person should be tried in the district in which he was alleged to have committed the cause of action. The justices of the peace admitted this was true, and Wall next urged them to go back down the creek to its mouth, so that the trial could have the benefit of the testimony of his aged uncle, Valentine Hatfield, and Dr. Jim Rutherford, both of whom had important evidence. He also mentioned that he would like to be close to his wounded brother.

After brief deliberation, the guards, all named Hatfield, consented to turn back.

At an old house at the mouth of Dials' Branch as they retraced their steps, they stopped and dragged out a corn sled, a boxed affair on runners. Into this the prisoners were placed, still untied.

Just after they had taken their seats, Wall sauntered over and put his foot on the sled. Suddenly, without apparent cause, the youngest of the McCoy boys began to cry. Hatfield looked at him without change of expression.

"I'm not going to hurt you," he said gruffly, and walked away.

Before they could get started again, Devil Anse and the group he had led out of Warm Hollow the night before came into view, all fully armed. They had stopped at the mouth of Blackberry Creek to get a few hours' sleep in an abandoned house and had been joined there by the Mahons.

With a horse pulling the sled along the rocky and uncertain path, the journey as it was resumed became more tedious. It was noon when the caravan got to Preacher Anse's and stopped for more food. Wall also took advantage of the halt to borrow the minister's razor and shave.

After everyone had eaten, Devil Anse walked into the clearing around the cabin and shouted in a loud voice: "All of Hatfield's friends form a line!"

So many men stepped forward that eyewitnesses later had trouble recalling them. In the group were Devil Anse's sons, Johnse and Cap, Alex Messer, Joe (Chuck) Murphy, the Mahons, Charley Carpenter, the neighborhood's only school teacher, Dan and Jeff Whitt, Mose Christian, Tom Mitchell, and others. Standing around, Most of them armed, were a number of mountaineers who took no interest in proceedings other than that induced by idle curiosity.

Wall and Elias brought the prisoners out and put them in the sled. They were now tied together with rope that Charley Carpenter had obtained at the home of Jerry Hatfield. When the three McCoy brothers appeared, Devil Anse announced loud enough for everyone to hear:

"We'll take charge of 'em now."

The law officers and guards stood by helplessly. Even

if they had wanted to interfere, it would have been foolish in the face of the Hatfields' advantage both in numbers and guns.

As the trek down the creek was resumed, Wall turned to Randolph McCoy, the boys' father.

"I understand we're to be bushwhacked down the creek," he said. "If we are, we'll kill yo' boys."

McCoy stared back in defiance without opening his mouth. A few minutes later he got on his horse and headed for Pikeville. He knew whatever trial was held would be dominated by the Hatfields and that his three sons would get justice only if he could enlist in their behalf what legal authority there was at the county seat. This conviction had been growing in his mind since they had turned back, even though Wall Hatfield repeatedly assured the officers all he wanted was the civil law.

Jim McCoy, thirty-three-year-old son of Randolph, who had been waiting at the minister's home when the prisoners came up, went along with them for more than a mile before Devil Anse turned to him and told him he had better go back, that he had no business farther down. The clan leader now had taken complete charge. He remarked as he turned away from McCoy that he had a notion to tell the officers there would be no further need for them.

A little later, the Hatfields gave more evidence that they had taken matters into their own hands. At the mouth of Blackberry, a skiff was pushed out of the bushes, the McCoys were told to get into it, and a slow journey was started across Tug Fork. In the boat were Devil Anse, Wall, Johnse, Charley Carpenter, and Chuck Murphy.

They landed along the opposite shore, moved upstream for a mile and a half, then turned left up Mate Creek, fast in the mountains. After going a short distance they stopped at an abandoned schoolhouse. It was moving toward dusk; clouds growing heavier along the ridges towering almost directly above gave promise of rain.

The McCoys, their hands still tied, were forced to lie on the floor of the one-room building. Some time later, a messenger arrived with a report that Ellison Hatfield had not much longer to live. As dark settled, the rain started in a heavy, beating downpour. Now the night drew in close around the schoolhouse, thick, clammy, and wet. To break the tenseness and to aid in guarding the prisoners, someone hung a lantern near the door. It smoked and flickered and gave out a mixed odor of carbon and kerosene.

Pretty soon, out of the darkness appeared two drenched women—Sarah McCoy and her daughter-in-law, Mary Butcher. Wall Hatfield, squatting on the porch with a rifle across his knees, recognized them and stopped them at the steps.

Sarah was frantic. Mary, drawn into this clan warfare only by her marriage to Tolbert, was more frightened over her own safety than that of her husband. The mother pleaded for a chance to see her boys, and Wall was all for allowing her the privilege, but Devil Anse objected. He stood silhouetted in the doorway, his stooped shoulders and long beard adding scores of years to his age. Behind him, the pale yellow glow from the lantern flickered despondently across the bodies of the prisoners lying on the floor, and a tongue of light escaped under Devil Anse's arm into the darkness of the porch and carved out the stark, business-like breech of Wall's rifle.

Sarah McCoy was a determined woman. For a long time she stood there in the rain, in front of her daughter-in-law, pleading, crying, addressing her words to Devil Anse. Once Wall spoke up, and what he had to say gave no comfort to the woman:

"You better go on off 'n leave us alone. If we're bothered with, we're a'goin' t' shoot yo' boys as full o' holes as a sifter bottom."

Devil Anse remained stolid in the doorway, with that tireless stand of the mountaineer. For nearly an hour he held this position; then he suddenly stepped out onto the porch and motioned for the women to enter.

The mother and the wife walked in, their clothes dripping and their sodden bonnets drooping over their faces. Devil Anse remained in the dark on the porch, and Wall, prodded by the stream of light that fell through the door after his brother moved, skidded back into the blackness. The only noise around the tiny building was the rain, still beating down hard, and the low talking between the women and the prisoners. There was nothing to indicate that other mountaineers squatted as guards at points in the surrounding trees.

The night advanced. Around ten o'clock, noise on the inside increased. Sarah McCoy had lost control of herself and was becoming hysterical. Tears were mixed with sob-pointed prayers. She knew the Hatfields; she knew their provocation; she knew the danger her sons faced. Wall had told her on the outside that, if Ellison died, her sons would die.

Her voice grew louder and louder as she knelt on the floor, praying and crying, and now and then above her supplications could be heard the soft, soothing words of Mary, standing over her.

This went on for several minutes until Charley Carpenter shouted out of the dark:

"Shut up, woman! We ain't a'goin' to have any mo' of this!"

A clamor of male voices now rose in protest from the trees. Devil Anse and Wall joined in, ordering the women out of the house.

Someone yelled that Randolph McCoy was across Tug Fork at that very moment trying to organize a party to rescue the boys.

Sarah McCoy raised up in protest.

"There ain't nothin' to that. That ain't so."

"You better go," Wall said from the outside. "If they do come, this house'll be set afire an' yo' boys'll be the first ones shot."

Sarah and Mary, now both sobbing, walked out into the rain, and the figures of the Hatfield brothers blocked the doorway behind them. The women turned back once to look at the prisoners; then walked off, miserable figures, and disappeared into the dark. Their footsteps were cushioned by the rain-soaked earth, but for a long time the men back at the schoolhouse imagined they could hear their sobs as they felt their way down the mountain trail to the home of Dr. Rutherford, nearest in that vicinity.

Around midnight, the guard around the McCoys was reduced. Devil Anse and a part of his followers departed to sleep until daylight at the home of Elias, leaving Wall and the others to take turns at guarding and napping.

The rain stopped during the night and the morning of August 9 dawned clear. Loiterers at the schoolhouse, waiting for the next developments, increased with the daylight, and so did the excitement. Latest reports from the bedside of Ellison Hatfield said he was sinking rapidly and that he could not live the day out.

In the middle of the morning, Sarah and Mary McCoy returned. They stood about on the outside, trying to peep through the open door at the prisoners. Once they heard Dock Mahon ask Tolbert for some tobacco and then take it from his pocket, and they thought maybe things between the two clans were not so strained after all.

Jim McCoy was there, too. Jim was calmer and more level-headed than his brothers. He was standing around, talking seldom, trying to attract as little attention as possible. Several times he had heard the Hatfields talking angrily and he thought once or twice they were going to shoot. At last Wall spied him and approached, delivering the same warning he had made to Sarah the night before—if Randolph attempted rescue, the boys would be the first to die. He added that the other McCoys would go the same way.

Later, Jim saw Wall with a writing in his hand, trying to get signatures to it. He thought he saw Wall actually signing some men's names, and once he tried to see what it was, but Charley Carpenter waved him back at the point of a gun.

Every hour or two a messenger appeared at the school with a new report on Ellison. Each time it was the same: he was dying.

The crowd continued to grow. Nearly everyone in the vicinity was there. Preacher Anse came up and urged Devil Anse and Wall to let the McCoys go. Their answer was repeated several times in reply to the minister's argument: "If Ellison lives, we'll let the la[illegible] course."

The person[illegible]

sagged like a sack of grain, slumped forward, swinging from the armpits. Young Randolph was in kneeling position, almost the entire top of his head shot away. Jim McCoy and his companions stared at the gaping hole in the boy's skull and recalled the single blast, louder than the others, that had come at the end of the firing.

The night of August 9, 1882, was etched for life in the memories of the mountaineers along Tug Fork. They remembered it for its sadness and its blight on a paralyzed family; for the bitterness and hatred and desire for revenge brewed in the early evening in the sinkhole on the Kentucky side of a low-water stream; and for the beauty that comes with a night in full bloom. Overhead was a bright moon and a blanket of stars, gold on blue-black, that gleamed and shimmered and looked down on the horrors hidden in the darkness covering the earth. Never before or since, it is said, have the people who noticed them that night seen so many stars at one time.

7

1882-1883
Indictments for Twenty

TUG FORK HAD NEVER BEEN AS SHEERLY THE DIVIDING line between West Virginia and Kentucky as on the morning of August 10, 1882. Although the steam rippled along with its same determined effort to get somewhere and the trees on the steep mountains rising from its banks still waved as gently in the rarified breeze, people were aware that at any minute a bullet might come plowing from either side. What had taken place in the last three days was as final as a formal declaration of war. There could be no peace now between Hatfields and McCoys. A leader of one clan had received his death wound in a fight with members of the opposing faction; three sons of the other side had been murdered.

Sometime during the forenoon, a sled similar to that in which the McCoy boys had been brought down Blackberry Creek was pulled by two yoke and oxen to a point near the sink-hole in which the brothers had been slain. The bodies were piled together in the crude vehicle and a slow journey started toward Randolph McCoy's cabin.*

* Allen Hatfield, who, at the time interviewed, was chief of police of Matewan, W. Va., said that his father, Wallace Hatfield, directed removal of the bodies and often commented in later years that it was the heaviest load he ever had hauled. When the author talked with him, Police Chief Hatfield lay on a glider on his porch in the morning sun, his shoes on the floor beside him. In his shoulder was a bullet

Arrangements at the home were not hampered by the confusion that might have been expected. Shock was cushioned by expectation. The mother and sisters, apprised hours earlier of the shooting, were tearfully making plans for the burial.

But another funeral was to come earlier. During the afternoon, while the sled with its tragic cargo still was being worked along precarious paths through mountain hollows, the homemade coffin bearing the knife-and-bullet-punctured body of Ellison Hatfield was taken up from the home of Elias and toted on the shoulders of men to an open grave near by. The assemblage of mourners was large, yet much smaller than it would have been had not the new deaths been added the night before.

On the following day, the burial scene shifted to the McCoy cabin on Blackberry Fork of Pond Creek, up near the backbone of the mountains where Hatfield Branch picks up and trickles on down to merge into Blackberry Creek at Jerry Hatfield's home. Three coffins, hastily constructed, were closed and nailed. One by one they were taken up and carried down the trail a few yards; then to the right, up a steep slope, to a shelf cleared of trees. There, under the eave of the mountain, overlooking a narrow pass, waited a single grave, three times as large as normal, and into it the boxes were lowered. Many people present were there because of the excitement.

Conversations among the McCoys were much more bitter, the threats more violent, than those at the Hatfield funeral. The burial across the river had been the final detail in a death that had been avenged; here, victims were being taken to their final resting place, but the penalty for their murder had not been administered, either by the law or by their survivors.

It was noticed during the burial that the mother stood beside the grave with her daughters; the father was miss-

hole and in his hip a bullet, both from a bawdy house raid he had staged the night before. In the manner of his heritage, he had stood in a rain of bullets in the upper hallway until he had got his man. He remarked lazily in the warm sun that day that "I'll go on down to the hospital in a few minutes and get them to take this bullet out of my hip."

ing. Many wondered if Randolph McCoy were off preparing his revenge. None knew he was slowly making his way back from Pikeville, disappointed, dejected, unaware that, even if all the civil authority in Pike County had come to his aid, it would have been too late.

A coroner's jury that had met over the bodies prior to the funeral served no purpose other than to fulfill a perfunctory act. It briefly reviewed what evidence there was —and this was circumstantial, because there were no eyewitnesses. Further investigation was dispensed with, everyone knowing and believing he knew who was guilty. The verdict: the McCoy brothers had been killed by persons unknown.

News of the murders swept the county, spread into other counties, was carried by word of mouth even to Louisville and Frankfort, but there it stopped. Pike County was so remote and so distant from these centers of population—not as the crow flies, but as the wayfarer was forced to travel along narrow, unbeaten passes of the mountains—that people who heard of the slaughter listened to the meager details impassively, chalking off part of the account as a fairy story from the hills. Newspapers paid no attention to it whatever. The report that came to them was so far removed from its source there was no one to quote; nor would the editors for a moment think at that time of sending a reporter so far out of the beaten path to check on its verity.

On the 4th of September, less than a month after the McCoys had been slain, the Circuit Court for Pike County convened with Judge G. N. Brown presiding. It was known throughout Kentucky and West Virginia that any judge who lifted his gavel in the mountain regions did so at the risk of his life, that civil authorities were not powerful enough to combat family or clan rule, that the instructions of the court could be carried out only if people to whom they applied were in a mood to comply. In the case of the McCoy boys, any legal pursuit of their murderers seemed foolhardy. First of all, they were across the river in another state, under a different jurisdiction. Furthermore, it would be a long and tedious task to stir up enough excitement at Frankfort to induce the governor of Kentucky to requisition return of the persons suspected of guilt, and it would be a still longer step to get necessary action from the governor of West Virginia.

This was not a new circumstance. For generations past and to come, thoughtful persons had talked and would talk over the great mistake of allowing the dividing line between the two states to extend through the heart of a mountainous region where guns were considered as essential as chewing tobacco and tempers were of a nature that provided no cooling-off period before the trigger was pulled. According to this wisdom, either one state or the other—and perhaps West Virginia preferably, because its topography was generally of that character—should have included all the mountain area within its borders.

Conscious of the dangers which went along with his robe, Judge Brown happened to be of sufficient experience to know when, and when not, to exert himself. Matters to be brought to the attention of the grand jury at this particular term of court had among them the murders of the McCoys, and the jurist was not one to shirk his duty, albeit fulfillment rarely exceeded a modicum. As required by law, he called together sixteen jurors, among whom was neither a Hatfield nor a McCoy, and placed in their hands the problem of deciding who fired the shots in the sink-hole on Tug Fork the night of August 9. For ten days the jury worked behind closed doors; then it emerged with indictments against Devil Anse, Cap, Johnse, Wall, and Elias Hatfield, Charley Carpenter, Joe Murphy, Dock, Plyant, and Sam Mahon, Selkirk and L. D. McCoy, Tom Chambers, Lark and Andy Varney, Dan and John Whitt, Alex Messer, and Elijah Mounts. Several names on this list, other than those of the two McCoys, caused surprise.

Each of the twenty men named in the indictments was accused of the crime of wilful murder and of "wilfully, feloniously and of their malice aforethought" conspiring to "kill, slay and murder" the McCoys by shooting them "with a gun or pistol loaded with powder and ball." It was admitted that the precise weapon, whether gun or pistol, was not known to the grand jurors.

On the 18th, four days after the indictments were returned, bench warrants were issued for these witnesses for the Commonwealth: Jacob Pucket, Mathew Hatfield, Anderson Hatfield, a son of George Hatfield, Richard Hatfield, James McCoy, Tolbert McCoy, an uncle of the murder victim, Lewis Farley, Joseph Hatfield, Samuel McCoy, James Francisco, Anderson T. Ferrell, John C. Frances, Samuel Simpkins, Uriah McCoy, George Sprouse, Floyd Hatfield, Harriett Simpkins, Mont Stafford, Scott Allen, and Sarah McCoy.

Next term of court was in Feburary. Shortly after it convened, the sheriff reported to the judge that he had been unable to arrest any of the individuals listed in the indictments. Accordingly, the clerk of the court wrote by each name: "Not found in this county February 19, 1883." For years this was stock phraseology, recorded by the same names whenever court was held. The sheriff and his deputies knew the whereabouts of the wanted, knew they occasionally, in strong and well-armed bands, slipped across the river into Kentucky, but no one would risk his life by attempting to arrest them. The same was true in West Virginia. Had requisition been granted, the next problem would have been to get someone to go up into the mountains after the Hatfields.

Eventually, Governor J. Proctor Knott was induced to offer a reward of $100 each for the arrest of the Hatfields. That, too, was futile. Civil and police authorities waited, hopeful that some day the West Virginians would become careless, would cross the state line in less formidable groups and lay themselves open to arrest. This was mere whistling in the dark. Most Kentuckians actually hoped Devil Anse and his crew would never come back.

odd name of O'Rear answered their questions as to his identity by informing them his name was Grant. The plan worked fine until he encountered a mountaineer who obligingly told him how far to the next place and then followed up the usual question concerning identity with "Any kin to the President?" "I am one of his brothers," replied the messenger. The mountaineer squinted at him more closely. "Yep," he accepted, "you favor him some. Well, good day. You will find the distance a leetel the rise of what I tell ye."

Railroad facilities available at that time, although limited, were a great aid to the reporters in their coverage. Chief of these were the Chattaroi, pushing up the east fork of the Big Sandy River, and the Eastern Kentucky, designed one day to extend up into the mountains as far as Pikeville. By the summer of '83, Kentucky had 2,000 miles of track, 500 of which had come during the last two years, and there was talk of more.

To stimulate rail development, the *Courier-Journal* centered attention more and more on the mountain area, on its coal, timber, ginseng, feathers, beeswax, dried fruits, sumac, sorghum, and other produce. Coal and timber were the main items, and New York capitalists were swarming into the country to buy in land titles.

Coal mining up in the Tug region had been held back by the uncertainties of river navigation. As early as 1847, investors from Cincinnati began mining coal near the border of Pike and Floyd counties, a hundred miles from the mouth of the Big Sandy. About the same time, another mine was opened at Prestonsburg. But both of these enterprises were suspended after brief trial. Some of the industrialists interested in them invested in other mines, closer to the Ohio, and continued mining operations until the outbreak of war in '61. By 1880, the fever had broken out anew and capital was pouring into the area. With it came renewed conviction that a profitable business would be assured only by development of some other method of transportation than water.

So the drive was on for more railroads. Each new rail spelled new progress, and each new tie, extending industry and growth of population farther and farther into the dangerous wilds of the mountains, represented the approach of new thought and a new method of living for the Hatfields and McCoys, then at the peak of their feuding.

The report Captain Pat Punch, U.S. marshal, and an outfit of soldiers brought back into Mount Sterling in the early part of the summer demonstrated how much people of the feud country opposed law enforcement. Mount Sterling was the "gate city of the mountains" and the first point at which a telegraph station could be reached coming out of the hills. Punch and his men were returning from a futile jaunt after a couple of bandits. For a time they had been confident of success. Three days in a row they knew they were within a mile of their quarry, but this gap could never be closed. Residents along the mountain slopes appeared to have risen in a body to assist the outlaws. Guns were fired and other signals were given to help the pair escape. Finally, in disgust, Punch and his men turned back. The best they had done was to round up two boys loaded with provisions for the fleeing men.

Naturally enough, incoming capitalists were impressed soon after arrival with the fact that there was something wrong with Kentucky's laws. Native Kentuckians themselves knew this to be true, and newspaper editors were crying for something to be done about it. But their cries were not to the benefit of the Commonwealth. Visitors could get little reassurance out of such editorials as this:

"From the sin of blood guiltiness no citizen of this Commonwealth is free. We do not deal with crime as we ought. We tolerate murder and pardon vice and honor criminals if they are brave. Physical prowess is the only virtue that appeals to us. We are passionate, unreasonable, unrestrained, lawless. Society protects no man either by its recognized rules of law or by that public sentiment which gives strength and force and vitality to all written laws. Unless we change all this; until murder is punished; until we educate men to look to the law for protection and vindication; until the law does what it pretends to do; what it is instituted for, we should cease our boasting, and no longer content ourselves with traits and achievements which equally distinguish the barbarous and half-civilized communities."

More and more as time went on and attention continued to be centered on the mountain counties, they became recognized as the hotbed of lawlessness. Story after story trickled down out of the hills and made its way into print. Many of these were about the famous hillbilly jurists, some widely known, who took their life in their hands by riding the circuits, trying to deal out justice to the hill country and still stay alive.

There was one story about Judge Finley of Williamsburg, who for two years had not dared to hold court in Whitesburg because of a threat made by one of the desperate men of the county that he would kill him if he ever entered it. This man finally fell victim to a plague and died, and the judge promptly convened court. One case on the docket involved a certain murder charge. On the day this was set for trial, the accused marched into town carrying a double-barreled shotgun and a belt full of revolvers, while behind him came a score of his friends, each armed in the same manner. The judge was in a spot. A day or two before the opening of court, the sheriff, drunk, fell and broke his leg while wrestling with a mountaineer carrying a fighting load of moonshine. Next day the jailer, who also was tipsy, shot himself in the leg as he went about the routine duty of locking up a refractory prisoner. Such mishaps left Finley without official aid; so, when the murder case was called, he refused to try it, knowing that if the accused were convicted his friends would not permit any order of the court to be carried out.

This condition of affairs brought newspaper comment that Judge Finley's court was "a special inquisition into an epidemic of murder." The *Courier-Journal,* in an editorial, June 30, 1885, turned its guns on the mountains and declared with vigor:

"There is practically no law in those counties; not even mob law; not even the law which in Italy and Spain relieves the vendetta of some of its most brutal features. In the 'bloody belt' of Kentucky a man is given really no chance for his life. Duelling is advanced civilization compared to assassination or street fighting, and in the counties mentioned assassination is the mode of warfare which finds most favor. A reign of terror prevails. The quieter citizens are cowed, and those peaceably disposed are leaving that section and coming down within the confines of civilization."

In rare instances, judges displayed enough courage to bluff the desperadoes, and immediately there was strong demand for them as substitutes for the regular jurists in counties in which trouble had reached a serious pitch. One of these courageous judges was William L. Jackson of Louisville, a city man with mountain ways. Called into a county in which no court had been held for nearly a year because of armed bands around the courthouse, he waded immediately into the murder cases on the docket. In the first to be called, all of the witnesses answered except one. The sheriff explained that it had been impossible for him to summon this particular witness. Jackson adjourned court for four hours to permit the man to be brought in; then he bravely walked out of the room without once looking back to see how many guns were pointed in his direction. At the expiration of the four hours, the sheriff reported he had found the witness barricaded in a house filled with armed mountaineers. This time the judge gave a stronger evidence that he meant business. He spoke in sharp language, well understood by the mountain people: the witness must be in court by ten o'clock next morning if he had to be brought on a litter—that, or the sheriff and his deputies would answer to the law. When court opened next day, half a dozen men appeared carrying the missing witness, one arm hanging limp at his side, a leg obviously unable to do duty, blood trickling from his head and an immense bandage concealing one eye. The trial went on and conviction resulted. Out of this grew a reputation that swept like fire through the mountains. Even the governor realized the value of Jackson. "I'd rather send him to try these lawless people than a regiment of soldiers," observed His Excellency.

Occasionally, people of reputation rose to the defense of the mountaineers and explained they were not as bad, nor as lawless, as painted; that they were like other people, if understood. Repeated newspaper publicity on the wickedness of the mountain region, for instance, induced its spokesman in Congress at Washington, Representative Taulbee, to explain to a reporter for the

Cleveland Leader the habits and peculiarities of his constituency:

"The ordinary house is a log one, consisting of two rooms, with boards shaved smooth with a drawing knife, or, split, nailed over the cracks between the logs. One of the rooms is used for a sleeping room, and the other is the living room, dining room, kitchen and parlor, all in one, in which the family stay during the daytime. There is but one sleeping room for a whole family, and when they have guests visiting them these turn in and sleep in the same room. There are a number of beds used, and a stranger always gets the best bed. They are very modest with it all. They turn their backs, if they are up, while the others of the family are undressing, or, if they are in bed, they will cover up their heads until you have completed your nightly toilet."

Taulbee tried to cushion the jolt of such a custom on people who never had been in the mountains. It must be all right, he said. Think of the large proportion of virtuous women in the region. "Virtue is as much respected in the mountains as anywhere else in the world, and though these women and men will undress together and sleep in the same room, they will be horrified at the exhibition of décolleté dresses seen at one of your receptions here, and would run away with shame from an exhibition of the modern ballet."

He named as a major redeeming feature their hospitality. "They entertain you and give you the best they have, and if you offer to pay they will refuse and say they do not make their money that way. The little money they do make comes from farming. They do not often grow wealthy, and they seem to be very well satisfied with their life."

Congressman Taulbee offered neither defense nor condemnation of their feuds. He said he had nearly half a score of murder cases to defend in one county alone on account of them. And then the Hatfields and McCoys came to his mind: "I know a place where two families have been fighting each other for a generation, and where the different families of the two tribes never go out to work except in squads and always carry Winchester rifles with them."

But fear and criticism of the mountaineers far outweighed any defense which could be built up in their behalf. A campaign of awareness to the failure of law in the mountains, as well as in other sections of Kentucky, definitely was on; yet too much stress still was placed on marksmanship and self-defense for an abrupt change to be brought about. While newspaper editors pleaded for more sternness, more rigor, more uprightness in law enforcement to stop murder, they at the same time cheered the Kentuckian who could place his bullets where he wanted them to go. They almost foamed at the mouth, for instance, when two factions in Morgan County fired nearly a hundred shots at each other and struck only one man. "The marksmanship was a disgrace to Kentucky," commented one editor. They choked, too, when they heard of B. F. Bisner, newly headed for Texas. Bisner was riding down the road one moonlit' night and saw someone lying by the roadside. Thinking it was his brother, who had recently been in that neighborhood, he called to him. To B. F.'s surprise, the man arose, holding to his trousers, helped a woman to her feet, and then started shooting at Bisner, who wasted a few shots himself before fleeing.

Crime got first place in the newspapers, large and small, and there was no effort to tone it down. For instance, over a roundup of state news in the *Courier-Journal* of December 30, 1885, appeared this headline:

STATE PISTOL PRACTICE
Thomas Haynes and W. S. Higgins
Perforate Each Other With
Bullets at Greendale

For Fun, William Brown Sends a
Toy Pistol Ball Into the
Body of Jane Miller

To Be up in Form, Jack Abney
Fires Two Bullets Into
Alex Poteet at Mt.
Vernon

A man's reputation was founded on his ability to handle shootin' irons. This was especially true far back in the mountains. One day a young fellow, in time to become a prominent lawyer of Baltimore, sat on the hotel steps at Pikeville. He was a newcomer to the area, a 130-pound legal expert looking up titles on coal land and much impressed, as well as somewhat awed, by the .45 he had taken to wearing on his hip since his arrival. It was a lovely day, and behind him lounged a group of natives who busied themselves by staring out at the Big Sandy River a few yards to the fore while they engaged in their favorite pastime—an oral evaluation of the men in the neighborhood who could shoot. This went on until the visitor on the steps could hold in no longer.

"They can shoot where I came from, too," he blurted, his youthful voice quavering with excitement. "See that leaf sticking out on that tree across the river yonder. Well, where I come from, they'd shoot that off with one shot."

Momentary silence followed, while the spokesman swallowed hard; then someone asked the question the visitor regretfully realized was certain to come: "Why don't yuh let us see some o' that shootin'?"

Cornered, the youth grabbed for his gun and blazed away at the leaf, taking no aim and expecting no bull's-eye, not even a nick. To his utter amazement, the leaf fell from the tree. There was more silence, and then the crowd gradually dispersed. Next day, mountaineers the young lawyer had never seen before stepped out of his path to let him by.

Public applause for men who refused to be backed down brought mountain feuds to Kentucky in growing numbers. They flared up in quick succession, and every short while throughout the '80's the names of new factions appeared in the headlines. Turner-Sizemore, Martin-Tolliver, Strong-Little, Turner-Sowders, Jones-Hall, and French-Eversole were some of the leading wars, and combinations of opposing factions like these became common to the tongues of people of that and adjoining states. But nowhere in public print was there mention of the Hatfield-McCoy vendetta. This had been—and for a few more years would continue to be—confined to the far side of Eastern Kentucky.

Since the death of the McCoy brothers, things along the Tug had remained under constant strain. Members of each clan roamed about in bands, and now and then there was firing back and forth across the river, or someone stole up into the hills to blaze away at the cabins of opposing clansmen, night or day. Sometimes the trail got hot and men hid out, and some of these never came back. Often human bones, uncovered by hunter or warrior in the heavy forests on the mountainsides, were ignored as those of some unfortunate animal, waylaid on routine prowl, or, if recognized as those of man, were passed by as better left undisturbed. Sometimes the Hatfields rode across into Kentucky to Pikeville in broad daylight, and occasionally the McCoys ventured over into West Virginia. But when either side did so, it was in large bands heavily armed. Risks were mutual.

Devil Anse took little part in the constant warfare. More and more as time went on, he turned over the leadership in his faction's hostilities to Cap, his second son.

Whatever may be said in defense of such factional wars as that between Hatfields and McCoys, there can be no claim to fairness or to refusal to employ foul play. The Hatfields, for instance, never bothered to propound an excuse for lying in wait to ambush Randolph McCoy in June of '84. They wanted very much to finish off the leader of the opposing clan. Not for once since the death of his sons had he ceased his efforts to bring the killers to trial. Time and again, he made his way to Pikeville and voiced his lament to the civil authorities, supported usually by a nephew by marriage, Perry A. Cline, tall, gaunt consumptive with long black hair and beard. Cline was an influential person, a man who had moved to town from a boyhood home near the Tug and had made good. Attorney by profession, he had been elected by the people to public office on several occasions. He was their choice for the House of Delegates and was sent to the important Democratic convention in '83. Moreover, he managed through political pull to supplement both his salary and his influence by serving as deputy jailer and deputy sheriff of Pike County.

The Hatfields knew that the sooner this league was broken up the better, that there could be no rest on the West Virginia side of the Tug as long as Randolph McCoy and Perry Cline were carrying on their campaign. So, when they got word that McCoy planned to make a trip to Pikeville on a particular day, they made their plans accordingly.

McCoy was late getting started that day, and later praised the Lord for his tardiness. He and his son Calvin were riding through the woods some distance from his home when they heard firing on the mountain side a mile or two ahead of them. Pretty soon they came upon their neighbors, John and Henderson Scott. One of them had been wounded and both of their horses had been killed by a volley from ambush.

Search of the neighborhood netted nothing, not even the empty cartridges from the shots that had been fired. The Scotts and the McCoys rode away from the scene, leaving another mystery of the mountains, another unclosed chapter in years of feuding. Their helplessness to avenge a deed of violence, murder or otherwise, even though it involved a case of mistaken identity, was known only too well to them.

In March of '85, an incident involving a Hatfield brought newspaper mention of the murder of the McCoy brothers. On the morning of the 5th, guards escorted a prisoner from Pikeville through Catlettsburg and on to the jail at Mount Sterling, where he was taken for safe keeping because of fear that his friends would attempt to release him from the Pike County jail. A newspaper correspondent identified him as Montaville Hatfield, arrested in Wolfe County and wanted in Pike on a charge of first degree murder.

"Hatfield," explained the reporter with grievous inaccuracy, "is also implicated in the murder of the three McCoy boys, who were taken from their home one night some two years since, and after being tied to a tree, were cruelly murdered by a band of five men, among whom was Hatfield. It is hoped that he will not be able to arouse the sympathy of the Mount Sterling people, and thereby prevent a speedy trial when the Pike Circuit Court meets."

Montaville Hatfield was not so closely allied with the clan on the West Virginia side of Tug Fork as the newspaper correspondent implied, and that may have accounted for his inability to avoid arrest. His father, Elexious Hatfield, was a brother of Parson Anse, which made the prisoner a distant cousin of Devil Anse. It was

Montaville's distinction that he was the first Hatfield to make the headlines, although others, long before him, were more deserving.

One morning, near the end of the month in which Montaville was arrested, the jailer's wife at Mount Sterling busied herself with the weekly wash. Out into the yard next to the jail she breezed, balancing a tub of freshly-wrung unmentionables and humming a tune through a mouthful of clothes pins. A pair of ruffled panties got first place on the line, and then came a second; but as the jailer's spouse reached for another pin, an object framed in the space between the two pairs of drawers caught her eye. From an opening on the upper floor of the jail hung a rope of blankets.

The wife had not been married to the jailer long enough to overlook such things. She screamed her discovery, and the townspeople came by the dozens. Upstairs they found a cell door torn loose by the hinges, a stone forming part of a grating yanked loose from the wall, and the rope of blankets swinging down like a trail through the weeds on a mountain slope. Missing were Floyd S. Williams, William F. Casky, and Montaville Hatfield.

"No clew can be obtained as to the means by which they forced the door of the cell," reported the alert newspaper correspondent at that point, "and nothing was found in the jail. They were probably assisted from without by some one. They no doubt have been planning their escape for several days, as Henry Watson, just released from jail, says that they told him they intended to make their escape and go to West Virginia and join their friends, where they would be secure from recapture."

But Montaville was not destined to reach the protecting wing of his kinsman, Devil Anse. A few hours after he slid down the blanket rope, U. S. Marshal Pat Punch was on his trail. For eight days the chase went on, until the marshal finally outsmarted the men he was following. Familiar with the cabins that lay in their path, he quickened his steps and was quietly waiting when the trio approached the home of friends in search of food. Hatfield was taken back to the jail at Mount Sterling, there to await trial and a sentence of life imprisonment.

9

1886-1887 Marriage Eliminates a Feudist

THE ROMANCE OF JOHNSE AND ROSE ANNE NEVER CEASED to be of major interest to their neighbors, even when the bitterest feuding was going on between the families. There was always speculation, among young and old alike, over whether and how often Johnse saw her; whether the families still kept watch on their woodland trysts, if such things took place, and whether the McCoys ever would loose their vengeance on Johnse for taking a mistress from their clan. It was never for once accepted that the love affair would be blighted by Devil Anse's refusal to consent to their marriage. By adage, it is understood that love always finds a way, and there was no reason to believe that Cupid would meet with rebuff in this instance.

So it was something of a surprise to people along the Tug when they heard that Johnse suddenly had taken unto himself a bride. The new Mrs. Hatfield was Rose Anne's cousin, Nancy, daughter of Harmon McCoy.

Johnse's marriage must not at first have been for Rose Anne the harsh jolt her neighbors assumed. Months back, she had heard, without proof, that Nancy and Johnse were seeing each other whenever the opportunity afforded. This news was a much harder blow to her than the eventual marriage. Not since the night her brothers had surprised them at Betty McCoy's had she seen Johnse. Then the killings in August, '82, had built up a still stouter wall between them; had given Nancy an advantage denied Rose Anne by her own previous behavior. The cousin had more freedom to go back and forth; nor were her movements and her actions those of a girl on probation in the eyesight of her father and brothers. Now, regardless of how much the disappointed girl hoped the report was false, there was no longer any doubt in her mind. Never again would she have reason to sit on the steps of the McCoy cabin and stare off toward the lonely ridges for some signal from her lover, some sign that he was trying to get in touch with her. And there would be no more lonely hours of sitting in the sun and imagining that he was staring at her longingly from the cover of trees along the mountain sides rising above her home. The end of her romance had come. The handsome mountain youth she had loved and whose mistress she had become finally had succumbed to the wiles of a girl who knew how to make her men marry her for what they got.

But the jilted Rose Anne could not escape the ultimate effects of such a blow to her hopes and longings. Openly, she was unaffected; inwardly, she was burning from the scars left by passion. Years would pass before the neighborhood would be able to tell what the disappointment had meant to her, what it took in toll from the years she had been allotted.

To the factions involved in the feud the marriage meant nothing. The McCoys long had known and resented Johnse's amorous powers over their women. That he should come within range of their guns and take from among them a bride, with love and affection granted, increased their hatred and bitterness, dampened their manly pride. But Randolph McCoy, perhaps alone of all his clan, was stirred to action. Bewailing the unhappy lot of men, especially those with seductive nieces, he renewed his vows for vengeance and made new plans for trips to Pikeville.

On the Hatfield side, the rejoicing was loud and sincere at first; then it slowly took on a rancid tinge. For, as the months went by, it gradually was realized that Johnse, the bold, domineering, and unrepulsed lover, was becoming the most henpecked husband along the Tug. His days as an active member of the clan were numbered and reduced. Nancy had taken the powder out of his gun. Devil Anse, once proud of the ways of his son with women, now chided him sourly and, behind his back, stamped the ground in disgust.

After a time, a more serious complaint was directed at Johnse's marriage. The Hatfields suddenly realized that someone in their clan was spying for the enemy. It was evident that the McCoys knew too much about Hatfield plans and actions for their knowledge to be laid to coincidence. More and More, as the Hatfields sought the leak, the finger of suspicion pointed toward the women and finally settled on Nancy, who must still have the welfare of her own family at heart. But before any guilt could be uncovered, the finger of suspicion jabbed in another spot.

The home of Bill Daniels, who had married Nancy's sister, was in Pike County, not far from the Tug. Its master was a peace-loving citizen, a man who minded his own business and took pride in his home, despite its simple construction and its simpler accoutrements. He was not given to fighting or to picking trouble; in fact, his interest in life went not too far away from the clearing around his cabin. He was by nature meek and shunned violence. When the feud reached the shooting stage, his first inclination was to flee the mountains in search of more peaceful living quarters, but his marriage to a McCoy who could henpeck in the fashion of her sister made this impossible. His wife was his opposite in many respects, chiefly in her curiosity about other people's affairs. This quality had been passed on to their daughter in generous degree, and they were a pair of busybodies whose ears and tongues spared no one. Developments in the feud were like a drug to them. They padded the neighborhood in search of gossip, and made the trip across the river to Nancy's so often that they wore a path to the bank of the stream on both sides.

One night as the Daniels family sat together at home, two men—one with a streak of prematurely gray hair down the center of his scalp—slunk out of the dark and shoved guns in their faces. Bill Daniels was helpless, by nature and by situation. One of the intruders backed him and his daughter against the wall and held them at bay while the other whipped the wife severely with a cow's tail. Then the pair changed tasks, and the one who first had administered the whipping held the gun while his confederate used the whip on the daughter. The father expected his turn to come next, but the assailants apparently had nothing against him. Without raising a hand in his direction, they left, throwing back a warning to the women that they would be better off if they stayed at home and did not cross the Tug so often.

The two men made no attempt at disguise, and the Danielses promptly broadcast that they were Cap Hatfield and Tom Wallace, the latter easily identified by the streaked scalp. There was some degree of revenge in the whipping Wallace administered. The Daniels girl had lived with him as his wife until she recently had learned he had tricked her with a mock wedding ceremony. No argument or pleading from Wallace so far had induced her to return.

Not long afterward, Jeff McCoy, brother of Nancy and Daniels' wife, killed Fred Wolford, Pike County mail carrier, and, on the advice of friends, took to his heels. To him the most appealing haven was the home of his sister across the river. There he would be out of reach of Kentucky authorities, and he knew Nancy would have no trouble forcing Johnse to permit him to hide out under their roof.

Matters developed as Jeff anticipated. He crossed the river and Nancy took him in with open arms, while Johnse looked on with the helplessness of a henpecked husband suddenly showered with in-laws.

But Jeff McCoy had a fault that would mean his end: he could not leave well enough alone. In time, as things were, the killing he had committed would have been forgotten and he would have been able to slip back into his native haunts unmolested. That was not the way Jeff would let it be; he had too much time on his hands at Johnse Hatfield's, and so his thoughts dwelt on revenge. He soon saw a chance to retaliate for the whippings administered to his sister and his niece. Word had come to him in direct fashion that one of the two men who had swung the cow's tail was Tom Wallace, working at the moment as a hand at the home of Cap Hatfield, not far away. It would be a clever stroke to capture Wallace and carry him off to the Pikeville jail.

Jeff's chance came one day when Cap was away from home and his wife was ill in bed. In company with Josiah Hurley, willing servant to the McCoys, he rode over to a point near the Hatfield cabin, tied his horse, and stole up to find Wallace working in the yard. Before the hired hand could take in what was happening, he was on his way to Pikeville.

But surprise was only a temporary setback to Wallace. Born and bred in the ways of the mountains, he quickly recovered from this sudden adversity. At the first opportunity, which came before they had ridden far, he leaped from horseback into the woods, receiving no more than a slight flesh wound in the hip from the bullets of his captors, and returned to barricade himself in the Hatfield cabin. McCoy and Hurley doubled back, too, and for some time futilely banged away at the home, on the inside of which Wallace unsuccessfully bided his time for a chance to get in a deadly shot.

When Cap Hatfield came home that night, he was furious. Doors and windows of his cabin were riddled with bullets, and the thing that made him maddest was that his wife, ill to the point of being bedridden, had been directly in the line of fire and had been forced to lie there throughout the attack. Next day he virtually dragged Wallace to a justice of the peace to swear out warrants. Then Cap got himself appointed special constable to serve them.

The service necessitated no long delay. Armed with his thorough knowledge of the intricate neighborhood, Cap quickly rounded up McCoy and Hurley and started with them to Logan Court House, accompanied by Wallace. The captives went along peacefully enough, so long as Cap and his touted rifle were at their backs.

The route toward the county seat led past the home of William Ferrell, near Thacker, on Tug Fork. There Cap suggested a halt, and he and Wallace went inside, leaving their prisoners, hands tied, in the saddle. In a few minutes, McCoy succeeded in freeing himself, leaped to the ground, and dashed off toward the river.

This would have been perfectly timed but for the fact that one of his captors happened to see him from a window.

Both Cap and Wallace hurried out of the house, firing their guns as they ran. Jeff McCoy had a good lead and might have escaped if he had not been so bent on getting back to the now safer Kentucky soil. In his flight, he took the most direct course across the field to the river and plunged in, thus giving his pursuers chance to close the gap between them. As he swam, bullets peppered the surface of the stream, but none hit their mark. He swam harder, past the mid point, and on toward the opposite bank.

His feet touched bottom, and he could feel the freedom for which he was struggling. But he remained low in the water as long as possible, even though the firing had died down. At the far bank, he reached for an overhanging root to give him support, got his hand around it and pulled his head and shoulders clear for the final leap to safety and escape. At that moment a rifle barked across the river, once, sharp and distinct, like the crack of a whip driving cattle back to pasture. The hand around the root tightened until the knuckles whitened, then jerked, loosened, and slid behind the head and shoulders out of sight into the water.

10

1887
Two Governors Take a Hand

AT THE START OF THE SUMMER OF '87, ATTENTION OF Kentuckians was turned suddenly to another war. In Rowan County, hostilities in the Martin-Tolliver feud, a conflict matching in bitterness and violence that of the Hatfields and McCoys, stirred anew. Temporary peace had been created by the voluntary exile of the two principal leaders on the opposing sides, but these men returned with warm weather, and soon their factions were restless and tense. Perhaps seventeen already had been killed, more than that wounded, several crippled. People in other sections of the state waited expectantly, confident more bloodshed was in the offing.

On the 7th of June, the town marshal at Morehead, Rowan County seat, went with a posse to a residence to arrest two members of the Martin faction. Bullets fired from inside the building killed the marshal and the posse killed the two men who fired them.

Two weeks later, the N. & W. solid train out of Norfolk, Virginia, was flagged, at 9:30 o'clock in the morning, a few miles east of Morehead. When it came to a stop, people running along the track told the conductor a bloody battle was going on in the town. The conductor waved the train into Martin's switch, two and a half miles short of the county seat, and sat there until someone informed him the fighting was over. It was then near noon.

A while later, when passengers stepped off the train at Morehead, they found the town under control of a 113-man sheriff's posse, made up of citizens who wanted to see the factions dispersed. This body of men had assembled in the dead of night, planted themselves at strategic points, and at dawn were waiting for a showdown. The hours since then had seen the worst. Up in the American House, principal hotel of the community, stretched the bodies of three Tollivers, leaders of the more troublesome faction, washed, dressed, and laid out for the public to see. Several men had been wounded in the furious battle that took place when the feudists refused to obey the orders of the posse, and these were getting treatment at private homes. Along the streets, people busied themselves in a search for cartridge shells as souvenirs, and up on the crest of the nearest mountain a blood-red flag fluttered in the breeze all day long.

Kentucky groaned over the unfavorable publicity brought on the state by this deadly fusillade at Morehead. Newspapers tried to shift the public attention to other subjects. Stated the *Courier-Journal* of September 1 with brave enthusiasm: "The mountainous section of the South, comprising Eastern Kentucky, Tennessee, Southwest Virginia and Western North Carolina, promises soon to be the scene of the greatest activity in railroad building ever known in the United States." A few days later, one of its emissaries to the hills wrote back: "Soon the neigh of the iron horse will startle the mountain solitudes, and long trains will flash to and fro like shuttles in the loom, weaving the woof of wealth and civilization."

One day toward the end of summer, Randolph McCoy sat beside the hearth in the main room of his cabin, pulling a greasy rag through the barrel of a rifle. Each time the cloth emerged, he refolded it in order to gauge the powder black on its surface. When he was satisfied with the gun's cleanliness, he swung the barrel toward the light of the open door, searching for specks, and the scene that shone through the hole at the end of the shiny cylinder gave him a nostalgic feeling that for a moment took his mind off his work.

He walked over to the door and leaned against the jamb. Before him the feud country of Eastern Kentucky roasted in the heat of a summer day. Foliage on the mountain slopes along Blackberry Fork of Pond Creek a few yards away barely stirred in the hot, dry air. It was a time of inactivity, of tasks laid aside to avoid the punishing rays of the sun, and this lethargy had spread to quarters other than daily routine. Throughout the whole of the hill section, along those ridges where the McCoys were plentiful and even across Tug Fork on the edge of West Virginia, in the region dominated by the Hatfields, there was peace. Not for months had a voice been raised in anger or a man gone down under a bullet fired by his neighbor.

Since the death of Jeff McCoy, the feudists seemed to have lost interests in their war. On both sides there were signs of fatigue, signs that some of the members were tiring of the ceaseless strain under which they lived, expecting a bullet to strike them any time they ventured from their homes. Some of this was stimulated by natural progression. In the young Hatfields in particular was developing a desire for education, for family improvement and individual betterment. Sons of both Devil 'Anse and Elias had their hearts set on such high professions as medicine and were studying hard. Elias' boy, Henry D., already was attending college.

This summer of 1887 it had got to the point at which members of the respective clans could cross the Tug without serious danger of battle. In time, a feeling of safety in enemy territory grew. Hatfields were seen in Pikeville in small groups, all openly armed, but apparently inapprehensive, while the McCoys sauntered just as frequently and just as confidently across the Tug in the opposite direction.

Only in two quarters was there reluctance to bury the hatchet. In Kentucky the battle flags still waved for the man who stood in the sunshine of his doorway, for his nephew, Bud McCoy, considered one of the most dangerous men in Pike County, and for Perry Cline, the lawyer nephew. And across the river, although they were more peacefully inclined than they had been in the past, Cap Hatfield and Jim Vance continued to broadcast throughout the region the supremacy of their clan.

These things were in the background of Randolph McCoy's mind as he leaned against the door and looked out on the green mountain side. It spread downward a few yards to the trail in front of the home; then turned almost straight upward and went out of sight before it reached the ridge scarcely half a mile away.

First glance at this hard-bitten, aging mountaineer would have put him down as a man who had no harm in his soul, no harsh thought in his mind. But folks knew that inside Randolph McCoy burned a fire of hatred that would die only when he died. In his eyes shone a look of sadness and resentment, a harsh bitterness that grew stronger when they turned in the direction of the huge grave, greening on a shelf of the mountain a few yards below the home. There lay the three sons the Hatfields had taken from him at one stroke.

McCoy looked to the left, down the sloping trail that led toward Pond Creek, distant three or four miles—hard miles, through thick forest and over rough terrain, rocky and terrible. Up the other way was Turkeytoe, on the ridge, and, from there on, the steep path downward to Blackberry Creek and the Tug and the Hatfields.

As Randolph McCoy basked in the sun, a gun barrel slid through the foliage of the mountain slope on the far side of the trail, steadied on the base branch of a tree, and belched forth a great volume of smoke and noise. A bullet whizzed with inches of the old man's head and splintered the door jamb.

For a moment he stood there, bewildered, unmoving, paralyzed. Then the meaning of the hole near his eyes brought him to life and, like an animal caught napping, he fell backward into the cabin, scrambled sidewise to his feet and slammed the heavy door. From a table he took his rifle and kneeled near the window. But across the way there was nothing but the green mountain side; no object to point out the whereabouts of an enemy; not even smoke from the powder that had hurled the bullet so near his head.

After a few minutes, Randolph McCoy put his gun in its rack above the door. Then he walked helplessly to the chair in which he had been sitting while cleaning the rifle and slumped into it heavily, a tired old man.

But his eyes were narrowed and his jaws were set. Tomorrow he would go to Pikeville to see Perry Cline.

On August 30 of that year of 1887, General Simon Bolivar Buckner,* the man who had surrendered Fort Donelson to Ulysses S. Grant, was inaugurated governor of Kentucky, replacing J. Proctor Knott. It was time of great rejoicing in certain sections of the state, especially at Pikeville. Perry Cline, stirred to new efforts by his brother-in-law's report of the bullet fired at him from ambush, saw in the change of administration a chance to avenge the McCoy murders. He had been laying plans for a long time. Early in the gubernatorial campaign, he had hurried to talk with Candidate Buckner. In return for assurance that every legal step to bring the Hatfields to justice would be taken at Frankfort, he, Perry Cline, lawyer, jailer, deputy sheriff, solon, and politician, would promise all the McCoy votes in Pike County and many votes from people who were not even affiliated with the clan. Buckner, grabbing at straws to gain political strength, gave his word.

The campaign activities of Perry Cline, champion of Randolph McCoy, were not lost to West Virginians in Logan County. They received word that the courthouse crowd at Pikeville was working at high pitch to see that the McCoys got revenge, that they were going about the effort with more determination than ever before, and that any night they might come storming across Tug Fork. Such a threat called for protection; so residents of Logan got busy and organized a band of vigilantes. This body of home guards was led by a Hatfield and operated under the fancy-sounding title of the Logan County Regulators. Shortly after their membership rolls were made up, they had cause to interfeere, for the public good, in a matter that in no way concerned the McCoys. This they handled with dispatch. It brought them favorable publicity, and it built up their morale and gave them pride in themselves.

* General Buckner was the father of the American general of the same name killed in the World War II battle for Okinawa, June 18, 1945.

Just before General Buckner took office, the leader of the vigilantes, signing himself president and secretary, wrote Cline this defiant letter, dated from Logan Court House August 29:

"My name is Nat Hatfield. I am not a single individual by a good many, and we do not live on Tug River, but we live all over this county. We have been told by men from your county that you and your men are fixing to invade this county for the purpose of taking the Hatfield boys, and now, sir, we, forty-nine in number at present, do notify you that if you come into this county to take or bother any of the Hatfields, we will follow you to hell or take your hide, and if any of the Hatfields are killed or bothered in any way, we will charge it up to you, and your hide will pay the penalty.

"We are not bothering you and neither are the Hatfields, and as long as you keep your hands off Logan County men, we will not do anything, but if you don't keep your hands off our men, there is not one of you will be left in six months. There is present at this time forty-nine of the men who regulated matters at this place a short time ago and we can get as many as we need in six hours. We have a habit of making one-horse lawyers keep their boots on and we have plenty of good strong rope left . . . and our hangman tied a knot for you and laid it quietly away until we see what you do. We have no particular pleasure in hanging dogs, but we know you and have counted the miles and marked the tree.

"Yours peacefully so long as you keep hands off, but with hell in our necks as soon as you make the *brake.*"

Cline ignored this letter and went on with his plans. The Hatfield indictments had been transferred from the Circuit Court to the new Criminal Court established by act of the General Assembly in 1884. These indictments Cline had managed to get the court clerk, G. W. Pinson, to copy for him, explaining that he wanted to use them to obtain from the governor a reward for the arrest of the West Virginians, as well as a requisition upon the governor of the adjoining state for their delivery to Kentucky. Pinson copied the indictments on September 6, and Cline immediately left with them for Frankfort, accompanied by two of his courthouse buddies—Lee Ferguson, county attorney, and Frank Phillips, deputy sheriff.

Governor Buckner kept his campaign promise. On the 10th, needled by the trio from Pikeville, he made requisition on Governor E. Willis (Windy) Wilson of West Virginia for the Hatfields and also offered a reward for their apprehension. This was the offer made for the arrest of Devil Anse:

"PROCLAMATION OF THE GOVERNOR
"$500 Reward
"Commonwealth of Kentucky
"Executive Department

"WHEREAS, it has been made known to me by Tobias Wagner, county judge of Pike County, that Anderson Hatfield stands charged in said county with the crime of murder and is now a fugitive from justice going at large; and the said judge having recommended that a reward be offered for the apprehension of said fugitive;

"Now, therefore, I, S. B. Buckner, Governor of the Commonwealth aforesaid, do hereby offer a reward of five hundred dollars for the apprehension of said Anderson Hatfield and his delivery to the jailer of Pike County.

"Dated at Frankfort, Sept. 10, 1887.

"S. B. BUCKNER, GOVERNOR.
"GEORGE M. ADAMS,
"SECRETARY OF STATE."

As his agent to receive the prisoners, assuming that they would be delivered by the state of West Virginia, the Governor appointed Deputy Sheriff Frank Phillips. This was done on the recommendation of Cline. In so doing, Buckner brought into his official service one of the most fearless and heartless men in the mountains, a cruel, quick-triggered officer just twenty-six years old. Phillips was a handsome little fellow, considered somewhat of a ladies' man, with ruddy cheeks, pleasant smile, black hair, dark complexion, and piercing black eyes the women considered "awfully pretty." He was handy with a six-shooter and loved an exhibition of firearms. His liquor he handled sometimes in too copious quantities, and it was on these occasions that the bully in him came out and he made some defenseless citizen dance in the streets while he peppered the ground at his feet with bullets. The deputy was widely recognized as a dangerous man.

Buckner's requisition remained in West Virginia just twenty days. It was September 30 when it came back, accompanied by a letter from Governor Wilson explaining that it would not be complied with unless an affidavit, as required by the statutes of the state, was attached.

On October 13, Buckner forwarded the requisition to Wilson again and, with it, the necessary affidavit. Three weeks went by without a reply. At the end of that period, Perry Cline kicked grammar and spelling to the winds and wrote the West Virginia governor a letter.

"Pikeville, Nov. 5, 1887.

"To His Excellency E. W. Wilson, Governor of W. Va.

"Dear Sir: Several days ago I had the required *affidavid* made out and sent with the *requision* for the Hatfields and have received no answer or have not heard from it since. Will your excellence be so kind as to inform as to the status of the case? I understand that Hatfields has *employd* counsel to prevent the warrant from being issued on the requisition, and that they have sent in a petition. They have and can make the people sign any kind of petition they want. I was *rased* near them men and know them; they are the worst band of *meroders* ever existed in the mountains, and have been in arms since the war; they will not live as citizens ought to; they stand indicted in the county in 4 bad cases of murder, and one of them which occurred about a year ago, and—last year's court was indicted for Ku-Kluxing and various other misdemeanor cases; in fact, we cannot hold our elections without them crossing the line and *rung* our citizens from the election grounds, and selling liquors in violation of the law, and these men has made good citizens leave their homes and forsake all they had, and refuse to let any person to even tend their lands. These facts are true and known to be true, both by the [word illegible] and Logan County, W. Va. I understand that they are trying to make it appear to you that we want them for the purpose of murdering them. That is—false as anything can be. We want peace and want the laws executed, & do not want our citizens butchered up like dogs, as these men is doing. This county has never [word illegible] any person, and *wont* do any harm to the Hatfields, except to see they get the law. We believe every person ought to answer for his conduct; that is the reason we ask the *requisision*. Our state has been compelled to *remain* [remand] these men and to ask the assistance of your excellency. I hope you will let me hear from this matter at your *earlest* convenience. You can find out all about myself by writing to any of our officers or to any of our state officers, and learn whether or not I am a man of my word. I want to know what has been done as soon as your excellency can let me know. Pleace excuse this letter, as I deem it of great importance.

"Yours, etc.,

"P. A. CLINE."

Cline's information that the Hatfields had taken action to prevent the requisition from being honored was correct. The West Virginians were doing all within their power to block the move. Supported by legal counsel, they were swamping the West Virginia governor's office with petitions, affidavits, and other material designed to convince him that justice was on their side. Moreover, they made it plain that, to deliver them to Frank Phillips for return to Pikeville, where the McCoys were in force, would be like leading lambs to slaughter. And while they were cautioning His Excellency in this respect, they also reminded him that the McCoys had never been punished for felonies committed by them in West Virginia.

The letter embracing the wholesale condemnation of the Hatfields got no answer from Wilson. On November 21, Henry S. Walker, Secretary of State for West Virginia, wrote the lawyer that the requisition had been honored as to all persons named except Elias Hatfield and Andrew Varney. These two men, he revealed, had proved to the satisfaction of Governor Wilson that they were in no wise connected with the murder for which they were indicted; that, according to evidence produced, they were miles away from the scene at the time of the McCoy killings. He advised that warrants for the other eighteen would be issued upon receipt of $54, the fees provided by law.

Cline waited no longer. By virtue of his influence and the political strings at his command, he got an order from the Pike County court having jurisdiction over the indictments. Under this order, bench warrants were issued for the arrest of each of the Hatfields listed in the indictments and were placed in the hands of the sheriff for service.

Within a week, Sheriff Basil Hatfield, one-time judge, and Perry Cline, acting as deputy sheriff, made this entry beside their names on the books of Pike County Criminal Court: "Executed the within warrant upon Selkirk McCoy by arresting him and delivering him, together with a copy of this B. warrant, to the jailer of Pike County this the 12th day of December, 1887."

It is odd that the first member of the Hatfield clan to be arrested in this wholesale drive to bring them to trial was a McCoy. Frank Phillips and a posse had gone across into West Virginia and gathered up Selkirk without the slightest warning. He it was who had turned traitor at the hog trial; he it was who had wedded a Hatfield and gone over to their side of the war. His name quite naturally came first to the minds of the McCoy adherents. At Pikeville, they slapped him in the hoosegow and, hours later, presented him with a bench warrant.

A day or two afterward, Governor Wilson received a letter from Frank Phillips. It was written on stationery with this letterhead: "Office of Perry A. Cline, Attorney and Counselor at Law, Office Back of Courthouse, Pikeville, Ky." The Governor assumed it was in the handwriting of Cline. It read:

"Dear Sir: Inclosed please find fifteen dollars to pay *feese* due your office upon the issue of state warrants for the following named *Parteys,* wan't [warrant] for Anderson Hatfield, Johnson Hatfield, Cap Hatfield, Daniel Whitt, Albert McCoy [Kirk's *sone*]. Please send warrant to this *Place* to Frank Phillips, the agent appointed by the governor of Kentucky. As to Elias Hatfield and Andy Varney, we do not care for. Did not intend to intercept them. Some of the *Parteys* is dead and sone *gon* and left the *contery*. The reason they all was named in the requisition *Was* they *Were* all jointly indicted and [word illegible] *Just Copyed* the indictment so if we want any others of the *Parteys* we will send for the warrants *heare* after.

"Yours *respectly*,
"FRANK PHILLIPS."

In a few days, a snappy letter, somewhat angry in tone, arrived at Pikeville addressed to "Frank Phillips, Esq." It was dated from Charleston, West Virginia, December 17 and was signed by Governor Wilson. "Yours of the 13th inst.," it stated, "enclosing fifteen dollars for fees in the matter of a requisition for Hatfields and others, rece'd. Information has come to me that certain parties have received a large sum of money from parties named in the requisition. The money for fees should be sent to the secretary of state—not to me. I herewith return the fifteen dollars, and shall make enquiry into this matter. Requisitions and warrants thereon are issued to subserve the ends of justice and for no other purpose."

Wilson's fury was occasioned by a well-founded report that had come to him only a few days before. Through petition, letter, and word of mouth, he had heard that Perry Cline, in his efforts to bring the Hatfields to justice, had his own financial interests at heart. It was said he had induced Buckner to offer rewards for the arrest of the West Virginians and then had extorted money from them on a promise that he would get the Kentucky governor off their necks. Some important men in Pike County were among Wilson's informers. Still later he heard that the Hatfields had sent an attorney to Governor Buckner to promise that they would stay out of his state if he would withdraw the requisitions and that this offer had been indorsed by Cline.

On December 22, A. J. Auxier, Pike County attorney, signed an important affidavit. It said he had been employed as counsel for some of the parties indicted in three cases for the murder of the McCoys. After the rewards and requisitions were offered for the arrest of Anderson Hatfield and others, it further stated, some money was left in his hands to pay fees and expenses connected with an effort to get Governor Buckner to withdraw the rewards. Out of this money, Cline was to have, as he remembered, $225—the amount he claimed had been spent by him in procuring the rewards and requisitions—if he would recommend the withdrawal. "Mr. Cline wrote to the secretary of state recommending the same on conditions, which was taken to the secretary and delivered to him," Auxier related.

This affidavit established the fact that a sum of money had changed hands. Next was added sworn assurance from G. W. Pinson, clerk of the court, that he had copied the indictments so that Cline could obtain from the Governor of Kentucky a reward for capture of the Hatfields and a requisition for their arrest and delivery. Then came this statement made on oath by Johnson Hatfield before John A. Sheppard, notary public for Logan County, West Virginia:

"That he is acquainted with the parties who stand indicted in the Criminal Court of Pike County, Ky., for the murder of the McCoys; that during the month of December, 1887, he, together with A. J. Auxier and James York, who were employed counsel for the parties so indicted, made a verbal agreement with one P. A. Cline, an attorney-at-law at Pike C. H., Ky., which was about as follows:

"Said Cline, upon his part, agreed that if Anderson Hatfield et al., who stood indicted as aforesaid, would deposit with A. J. Auxier the sum of $225, to be paid him (Cline) if he succeeded in his undertaking, that he would recommend to and use all his influence with the Governor of Kentucky to have him take no further steps for the arrest of the said parties indicted as aforesaid; and this affiant, upon the part of the said Anderson Hatfield et al., agreed and did deposit with said Auxier the said sum of $225, to be paid said Cline if he succeeded in getting the Governor to take no further steps for the arrest of the said parties. Said Cline claimed that he had spent $225 in procuring rewards and a requisition upon the Governor of West Virginia for the arrest of the said Anderson Hatfield et al.

"This affiant further states that it was well understood at the time of the making of said agreement by all parties interested that the said Cline had not spent any such sum of money in the manner stated by him, but that it was only an excuse for him to take shelter behind."

The year 1887 came to a close with the Hatfield-McCoy feud on the brink of its worst stage of killings. It still had attracted virtually no attention in the newspapers of the country, but it had at last made its way into the official records at Frankfort, largely because of the efforts of Perry Cline, whether he did so to reap rewards from the Governor and extort money from the Hatfields, or whether he did so with the honest intention of helping his brother-in-law obtain legal retribution for the grievances brought upon his family. On the last day of the year, the press of the state carried as its foremost news of the moment the first message of Simon Bolivar Buckner, delivered before the General Assembly. "A straightforward, manly, deliberate document," characterized the editors, a statement with "a grateful sound to those who have long witnessed the unchecked deeds of lawless men in certain sections of Kentucky and mourned because means of bringing them to justice were useless in the hands of incapable or unwilling officials."

Buckner had voiced strong disapproval of the behavior in the mountain counties. Numerous acts of violence and defiance of law in this section, he reminded, gave color to the prevailing belief that Kentuckians were not law-abiding people. This circumstance must end, he declared, adding: "As the reputation of a community is often popularly judged by the conduct of its worst elements, so likewise is the law-abiding character of the people of Kentucky estimated by others, in a great measure, not from the general disposition of its citizens to obey the laws, but from the violent conduct of comparatively a few lawless individuals. If, from neglect or inefficiency, we fail to repress this lawlessness, or to bring the offenders to justice, we have no right to complain of the fasle estimation in which we are held by the people of other states."

Buckner's message was received with cheers by the people outside of Eastern Kentucky. They read it over and prided themselves on having at last a governor who had no hesitancy about removing a wrong. But in the mountains it created no effect at all, not even a slight qualm. The Hatfields at the moment were madder than they had been since August, '82.

11

1888
Fire and Murder Mixed

THE FIRST DAY OF '88 DAWNED CLEAR AND COLD, WITH air briskly sharp and invigorating. Ridges in all directions looked skinned and barren, shorn of their foliage except for an occasion fir or pine. Along the slopes trees fraternized in their nudity and swayed lonesomely in the clutches of the freezing breezes. They had won a slanting victory over the wind, and at their feet lay the toll of their triumph—summer raiment, discarded, forgotten, browned by frost, untóuched except by feet of wild animals and birds or nuts dropped from the paws of ravenous and eager squirrels. For better or worse, nature was caught with her curtains down.

That morning, smoke climbed early from the Hatfield chimneys, indicating the birth of a busy day. It was Sunday and New Year's, a time for worship, but the West Virginians had other things in mind, other respects to pay. Devil Anse, Jim Vance, and Cap Hatfield put their heads together soon after dawn, and in a short while messengers were spreading the word that the clan was gathering.

Recruits were hard to find. News of the raid the Kentuckians had made to capture Selkirk McCoy had spread, and the more cautious clansmen, especially those drawn into the trouble by family ties rather than personal animosity, were hiding out.

One of the messengers that day was Johnse Hatfield, enjoying temporary marital freedom because of a quarrel with Nancy and her subsequent disappearance from home. Another was Tom Chambers, alias Mitchell, nicknamed "Guerrilla." These two made a wide circuit of the countryside, spurred on by thoughts of the task ahead. Their first stop was Guyandotte River, where they found the undevout Ellison Mounts busy making repairs on his mother's home. Mounts' impiety was pardonable. He was looked upon by his neighbors as a halfwit, a person whose intelligence had been stunted at some time during the early part of his twenty-four years. But what he lacked in brains he made up for in brawn. He stood better than six feet, a little over 180 pounds of muscle made hard by the rough life of the mountains. There had never been the slightest secrecy to the bastardy associated with his origin and to the fact that his father was a Hatfield. Instead, secrecy and conflicting rumors had been confined to the identification of the particular Hatfield who had impregnated the mother. Some said it was Ellison, thought to be the source also of the son's name; others that it was Wall, who, after all, was admittedly the most prolific member of the family. At any rate, whether the given name came from father or uncle, it was little in use. A head of light blond hair had early in life earned for this offspring the nickname "Cotton Top."

Johnse and Mitchell, imbued with the spirit of their enterprise, put the house repairer through a quick bill of sale. The told him first of all that Cap Hatfield had sent for him. Cap was a hero to the dull-witted Cotton Top, and they knew that use of his name would be persuasive. But Mounts was slow to react; so they reminded him that the Kentucky people already had offered $500 reward for him and that the best thing he could do to save his neck would be to stand in with the Hatfields. The dullard threw down his hammer and reached for his gun.

At Dow Steele's, on Island Creek, they met Devil Anse and his sons, Cap and Bob. The latter was little more than a youth, just at the age at which he could take part in the feud. In the family Bible his name was listed as Robert E. Lee Hatfield.

From Stelle's, they went on to the homes of Henry Vance, Floyd Hatfield, and other factionalists, arriving finally at the cabin of old Jim Vance.* There they stayed for a while, waiting for Anse, Cap, and Vance to finish a council of war held off to one side. When it was over, the program for the day was laid out: some of the Kentucky people must be eliminated.

The group set their minds on the journey into enemy territory. All except one expressed willingness to go. The one who held back was Devil Anse. Without apology, he announced to his followers that he was sick, too much so to make the trip, and that he was turning over command of the party to Jim Vance.

Standing beside his nephew, the grizzled Vance immediately assumed leadership. He summoned the others more closely about him. There were only eight—Cap, Johnse, Bob, and Elliott Hatfield, the last of these the son of the ill-fated Ellison and newly admitted to the feud ranks; Chambers, Mounts, Charles Gillespie, and French (Doc) Ellis. The man whose presence excited the most interest was Johnse. It was common gossip around the neighborhood that he and Nancy were not getting along, that they quarreled constantly, even though one child had been born of their wedlock. Friends knew that this marriage could not last; that, whether Nancy had become Johnse's wife through love or convenience, his attraction to her had disappeared. Latest reports said she was making eyes at Frank Phillips, Eastern Kentucky's newest hero.

With the other men gathered around him, Vance raised his arms above his head. "May hell be my heaven," he said solemnly and portentously, "I will kill the man that goes back on me tonight, if powder will burn."†

The tiny band moved up the Tug, heavy with arms. Between four and five o'clock in the afternoon, they arrived at Cap Hatfield's cabin and stopped for food. It got dark early these days and the gloom of the mountain hollows was settling fast. While this was a circumstance

* The route they followed was recorded fully in a confession made later by Ellison Mounts.

† Ellison Mounts and Cap Hatfield at later dates both quoted this statement as made by Jim Vance, on this occasion.

that fitted in with their enterprise, offering better concealment, they looked toward the crest of the ridges with apprehension. The moon had been full the night before. It meant they would have to travel in the shadows and keep their heads down.

It was well after dark when the band started off again, heading for the home of Amos Hatfield, across from the mouth of Peter Creek. There they swung directly down to the bank of the Tug, rode into the water and came out on the Kentucky side near the mouth of Pounding Mill Branch, went on up it and over the ridge to Peter Branch, and down that to Blackberry Creek, following almost the indentical route taken by Wall Hatfield and the Mahons the night Ellison Hatfield was stabbed. Once on Blackberry, they followed the stream up to Jerry Hatfield's and the election site, swung to the right up Hatfield Branch to the crest of the mountain, and down Blackberry Fork of Pond Creek on the other side. Only a mile or so down the steep trail, they halted until they could tie their horses and until Cap, Johnse, and Vance could put on masks. Randolph McCoy's cabin was only a few yards away, up to the left, atop a shelf on a hillside heavy with trees.

Before they closed in, Vance told each man where to go and what to do. The McCoy home was a twin cabin affair, with a roofed passageway connecting the two parts of the structure. The main part, or big house as it was called, was a story and a half high, while the other, used as a kitchen and bedroom, was only a single story. Cap and Mounts were assigned to the back door of the kitchen, and Bob and Elliott Hatfield to the kitchen door opening on the passageway. Chambers, Gillespie, and Ellis were told to surround the front of the big house, and Vance said he and Johnse would watch the other door in that part of the building.

Before they separated Vance impressed upon the group the importance of the undertaking. If Randolph and Calvin McCoy were out of the way, the last material witness who could speak up against the men who had taken part in the murders back in '82 would be removed. There could be no conviction of any of the Hatfields, even if they at some time were arrested.

"All of us have become tired o' dodgin' th' officers o'

th' law," reminded Vance. "We wanna be able t' sleep at home with better bedfellows than Winchester rifles. An' we wouldn't mind takin' off our boots now'n then when we go t' bed."

Cap and Johnse spoke up in approval.

Some of the men moved to go, but Vance held them. One more thing:

"You gotta be keerful an' not let the men escape in women's clothes."

They made the remainder of the distance in single file. As they neared the edge of the clearing around the home, they saw the cabin, standing dark and throwing a shadow down the slope of the mountain. Windows were black. On the roof, frost lay white and heavy, sparkling like a million diamonds in the white moonlight.

The men stole to their positions, moving silently. It was half past ten o'clock.

They waited until Jim Vance got in place. They saw the big man straighten and heard his voice boom toward the cabin.

"Come out, you McCoys, an' surrender as prisoners o' war!"

For close to a minute the West Virginians stood by in silence, listening for the answer from within. It did not come, and from around the kitchen Cap called in a whisper:

"Are they comin' out?"

There still was no response from inside. Then Cap, his trigger finger itching, said in a louder tone:

"Goddamn it, fire it! Fire it!"

Johnse could hold in no longer. He let go with his rifle at the nearest doorway. This was a breach of plans, of Jim Vance's instructions. It was understood the shooting would not start until the old man gave the word.

Other guns followed in quick succession, aimed at the doors of the main part of the house. The sound of falling glass was added as someone turned his aim toward a window. Now came the answer from within—the blinding flare of mountain rifles barking back from the openings.

The McCoys had been preparing for action. At the first shout from outside, Calvin McCoy, sleeping upstairs in the main part of the cabin, put on his trousers and suspenders and went down to the bed of his parents directly below. His hand first touched his mother lying in the dark, and he patted her and told her to lie still or they would all be killed. Then came the warning from outside that the cabin was to be fired. He pulled out a trunk, got his gun and cartridges, and climbed back up the ladder to the loft.

The Hatfields held close to the shadows. They heard Calvin go upstairs, calling back directions to his mother and father as he climbed. It was a few seconds later before his gun blasted out defiantly from above. One of the attackers grabbed himself in pain. It was Johnse, wounded in the top of the right shoulder with bird shot.

Jim Vance ran toward the house from a side on which there were no openings. He got up close, next to some cotton drying against the building. He lit a match. The cotton blazed up, and he jerked it loose, tore it into two pieces, placing one in a joist hole and the other against the shutter of the door. Then he fired two shots through the portal.

Tom Chambers saw what Vance had done. It gave him an idea. He found a pine knot at the woodpile behind the kitchen and lit it. The fat of the knot blazed up, sputtering and sizzling. With this in hand, he ran toward the kitchen, leaped upon a pile of logs stacked against the house and from there to the roof. He worked his way over, across the top of the passageway, to the big house, and tried to pry a shingle loose to create a good place for the blazing brand. At that moment, a gun went off directly below him, blowing a hole in the shingles and blinding him. One hand hung limply at his side, and he suddenly realized it was numb. He held it up. In the glow of the pine knot he could see three fingers were missing. He dropped the torch, rolled off to the ground, his body striking with a heavy thud, and ran. The pine knot rolled behind him, a meteor on the dark side of the house, landed at the base of the log wall, and lay there flickering, helpless and harmless.

Calvin McCoy called to his sisters in the kitchen: "Josephine! Allifair! Addie! Go outdoors an' put out thet foire!"

Vance called out, too. "Boys, if they come out, damn 'em, shoot 'em!"

From somewhere was thrown a bucket of water, aimed at the fire licking at the door shutter. The blaze faltered and flickered, but continued to burn.

"That's all the water!" a woman screamed.

"Use the buttermilk in the churn by the hearth!" yelled Calvin.

The buttermilk followed, with no better results.

At that moment, a girl in night dress opened the door of the kitchen. She spied the masks over the faces of some of the attackers.

"Cap Hatfield," she yelled, "I heered your voice. I know you're here!"

Cap and Johnse saw her simultaneously and shouted to Mounts, closest to her at the time.

"Damn her, kill her!"

Cotton Top raised his rifle and fired. The girl staggered and fell in the doorway.

Josephine called from inside.

"Are you hurt?"

The wounded girl muttered something the men in the shadows could not understand. But one of the McCoys on the inside heard and answered.

"Farewell, sister!"

Calvin McCoy seemed to sense that something tragic had taken place.

"Has anybody been hurt?" he called.

Josephine screamed back. "They kilt Allifair!"

The back door to the big house opened and out rushed Sarah McCoy, stooped over, hair flying loose. Jim Vance, crouching in the safety of the passageway, saw her and yelled for her to go back, raising his rifle as if to shoot her. But Sarah saw that the gun had the wrongend turned toward her and kept going. Vance lunged forward, striking her with the butt of the weapon. It caught her in the side and sent her reeling to the ground. For a moment she lay stunned; then, groaning and crying, raised herself up on her hands and knees and tried to crawl to the prostrate body of her daughter.

"For the Lord's sake, let me go to my girl!" she cried. "Oh, she's dead. For the love of the Lord let me go to her!"

She put out her hand. She could almost touch the feet of her daughter, and she could see the blood from Allifair's wound running down from the sill of the door in which she had fallen.

Johnse was standing against the wall of the kitchen, close to the logs. He reached out with his revolver in the hand unaffected by the shoulder wound and clubbed her on the head. The revolver struck with resounding thud against the skull of the woman and she dropped, face down, and lay as motionless as a felled tree.

The fire was spreading along the front and one side of the big house, roaring as it lapped at the seasoned logs. On the inside, Calvin McCoy gagged with smoke and realized the situation was hopeless. He felt for the ladder and dropped down beside his father.

"Pa, I'm gonna run fer it. I'll git out next the corn house an' then hold 'em off whilst you run past 'em."

He grabbed a box of shells from a table, turned, took two long strides to the door and was gone.

Randolph McCoy held his breath. He heard his son's boots on the frozen ground outside, and then they were drowned out by the shouts of the Hatfields. A fusillade of gunfire followed. There were hurrying feet, after which more yelling and loud talk came from the direction of the corn house. The father grabbed up gun and cartridges and ducked out through the smoke.

Shortly afterward, the Hatfields left the scene. They were dejected, for they realized trouble would come out of what they had done. One of the men they had intended to silence had been killed, but the other—old Randolph McCoy—was off hiding somewhere in the woods, free to cry anew for vengeance. Johnse's impulsiveness in firing that first shot was blamed largely for the failure.

Back where their horses were tied, they found that Charley Gillespie's mount had broken loose and gone home. They swung into their saddles, with Gillespie riding behind Mounts (who fainted from loss of blood before the ride was over) and headed on up the trail toward the ridge. Behind they could see the reflection from the burning cabin on the tops of the trees, and faintly to them came the voices of the McCoy girls crying for help. Mixed with the noise was the childish wail of young Cora, whose father, Tolbert, had died with his brothers in '82.

The riders spurred on, impatient to get away. Before they reached the ridge, Vance cautioned them to be quiet. They were nearing the home of Aly Farley. But their precautions were wasted. Farley's wife, Nancy Jane Burns, was awake and watched the cavalcade as it passed. She could see their guns glistening in the moonlight and she wondered what they were up to. It had been whispered about in recent weeks that the Hatfield-McCoy trouble was breaking out anew.

12

1888
The McCoys Turn to Kidnapping

PIKEVILLE HAS NEVER FORGOTTEN THE PITIFUL GROUP OF refugees who straggled into town from the Tug the second day of '88. The weather was bitterly cold, and the misery that emanated from the travelers was augmented by the somberness of the wintry skies. Riding in front were Randolph McCoy and his son Jim. Jim had hurried over from his own home as soon as he heard of the disaster. Behind the men rolled a wagon in which lay the battered form of Sarah McCoy. She was tended by her weeping daughters, including Rose Anne, who had been visiting a few miles down the hollow at the time of the attack. Back on the mountain slope, beside the ashes of the cabin, they had left the bodies of Calvin and Allifair, to be buried by neighbors near the triple grave opened for their brothers six years before.

As details of the house burning were unfolded, the town stirred with indignation. Relatives took the stricken family into their homes, and to them soon came gifts of food and clothing. The women were silent, and this the townspeople understood. It was the way of the mountains; females were brought up to bear the burdens and sorrows of a primitive life. But the wails of the father were uncontrolled. He moved about the streets, a broken old man, talking freely of the attack, cursing the Hatfields, and recalling that, when he returned in his night clothes to the home site, after spending the rest of the night concealed in a neighbor's pigsty, he had found his wife's bloody hair frozen to the ground. The thought drove him to fury.

It was the following week-end before the newspapers heard of the tragedy. Sunday editions blazoned the story, with certain erroneous details:

"A letter has been received by Senator A. H. Stewart from a friend in Pikeville, Ky., giving account of a terrible tragedy in Pike County on January 1. It appears that in 1882 parties, led by a man named Hatfield, abducted three boys named McCoy and conveyed them to West Virginia. A reward was offered for the arrest of the Hatfield party, and one of the gang was captured, who is now in the Pike County jail. On Sunday last others of the same party went to the residence of Randolph McCoy, in Pike County, and killed his wife, mother of the three boys mentioned, and his son; also set fire to the house, which, with its contents, was entirely consumed.

"Two little girls, daughters of McCoy, escaped and succeeded in recovering the dead bodies from the flames. McCoy escaped in his night clothes under fire of the murderers, shooting as he went, but without effect so far as ascertained.

"The Pikeville jail is strongly guarded, but fears were entertained at the hour of writing that an attempt would be made to release the member of the gang confined there."

Label headlines ranged all the way from "A MURDEROUS GANG" to "A TERRIBLE STORY." Newspapers were positive that Sarah McCoy was going to die, and they freely predicted her death. But they held little hope for bringing the Hatfields to justice.

"There are rewards aggregating $2,700 offered by the state of Kentucky for the arrest of the Hatfields and their delivery to the jailer of Pike County for the murder of the three McCoy boys," reminded a news article from Catlettsburg, "but no one seems anxious to make the attempt to take them, as they are strongly barricaded in the wilds of West Virginia. One of their number constantly stands guard, and they defy the authorities, but retributive justice is now likely to speedily follow, as their last acts have stirred up that whole section. This gang of outlaws has killed Mr. McCoy's wife, three of his sons and one daughter, besides burning his house, leaving only three daughters; but, if the Hatfields are taken, dead or alive, the men who undertake the job will experience some fun, as this set of West Virginia toughs is a determined and desperate band."

Frank Phillips was the sort of man who liked the fun this story mentioned. On Monday, posing as a "state agent" with full authority for what he was doing, he led a posse across the Tug in search of Hatfields to keep company with Selkirk McCoy.

The Hatfields were not expecting him. They were more concerned at the moment with the reaction of Simon Bolivar Buckner, for only a few days after the incident those who had taken part in the house burning went to the home of Harve Duty to make up alibis which could be sent "Windy" Wilson by affidavit and induce him to refuse the requisitions from Kentucky. Joe Simpkins, justice of the peace, was present, and they all took oath as to their whereabouts at the time the McCoy cabin went up in flames. According to their accounts, not one of them was within miles of the blazing house on New Year's night.

Phillips and his posse reached West Virginia at a time when the two worst enemies of the McCoys—Cap Hatfield and Jim Vance—were together. The two leaders had left others of the clan on Guyandotte River the day before and had walked to Vance's home. On the way, they bagged two coons and brought them along for Jim's wife to cook.

Next day they proceeded with plans to go on to Cap's home, but delayed their departure to allow Vance to recover from certain gastronomic troubles; the coon meat he had eaten the night before had upset his stomach. It was early afternoon before they got started, despite Jim's bellyache, and, when they were ready to leave the house, his wife decided to accompany them.

By the time they began the ascent of Thacker Mountain, Vance was in severe pain and also in a foul humor. Cap tarried along the trail with him, but Mary Vance, knowing the mood of her mate and preferring not to test it, walked ahead.

The climb was steep and rocky, and progress was slow. Further delay was occasioned by the frequent halts

Vance demanded to help him bear the torture of his rebellious midriff. Near the crest of the mountain, they suddenly heard Mrs. Vance running back down the path. She shouted before she got to them: "They's a-comin'—Frank Phillips an' his men. I seen a whole passel o' 'em on t'other side o' th' mountin!"

She reached them and stopped, breathless. Her husband motioned her on down the path.

"I don't feel like runnin'," he said. "I'm a-goin' t' fight."

He and Cap crawled behind rocks and waited, their guns ready for action. Soon they heard Phillips and his posse advancing cautiously down the mountain slope.

The first bullets sang out through the trees. Then there was a fusillade from both sides. Jim and Cap were shooting rapidly, hoping to give a false impression of strength. But Phillips was too much of a mountain fighter to be fooled. He directed his men in a flank movement. They spread out in a fan-shaped line and closed in, slowly, carefully. Presently one of them got a bead on Vance and sent toward the grizzled veteran a bullet that found its mark.

Vance grabbed his stomach. On his face was agony different from that caused by the coon meat. He knew the seriousness of his wound and yelled to his younger companion.

"Git, Cap! Git while ye can!"

Cap turned, stooping low behind the rocks, and ran off down the mountain.

Phillips and his posse respected the prowess of Jim Vance, even as a dying man. It was several minutes before they worked up close enough to make sure he had been finished. He was lying on his back, his eyes closed, and they could see his right forefinger jerking feebly against the trigger of his rifle. The deputy sheriff took no chances. He walked up and, at close range, fired a bullet into the veteran's head.

The *Huntington Advertiser* got coverage on the Phillips raid through its correspondent at Catlettsburg. Details were combed from passengers and crewmen on boats coming down the Big Sandy, which meant that they had passed through several hands before they reached the reporter. By Wednesday, this story, complete with prevarications and erroneous information, could be assembled:

"The war of extermination goes bravely on between the McCoys of Pike County, Kentucky, and the Hatfields of Logan County, West Virginia. As soon as the last sad rites of the recent butchery were over, the McCoys organized a posse and visited the Hatfield settlement in West Virginia for the purpose of annihilating the gang. The posse visited the Hatfiled house and, finding no one at home, they repaired to the woods to meditate for a few moments. Their secrecy was of short duration, for the Hatfield gang was soon upon them, and a regular war ensued.

"After the smoke of battle had cleared, it was found that the Hatfield party was badly worsted, and three of their number were killed, while none of the McCoy posse were hurt. Those known to be killed were Johnson Hatfield, Thomas Chambers and James Vance. Vance was shot seven times. Satisfied with their day's work, the McCoy posse returned to their settlement to await developments. Vance has killed several men in the McCoy neighborhood, and had to leave in consequence. He has been a bold, daring, desperate fellow. The authorities are powerless, and the war will doubtless be waged until one side or the other is completely exterminated, as no one in authority seems to care. . . . The greatest excitement prevails in the neighborhood, and the end is not yet, as there is bad blood on both sides."

While the newspapers were circulating this story, Phillips was making more raids into West Virginia. Three days in succession he crossed the Tug with a large posse, and each time he came back with additional prisoners to await trial in the Pikeville jail beside Selkirk McCoy.

Little sleeping was done on either side of the river. The Kentucky press, fearing reprisal, warned that the Hatfields might swoop down at any hour to free the members of their clan, burn the town of Pikeville, and kill the people who got in their way. "The Hatfields are known to be well organized," it was announced. "Winchester rifles are in great demand and command good prices. . . . You may listen for music from that quarter now at any time."

The music came from the direction of Logan Court House and reached its crescendo at the mouth of Grapevine Creek. That point was the meeting place on January 19 of a band of eighteen men under Phillips, still beating the bushes in search of West Virginia clansmen, and a thirteen-man Logan County force, led by Constable J. R. Thompson and armed with warrants for the arrest of the slayers of Jim Vance. The two groups came upon each other unexpectedly. A woman, standing in the middle of the road, first detected the approach of the Kentuckians and gave an alarm that alerted both sides.

Riding with Phillips were a number of McCoys; with Thompson, a number of Hatfields. The shooting became fierce as the bands spread out in skirmish formation, a part of them behind a rock fence. Men on both sides were wounded. Cap Hatfield got a quick bead on Bud McCoy and blazed away, wounding him. Bill Dempsey, youthful member of Thompson's posse, went down with a shattered leg. Devil Anse Hatfield, also in the group, gave this report, obviously paraphrased, of Dempsey's fate:

"Dempsey crawled into a shuck pen with his broken limb and was crying for water when Dave Stratton, James McCoy, Sam Miller, Frank Phillips and two other men came up. They began to abuse the wounded man. He told them he was summoned by the sheriff as a guard, and had to pursue them. Frank Phillips walked up close to where he was lying, drew his revolver and shot his brains out with one shot. . . ."

It was days before details of this encounter, identified as the battle of Grapevine Creek, reached other sections of Kentucky and West Virginia. John B. Floyd, state senator from Logan and secretary to Governor Wilson, got his information through a letter that came to his desk at Charleston from a friend back home and was later published in the *Cincinnati Enquirer*, January 30. His informer reported that "the hilltops have not been made to ring so since the year 1865." He also related that the Kentuckians had taken a silk handkerchief and $2.50 from Dempsey's pocket. When they prepared to return to Kentucky, he reported, they gathered up a feeble-minded youth near the scene of batle and took him across the Tug to question him regarding the rumored death of Johnse Hatfield. This boy had on an overcoat that caught their attention. He told them it had been left on the battlefield by one of Thompson's posse, but they took it away from him, claiming that it was one they had shot at the day before and, by God, were entitled to wear.

Floyd's informer had still other news. It had come to him on good authority, he wrote, that the Kentuckians as they left the battle scene fired at the wife of French Ellis, one of the Hatfield feudists, while she stood in the doorway of her home. They also for some time past, he charged, had prevented the tri-weekly mail from passing between Pikeville and Logan.

The tone of the letter received by Floyd in no way exaggerated the excitement along the Tug. Pike County heard that the Hatfields had warned people on the Kentucky side of the river that they proposed to kill them and burn their property, and it was widely rumored that the West Virginians were organizing for such a raid. The jail at Pikeville was surrounded by a strong guard night and day. Even the town itself looked to its security. Each evening as dark approached, pickets went out in all directions to remain on duty until dawn.

Effects of this wholesale scare were felt at Catlettsburg, the shopping center down at the mouth of the Big Sandy. On the 24th, a group of men from Pike County came into town and bought sixteen Winchester rifles, .38- and .44-caliber, all they could find at the hardware store. They trailed by a day or two a Hatfield delegation that had confined its purchases to ammunition. "This, coupled with the fact that the county judge and county attorney of Pike County have gone to Frankfort in quest of arms," reported the *Cincinnati Enquirer* on January 25, "looks very much like the war is on in earnest and that the wilds of West Virginia will ring with music during the coming week. Almost everybody is up in arms in the two counties named above, and the excitement increases daily. There is big fun ahead."

Newspapers of both states beat the war drums with fury. They were strongly partisan, those in West Virginia championing the Hatfields, those in Kentucky the McCoys. The pro-Hatfield press was not satisfied with stark and simple murder; it dressed up the killings with theft and arson and all the other trimmings connected with villainy and ruffianism. It was said that after the death of Jim Vance his assassins shook hands over his body. Moreover, Randolph McCoy was reported to have sent Cap Hatfield word that he intended to kill him, cut out a piexe of his flesh, and broil and eat it.

Occasionally an editor listened with a grain of salt to the many rumors of ferocity and desperation. One West Virginia journalist wrote in the *Wheeling Intelligencer* of January 25 that "if one-half the stories of brutality and murder are true, the case would seem to warrant the authorities of both states in taking hold and ending the trouble, even if it is necessary to call the state troops into action." On the other hand, if they were not true, he added, then the enterprising newspaper correspondents guilty of bringing reproach upon the good name and fame of the state should be called to account in some way.

Meanwhile the raids of Frank Phillips, although staged without the formality of proper official dictation, had stunned the Hatfields rather than incited them to repeated atrocities. Their confidence in their impregnability suddenly waned. Behind the bars at Pikeville by this time rested nine of their members, all "kidnapped" by the deputy sheriff and his posse made up largely of McCoys. Most important of the prisoners was Wall Hatfield, the justice of the peace. Others were Tom (Guerrilla) Chambers, alias Mitchell, his hand still bound as a result of the gunshot wound he received New Year's night; Andrew Varney; Selkirk McCoy, and his son L. S.; Moses Christian and three Mahon brothers, Sam, D. D. (Dock), and Plyant.

Perhaps the most complacent of the group behind bars was Wall. Only a few days earlier, he had written letters to Jim McCoy and Frank Phillips, telling them he wanted to surrender and would be found at his home. He advised them further, however, that he would rather not be taken until just before court convened.

But no matter how willingly the prisoners had come into the hands of the law, Kentucky authorities said they were there to stay. To this adamant attiude, West Virginia replied by offering rewards for the capture of Phillips and members of his posse—all twenty-two of them.

13

1888 West Virginia Files Suit

WORD PASSED ALONG THE BIG SANDY THE 24TH OF January that the steamer *Frank Preston* was coming down stream with a Frankfort-bound delegation from Pikeville. Catlettsburg identified the emissaries as Judge Tobias Wagner and County Attorney Lee Ferguson, two officials who had had a hand in stimulating action at the state capital back in the early fall. They were on their way to lay the case again before Governor Buckner and to ask him for arms with which to protect themselves and their property.

Pike County's spokesmen got to Buckner's offices only a few hours before a similar group from Logan County was rapping at the door of Governor Windy Wilson in West Virginia. Their requests were similar to those made in Kentucky. Either they must have troops to defend them or arms with which to defend themselves.

At Frankfurt, Governor Buckner listened to his visitors, but refused to recognize sufficient provocation to warrant dispatch of state militia to Pike County. Instead, he suggested that a local military company be organized and that responsible men be placed in command. Such a force, backed by civil authorities, he felt sure, would be equal to the emergency. It was his belief that a community should do all in its power to protect itself before it called on the state for assistance.

Wilson gave better response to the delegates on his side of the Tug. In his hands was placed a petition signed by some of the best people of Logan County. It told of the death of two of their citizens, one of them a deputized official in the discharge of his duties at the time he was killed. It also revealed that these men had been shot down in cold blood on West Virginia soil, without provocation, by Kentucky desperadoes who still were making lawless raids into Logan and were too powerful to be suppressed by civil authorities. The Governor ordered two companies of militia to report to Charleston for duty at once.

Reaction in the two states differed according to their respective adherences. S. G. Kinner, Commonwealth's attorney in the Sixteenth Judicial District and thoroughly acquainted with details of the feud, spoke up in Kentucky. He had visited Governor Buckner and was in a position to talk. He reported that on each side in the feud were engaged about thirty men, a majority of them the best people in their section. The Hatfields, he said, were men of considerable means and fair standing, but terribly vindictive, while the Pike County faction was made up of "as good people as you will find anywhere."

State Senator John B. Floyd was spokesman in West Virginia. He denied that the conflict was confined to the Hatfields and McCoys, claiming it was a fight between the civil authorities of Logan County and the murderers of Jim Vance. "The Hatfields," he said, "are not interested in the difficulty more than other citizens of Logan County and, while the McCoys are among the Kentucky men, they constitute but a small portion of the gang."

Floyd, who said he had lived within eighteen miles of the Hatfields for twenty years, also attempted to give a history of the feud, which was printed in the *Wheeling Intelligencer* of January 27. The trouble, he related, began during the Civil War and continued up into the 80's.

"Everyone thought the trouble was over; but a few months ago a man named P. A. Cline, a lawyer, and I am told the jailer of Pike County, concluded that he would stir up the thing again and make some money out of it, knowing that the Hatfields owned some good property in Logan County, West Virginia. He therefore looked up the old indictments and by misrepresentations induced the Governor of Kentucky to offer a reward of $2,700 for the capture of the Hatfields and to grant a requisition for them.

"This done, he let the Hatfields know of the fact, and at the same time intimated that, if he could get some $400 or $500, he would have the proceedings put an end to. Well, he agreed to take $225, and the money was placed in the hands of A. J. Auxier, a prominent lawyer of Pike Court House, for Cline, when he had fulfilled his agreement.

"Cline made a pretense of having the reward and requisition recalled, but in the meantime his co-workers, John Kite, who is one of the most notorious murderers in West Virginia or Kentucky, and Frank Phillips have been making desperate efforts to get hold of the Hatfields so as to secure the reward."

Some newspapers were bitter in their condemnation of the faction in the adjoining state, charging invariably that they were the aggressors. They also were unanimous in the thought that the respective governors should intercede. Said a West Virginia editor in the *Wheeling Intelligencer* of January 27: "The West Virginia authorities should, for the sake of the credit of the state, take some action in the matter of the alleged outrages in Logan County. A thorough investigation seems to be a necessity. If the reports of lawlessness are true, no expense should be spared to rid the state of the disgrace. If they are not true, then an official statement to that effect should be given as wide circulation as the sensational newpaper accounts have received. The notoriety West Virginia is acquiring by reason of the reports is decidedly unpleasant, and is very damaging to the welfare of the state."

The press of West Virginia grew sensitive over the things that were written about the state's part in the feud. In time, the *Wheeling Intelligencer* sought to counteract them. It reminded that, with one or two exceptions, all the press dispatches concerning the trouble had come from Kentucky sources. The *Pittsburgh Times*, meanwhile, made the Wheeling editors indignant by suggesting that the governors refused to intercede because, if kept up, "the conflict would in time exterminate a lot of citizens of no earthly use and that had better be killed off for the good of the state." Soon afterward came a geographical error in the *New York World.* This paper reported that, "among the neighboring wilds of Pike County, W. Va., the war of extermination between the Hatfields and McCoys proceeds with unflagging energy and tenacity." The *Intelligencer* retorted on Page 1, Column 1: "West Virginia has many sins to answer for, but one of them is not the possession of the notorious Pike County alluded to. If something is not done soon to muzzle a few of the sensational liars who furnish, for pay, specials to the Eastern press, West Virginia may look soon to see the scene of Texas cowboy raids and Mexican outrages located within her borders."

By the latter part of January, newspapers all over the country were carrying front-page stories of the feud, many of them with artists' conception of the feudists. Kentucky and West Virginia string men for Eastern journals were having a heyday. They wrote until their arms got tired, and the editors accepted their copy without a murmur. Some of the larger papers sent their own correspondents to pry into the situation. One of these, Charles S. Howell of the *Pittsburgh Times,* managed to interview Randolph McCoy and his wife at Pikeville. He found the old man especially broken up over the recent killings. "I used to be on very friendly terms with the Hatfields before and after the war," the reporter quoted McCoy as saying. "We never had any trouble until six years ago. I hope no more of us will have to die. I'll be glad when it's all over."

On the strength of this interview, Howell wrote a five-column account of the feud, in which he said: "The Hatfield-McCoy war, divested of the coloring with which assiduous correspondents have clothed it, and of all the sentiment with which the representatives of the two states have invested it, is simply a succession of cowardly murders by day and assassinations and house-burnings by night. All of the murders have been cruel, heartless and almost without the shadow of provocation. Given, on the one hand, a family with its contingents of the same blood, allied and cemented by a common desire to avenge an imaginary affront, and on the other another family, small in the matter of alliance and collateral sympathies, doomed to destruction by the larger one, and the case is stated."

Howell also got in to see the prisoners in the Pike jail and found them all confined in two small cells. He took a good look at Wall Hatfield and noticed particularly his shaggy eyebrows, which he said almost concealed "eyes of a greenish gray that are forever evading the person with whom the owner may be talking." The owner of these eyes, however, seemed cool and possessed at all times, and never allowed himself to be led into any entangling statements. It was said around Pikeville that Devil Anse had fallen out with him because he refused to participate in the New Year's night raid.

The Pittsburgh reporter ran into other news. He learned that Frank Phillips had been ousted as deputy sheriff and that Basil Hatfield, the sheriff, was accused of influencing his discharge. The severance interfered with Phillips' career as a police officer, but not with his determination to aid in bringing the Hatfields to trial. The West Virginians evidently believed Phillips was in earnest, Howell said, because Devil Anse, Johnse, and Cap had gone to Logan Court House, and other members of the clan had set out for Virginia to wait until Pike County authorities had had time to file away the indictments against them.

Howell thought it a mistake to order out troops. He explained that the governors should know the militia could do no good in the passes and defiles of the mountains or in the narrow bottoms of the Tug and its influent creeks. One agency, and one agency alone, could do the job—special detectives. Twenty or twenty-five of these trained men—none of the fakirs from Charleston, Fairmont, and other West Virginia towns—would arrest the suspected persons without noise or comment, in the opinion of the reporter, who made it plain that his findings were based on careful investigation.

Governors Buckner and Wilson, as early as January 9, had resumed their exchange of feud correspondence started during the early fall. On that date, the Kentucky executive wrote his neighbor that he had received information of the New Year's Day slaughter and would like to be advised if there was anything which prevented the criminals from being rendered. Wilson replied on the 21st, explaining that his delay in answering was occasioned by sickness in his family and his own absence from his desk. He recalled to Buckner's attention that, while the application for requisition did not appear to be supported by any official authority of Pike County, he had directed issuance of warrants against all the people named except Elias Hatfield and Andrew Varney. These were withheld, as West Virginia's Secretary of State Henry S. Walker had explained by letter to Perry Cline months earlier, because he had evidence showing they were nowhere near the scene at the time of the killings back in '82. Shortly afterward, he added, he was reliably informed that the requisition was being used to extort money from the accused, rather than to secure the ends of public justice. He enclosed copies of affidavits to prove it. "I would be glad," he concluded, "if such enquiry were directed as to your Excellency may seem proper, so that warrants may issue only for those against whom there is some evidence of guilt."

As soon as Wilson heard of the battle of Grapevine Creek, he wired Buckner: "You have probably noticed in yesterday's papers an alleged conflict in this state between the McCoy and Hatfield parties, in which William Dempsey was killed. My information is that Dempsey was killed while acting as a deputy in assisting the officers of the law in arresting Frank Phillips and three of the McCoys on a warrant for the murder of James Vance."

Buckner replied the same day: "My information differs from your excellency's in reference to the alleged conflict on the Sandy. Steps are being taken to prevent any aggression by Kentucky citizens on those of West Virginia. I will communicate by mail."

Wilson resorted to the mails before Buckner. The following day, he wrote that he had positive information Dempsey had come to his death while acting as a deputy; that Vance had been killed only a short time before. From what he could learn, he said, the feud dated back to the early years of the Civil War, the two families representing opposite sides. Recently, the hope of reward had prompted a set of men just as lawless as either the Hatfields or the McCoys to commit heinous crimes while discharging their duty as officers of the law. He also had been informed, though not officially, he added, that a number of persons, without warrant, had been forcibly seized and taken from West Virginia by the same band and placed in the Pike County jail. "I have sent a reliable agent to Logan County to ascertain and report the whole facts of the matter," he reported. "If you will pursue that course would it not enable us to adopt similar measures for the suppression of the lawless on both sides of the lines?"

This letter brought notice from Buckner that he had sent his adjutant general to Pike County to confer with Wilson's agent. He asked the West Virginia Governor to give similar instructions to his emissary in the hope of quieting public excitement in both states.

At the same time that he was corresponding with Buckner about the agent, Wilson sent a telegram to Colonel L. T. Moore, lawyer of Catlettsburg, asking him to come to the state capital to confer on the manner in which the Hatfields had been arrested and jailed. Moore at the moment was in Frankfort, trying to defeat a move to transfer the Boyd County courthouse from Catlettsburg to Ashland, but he at once made plans to go to Charleston.

In the meantime, the *Courier-Journal* published on January 28 news that brought cheers from Kentuckians. Under the heading "Hatfield in Hock," it announced: "Information reached here tonight that *Anson* Hatfield, the leader of the West Virginia gang of outlaws that has made war on the McCoys of Pike County, had been arrested and conducted to jail at Pikeville. There are now ten of the Hatfields in jail, and indictiments are pending against all of them." Readers watched papers for further news on the development and then gradually forgot about it, taking it for granted that some reporter had placed too much credence in idle rumor.

While the exchange of telegrams was going on between governors, troops were standing by in each state ready to go to Tug Fork. Although he denied to the Pike delegation that he saw the need for it, Buckner had followed Wilson's earlier move in alerting the militia. At the same time, the Kentucky General Assembly was gingerly handling a Senate bill authorizing the Governor to organize six additional troops for the state guard. But amendments were hamstringing the measure. One proposal specified that nothing in the bill should be construed as a declaration of war on the part of the Commonwealth; another, that provisions for sending guns to the counties where the companies were to be organized be stricken out and in its place be inserted "that six good school teachers and two evangelists be sent to said counties, to remain until the disturbances are quelled."

The militia bill was recommended by both the Governor and the Adjutant General. It was understood one of the six companies would be located in Pike County, and on this provision the House refused to agree. The measure went down 33 to 53.

On the 30th, Wilson wired Buckner that citizens of Logan County, assembled in a mass meeting, had passed a resolution asking the governors of both states to send troops to the border. "I have ordered sixty to Logan County to assist the civil authorities," he added. "They will report here tomorrow night, but cannot reach the scene of the trouble before the 3rd prox. May I request that your excellency send a like number of troops to the scene of the trouble?"

The troops Wilson had called out were the Goff and Auburn Guards of Ritchie County, first to offer their services. They left Pennsboro at 5:00 P.M on the 30th and headed for Parkersburg, expecting to go on on to Charleston the next day. Other companies from various sections of the state also volunteered for immediate duty.

Shortly after the telegram about the militia was dispatched, Wilson's agent, Colonel W. L. Mahan, returned from Logan. He had found the Hatfields "good, law-abiding citizens," possessing the respect and confidence of everyone in the neighborhood. According to his information, the recent outbreak had been caused by a resurrection of the old indictments against the family by certain people in Kentucky. These people had come across into West Virginia and "kidnapped" nine men, had killed old man Vance "without as much as calling on him to surrender" and also had slain Dempsey. Residents of Logan were confident that, if the task of making the arrests had been assigned to people other than the McCoys, who "had sworn to kill the Hatfields and would have done so after they were disarmed," no blood would have been shed. But, said Mahan, even though the surrounding country had been in a state of excitement and tumult bordering on a genuine young war, he was able to report that peace had been restored, "at least temporarily."

Mahan's assurance that the clans had disbanded induced Wilson to send a second telegram on the 30th. It informed Buckner that he had countermanded the order directing troops to Logan.

Buckner's agent, Adjutant General Sam E. Hill, had been slow starting for Pikeville. Colonel Mahan was back before the Kentucky representative got to Catlettsburg, and it was there he caught up with Pike County Judge Wagner and County Attorney Ferguson, on their way home after laying their troubles before the Governor. At the railway station, there was for a time danger that the feud would be extended to that town. Some West Virginian asserted within hearing of Ferguson that Kentucky had invaded his state and murdered its citizens. The attorney was in no mood to let such a statement pass unchallenged. He flared up with more pluck than physical stature and called the charge a "goddamn lie." The crowd swarmed around, expecting a good fight, but the man from the neighboring state had no desire to push the matter.

The newspaper correspondent at Catlettsburg was on his toes. He was standing by when the exchange at the depot took place and he was on hand that same day when certain suspicious-looking boxes were labeled for shipment. He identified the contents as "Winchesters and ammunition" for Pikeville.

Adjutant General Hill was back in Frankfort by the following week-end. He had found conditions along the Tug much as Mahan had described them, except that blame for the hostilities seemed to him to lie in West Virginia, rather than in Kentucky. To begin with, as he saw it, John B. Floyd, a friend of the Hatfields and secretary to Governor Wilson, was obstructing the ends of justice by influencing the executive to ignore the Kentucky requisitions. The trouble would end, he predicted, if Devil Anse and his sons were brought to town and convicted. In the meantime, there seemed to be no danger in his opinion that the prisoners in the Pike County jail would be released except by writ of habeas corpus.

Along the Tug, Hill had noticed a condition of the most intense excitement. Many families, he found, had abandoned their homes temporarily and moved into Pikeville. "The Hatfields are laying low for the time," he reported. "I was shown some private correspondence which said they were at Logan Court House and only named eight in the party. I also had other information which was to the effect that they were bivouacked on the east bank of the Tug, and were twenty strong. But I am inclined to believe that numerically they do not amount to much."

At Pikeville, Hill talked with Perry Cline and was much impressed. He found the lawyer a man of great courage, an impression difficult to understand in view of the fact that he was seen going about at all times with three guards armed with Winchesters and revolvers.

Days before his agent returned, Buckner wrote Wilson a long letter in which he reviewed both the history of their correspondence and the history of the Hatfield-McCoy troubles. His information on the feud, he admitted, had come from the Pike County attorney.

This letter from Buckner, more than anything else, convinced Wilson that his efforts to get the Hatfields released without legal procedure were futile. He waited no longer. On the 1st, he prepared a requisition upon Buckner asking him to release the nine prisoners, who, he said, were forcibly taken from West Virginia without any legal process and in violation of the laws of the state. This was sent to Frankfort by Colonel Mahan, who had instructions to get an answer before he returned.

Mahan was back in less than a week. In his valise he packed a letter from Buckner explaining in detail that authority for release of the prisoners rested alone in the jurisdiction of the courts.

Wilson immediately commissioned ex-Congressman Eustace Gibson, prominent attorney of Huntington, to represent the state of West Virginia in habeas corpus proceedings. The case was scheduled to come up in the U. S. District Court, in session at Louisville, so Gibson headed for that city on the 7th of February. In his heart he carried determination to get the Hatfields back or know the reason why; in his heart also he tucked fear that the McCoys would assassinate the captives before he could accomplish his purpose.

The same day Gibson arrived in Louisville, the *Courier-Journal* announced without apology: "If the Hatfields would move to Dakota and the McCoys would move to Venezuela, West Virginia and Kentucky could afford to give them free passes."

Judge Barr of the U.S. Court set the Hatfield case for hearing at noon February 9. The press pointed out that the trial was expected to be very interesting because it would decide "some very fine points" regarding the relation of adjoining states to each other.

Gibson's strongest argument was that the prisoners had been illegally "kidnapped" from West Virginia. He said in his petition he believed the Commonwealth of Kentucky had been the first in the history of the country to seize and enjoy an opportunity for the invasion of a sister state and the seizure of her citizens by a band of outlaws.

Ex-Governor J. Proctor Knott and Attorney General T. Watt Hardin presented the defense. They argued that the proceeding should be before the U.S. Supreme Court, citing that that court alone had jurisdiction in controversies between states.

This case had no precedent, a fact Judge Barr took into consideration, along with a lot of other points, when he reached his decision. It was to the effect that the petition for a writ of habeas corpus should be admitted, returnable on February 20.

The Kentucky press was indignant that West Virginia was to be permitted to take up the time of the courts. Commented the *Courier-Journal:* "For years the press and the officers of the state have been earnestly endeavoring to make the law a terror to evil-doers, and now for the first time in the history of any civilized community the power of a 'sovereign state' is invoked to give protection, license, immunity for the past and assurances for the future to a band of white savages whose brutalities, whose inhuman tortures have not been paralleled in Kentucky since Boone and his followers drove the Indians to other hunting fields."

Wilson was denounced unmercifully for taking the side of the Hatfields. "The Governor of West Virginia has not yet issued a proclamation offering a reward for Kentucky scalps," sarcastically quipped one newspaper. And again: "The Governor of North Carolina and the Governor of South Carolina no doubt agree, between refreshments, that the Governor of West Virginia ought to be sent to some other state."

The judge's ruling gave Governor Wilson courage. Two days later he issued a requisition on Governor Buckner for twenty-eight men, all of whom he identified as participants in the murder of William Dempsey. This constituted no more than a rehearsal of effort. Buckner at the moment was too busy with legal proceedings to think about giving up any of his citizens.

14

1888
Kentucky the Winner

THE DAY JUDGE BARR GAVE HIS DECISION, U.S. DEPUTY Marshal J. V. McDonald left for Pikeville to serve the writs of habeas corpus. There he found the jail still well guarded, the town quiet, the feud in status quo. In fact, Wall Hatfield had not even been locked up. He was allowed the liberty of the streets and frequently engaged in discussions with those who were most anxious to prosecute him. Once he had gone before Sarah McCoy, lying sick abed at the home of Perry Cline, and, in the presence of witnesses, had discussed details leading up to the slaughter of her sons in '82.

McDonald was preparing to move the prisoners when word came for him to delay his departure. There were rumors the Hatfields planned to attempt a rescue. He was told to wait until more deputies could arrive.

The deputies were ready to start from Louisville the evening of the 15th. Their path was marked out for them: by rail through Catlettsburg to Richardson, thence by water the remaining forty-six miles to Pikeville if a steamboat were available, or by mountain stage or horseback over the circuitous and rocky route by land. But the trip was never made. Before the deputies could entrain, the telegraph at Louisville clicked out a message from McDonald that he had arrived at Catlettsburg with all his charges.

Louisville waited breathlessly. Newspapers announced that the famed "Hatfield gang" would be placed aboard the Chesapeake & Ohio train scheduled to leave Catlettsburg at ten o'clock next morning and would arrive in the city at 7:15 P.M.

The *Courier-Journal* rushed a reporter to Catlettsburg and managed to get him aboard the train, where he could interview the prisoners en route. This newsman found the captives willing talkers and conversed with them at length. They all informed him that they were entirely innocent of the crimes charged to them. Wall Hatfield impressed the fourth estater as a quiet, inoffensive citizen and by far the most intelligent of the group. He gave out a detailed statement, which the reporter translated into these words:

"I know nothing about the crimes that have been committed in the quarrel between the McCoys and Hatfields, and I don't think any of the men with me know, or had anything more to do with the killings and fighting than I did. We were taken away from our homes by armed men from Pike County and, as it seemed safer to submit than to resist and risk being murdered, we went with the men who came after us.

"I know that several people have been killed, but except what has been told me, I know nothing of who killed them or why it was done. When we were arrested, the men who, from all that I have been told, committed all the crimes were not taken, but those of us who did not expect any trouble and who remained quietly at home, were taken by the party from Pikeville and put in the Pike County jail.

"They say that, after we were over the boundary line of West Virginia, we were legally arrested, but I have never been aware of any legal steps to confine us being made. We were well treated in jail and I was not locked up at all, but threats were made against us and some of the men thought the jail would be attacked and that we would be killed. Mr. Cline, the jailer, told us, however, that he would not give us up and that, before we were taken, he would be dead, and I was not much disturbed after that.

"I was permitted to go wherever I pleased and had nearly all the privileges I would have enjoyed had I been at liberty. When we were first taken, old Randolph McCoy, whose sons and daughter were killed, said that he could not desire us in a better place than the jail, as he could blow us all to pieces with dynamite. He threatened to do this and, as he could have done it if he wished, that caused me some uneasiness. When we were to be taken away, McCoy said he would get his gun and shoot me if he saw me. I thought he might carry out his threat, but he did not. He made the same threat when the liberty of the jail was given me. I tried to give bond, and Colonel John Dills offered $50,000 surety, but they wouldn't take it and, while not exactly confined, I was kept prisoner."

Seated with the group from Pikeville was a sixty-two-year-old man whose age the reporter far underestimated. He had very little to say to anyone and appeared more typically mountaineer than the others. When the newsman asked him if he was Randolph McCoy, he readily admitted his identity and, in answer to questions, briefly reviewed details of the merciless war he charged to the Hatfields.

A large crowd was on hand at the Louisville railway station at Eighth and Water streets when the train arrived, a few minutes late. Mingling with the bystanders was a special delegation from the U.S. marshal's office, fully armed, to see that no rush was made on the prisoners as they detrained.

After all the other passengers had left the coaches, the marshal's deputies gathered around the car immediately behind the smoker. Through the windows, the crowd on the platform could see the prisoners, seated two to a seat on the same side of the aisle, while directly across from them were members of the guard.

Jailer Perry Cline gave directions. Two guards came out and took positions beside the coach steps on one side of the train; two more emerged behind them and took their stand on the opposite side. These guards, as well as those waiting inside with the prisoners, were specially picked. The group included Lee Ferguson, the Pike County attorney; Jim York, attorney for Randolph McCoy; Charley Yoste, deputy sheriff of Pike County; Jim Sauers, first lietenant, and Allen Cline, second lieutenant, of the Pikeville militia; Link Cline and Dan Marrs. Each carried a Winchester rifle and wore a belt of cartridges from which dangled a heavy revolver.

When the prisoners marched out and down the steps, the crowd pushed up. It was the first chance Louisville had had to see the much-publicized feudists, and there was some degree of disappointment. To begin with, most of these strange visitors seemed to be young men, all very different from the type of mountaineer frequently brought into the city to answer to charges of moonshining. Several had on white shirts and three sported collars around their unshaven necks. All wore soft felt hats. There were nine captives and nine mustaches.

As the guards prepared to move off, the throng threatened disorder; so a halt was called until the bystanders could be pushed back. Then the march to the county jail started, with two prisoners locking arms between two guards and with other deputies in front and rear. Out Seventh Street to Main they walked, up Main to Sixth, and then out Sixth and around Jefferson to the bastille. At their heels trotted an escort of small boys that got larger as the procession advanced.

At the jail, Perry Cline formally surrendered his charges to U.S. Marshal Gross. The mountain men, in the meantime, quietly gave their names and then filed off to the cells. When the last lock clicked behind them, the rifles of the guards were stacked in the jail office, and in half an hour all was quiet behind the barred windows.

From the jail the newspaper fraternity turned its attention to some of the other mountain visitors. Lee Ferguson was cornered as he prepared to go into consultation with ex-Governor Knott. He talked readily enough, laughing heartily when he was reminded of the claim of the nine men just locked up that they were innocent. He did not deny that the West Virginians were forcibly taken from their homes, but maintained that the Kentucky posse was justified in its action because authorities of the neighboring state refused to punish the guilty persons. The attorney said he had creditable information that a state official of West Virginia (referring anonymously to John B. Floyd) had been retained with a fee of $500 to prevent Governor Wilson from recognizing the requisition of Governor Buckner.

Devil Anse Hatfield, Ferguson related, was a man of

considerable means. In this connection, he gave the reporters a choice bit of information. The clan leader had sold the 5,000 acres of land he owned along the Tug and had moved miles nearer Logan Court House. His property, by the attorney's estimate, easily was worth $15,000, but it had brought him only $7,000.

Ferguson also had something to say about Wall Hatfield. This member of the clan, he related, recently confessed that he had five living wives and thirty-three living children. Nine of his children had died, according to this confession. The attorney explained that Wall had "peculiar" ideas of polygamy, not marrying his wives by law, but taking them and apportioning his time out among them.

The *Courier-Journal* of February 17 was made up almost entirely of feud news. On the front page were ten artist's drawings of men, including those of the nine prisoners and of Randolph McCoy, copies of which the newspaper proudly sent Governor Wilson. A large part of the accompanying news story was devoted to a history of the trouble and to an account of the manner in which the Hatfields tried to dominate the McCoys. The paper announced that Pikeville had organized a new militia company to protect itself in case further violence resulted from the war.

Throughout the day, reporters kept as close watch on the prisoners as jail authorities would allow. The captives remained quietly in their cells in Apartment 5. Some of them sauntered occasionally to the outer corridor to talk with visitors allowed in the building, but most of them remained out of sight. They would have nothing to do with the other inmates. Among themselves they talked in subdued tones. No one could tell what was on their minds, except for the fact that Wall Hatfield made it evident he wanted to see his lawyer, Eustace Gibson.

A couple of days later it was noticed that the manner of the mountain men had changed. Gone was their diffidence, and they were beginning to converse with the other prisoners, some of whom already had applied the nickname of "Judge" to Wall, the justice of the peace. This sobriquet seemed to please the clan leader and he conversed freely with those who so addressed him.

Much of the day the mountain men listened while other prisoners read to them. They took part in divine sercices on Sunday and joined heartily in the songs. Wall held one side of a hymn book with a convicted swindler and sang loudly the words of "One More River to Cross." All who were present noticed that the newcomers from the Tug had fine voices.

Morning in jail was a bedlam since the Hatfields had come. By 4:30 or 5:00, these fellows who went to sleep as soon as they were locked in their cells at dark were up and serenading the other prisoners. They were the first on hand for their daily rations.

Judge Barr called the habeas corpus case Saturday morning, the 25th. The U.S. District Court building was packed, and deputy marshals had trouble escorting in the captives. They were seated in two rows of chairs, five in front, four behind. Their appearance was unchanged except that one of the white shirts worn at the time of their arrival had given way to flannel. From the start, they were stoical and indifferent, and in time the spectators in the room began to hope that their expressions would change, if only to break the monotony for a moment.

Throughout the opening day there was much wrangling. The attorneys could agree on nothing. In one instance, Judge Barr announced he would admit a petition and would himself eliminate such of the facts as were irrelevant. That afternoon, late, he adjourned court until Monday morning.

When the case was resumed, the West Virginia delegation was strengthened by the presence of Governor Wilson and his secretary, John B. Floyd, armed with books and official records. Wilson sat directly behind Gibson, who was assisted by Colonel J. W. St. Clair. Reporters noticed that the Governor was small, rather slender, a man whose wrinkled face was that of a person habitually in ill health. Over his mouth was a bushy red mustache at which he nibbled nervously. Throughout the day he frequently consulted the attorneys and gave ample evidence that he was a man of unusual ability.

It was Tuesday before arguments by the opposing counsel were completed. Kentucky's defense of her action was based on the claim that a prisoner could not escape prosecution by pleading illegality or irregularity of arrest; that Frank Phillips had been acting as an individual under his own responsiiblity and not that of an agent of the Commonwealth; also that, with the state no party to the violation, the violation did not suspend the power of the state to make an arrest when the wanted person was found within her borders.

When both sides had been presented, Judge Barr announced that the case was one of too much importance to be decided at once. He realized that, for the first time in the history of the nation, its courts had been called on to stop the bullets of murderers on the border line of two of its states. His decision would come as soon as he could consult the authorities on such matters.

In the intervening period, th prisoners were turned over to the U.S. marshal. Before they left the court room, Colonel St. Clair called the attention of the judge to Wall Hatfield, whom he described as an aged man, in poor health. The confinement and prison fare, he said, had caused the captive to become ill and in need of medical attention. It was promised.

Judge Barr rendered his decision at the opening of court March 3 in an oral statement that took him half an hour to deliver. It decreed that the proceeding was beyond the jurisdiction of his court because it concerned a controversy between states, a matter that rightly could be decided exclusively by the Supreme Court.

Under this decision, the prisoners were remanded to the custody of the Kentucky authorities. Gibson asked that they be allowed to give bail for their appearance, but the judge held that the offense charged was not bailable. The next question was to what jail they should be sent, and this provoked so much discussion Barr finally adopted a temporary expedient and ordered them locked up for the night.

Just before the judge settled on this disposition, a new and strange voice was added to the din. It was that of the thirty-three-year-old Andrew Varney, standing limply beside the other captives.

"Judge, I wanna go back to Pike," he said.

The judge studied him uncertainly, speechless for the moment; then he asked: "Why?"

"Cause, the court thar are gonna be aholden for a week, an' I wanna go back and show I ain't guilty."

The judge spoke calmly. "If you had not made application for a writ of habeas corpus, you would be there now."

"It warn't on my account I were brought here," replied the mountaineer. "I didn't know nothin' 'bout it till I got here."

"I wish I had known that before," commented the judge, dryly, and joined in the exchange of glances then going on among the attorneys.

That night reporters found Eustace Gibson at the Gault House. He admitted he was preparing an order of appeal in the case and said it would be presented in court Monday. In the meantime, he was expecting Governor Wilson, temporarily called away from the city, to return and assist him. "The prisoners," said the attorney, "are, some of them, very anxious to be taken back to Pike County, and I believe they have been tampered with in some way and false hopes held out to them as to bail being furnished for them. I do not wish them to be sent back there to remain in jail, for I don't believe they would be safe there."

With the prisoners it was a case of plain homesickness, brought on mainly by the realization that their families could reach them at Pikeville and supply clothing and other comforts not available to them at Louisville. They filed into court on Monday morning and sat placidly while Governor Wilson, who had returned the evening before, went through a fiery speech in which he charged that the honor of his state had been impugned. He also, in filing a motion of appeal, told the court that the case was of great consequence because it involved a decision as to whether kidnapping was a legal means of arresting citizens of one state in order to bring them to justice in another. Then he swung about and pointed to the nine captives. His next words belied the expression on their faces, the hope in their hearts. Only one of them, he maintained—Varney, who was ill—wanted to return to Pike.

Judge Barr gave his decision in the afternoon. He admitted the appeal and ordered the prisoners held until local authorities could return them to the Pikeville jail. "To be murdered!" stormed Gibson.

The West Virginia representatives indicated they planned to take the case to the Supreme Court of the United States before they would be convinced they had obtained justice. Before he got out of the city, Gibson voiced his feelings to a reporter.

"We have been treated badly," he said. "Your papers have not treated us fairly, and we have not received a damned bit of courtesy from the opposing counsel. I don't think much of either Governor Knott or Attorney General Hardin, both of whom have been contrary and unaccommodating throughout the trial."

Kentucky newspapers accepted Mr. Gibson's irritation magnanimously. Commented one: "Mr. Gibson was mad and probably didn't mean all he said. He should revisit Kentucky when she has donned her bluegrass garments, and her mint julep crop is ready for the harvest. Then he cannot help loving us."

Nearly ten days passed before there was any move to return the prisoners. At the end of that period, Perry Cline appeared in Louisville with three guards, remained long enough to make known his plans to court officials, and went on toward Frankfort.

Cline had serious business at the state capital. On his official head suddenly had descended a debt of $900, the cost of transporting the prisoners. So far no one had consented to assume this financial burden. U.S. Marshal Gross maintained it was not his expense and refused to listen to any argument to the contrary, which left the responsibility up to Pike County, under whose charge the Hatfields remained. At Frankfort, Cline talked directly to Governor Buckner. The legislature must make an appropriation or he would have to foot the bill himself. Buckner was sympathetic and promised to recommend that the state take over the debt.

The Pike County attorney and deputy jailer returned to Louisville in the late afternoon of March 16.

Back in the cells of the Louisville jail, the prisoners were in a joyous state. A reporter, admitted at the right moment, found Wall in a talkative mood. Questions regarding their guilt the old man brushed off with a squirt of tobacco juice. They were not the ones who had committed the dastardly crimes in Pike, he scoffed.

"Nary a man in our party ever had anything to do with the murders. Nary a man in our party ever harmed any man."

"Who did, then?" asked the reporter.

"My brother Anse and his sons, Bob, Johnse, and Cap, and four or five others. They are all bad men."

Wall studied the reporter seriously for a moment, and then said with a touch of humor: "I wisht you'd contredick the piece about my having seven wives. I ain't never had but one and I don't want any more."

The Hatfield case came before Judge Howell E. Jackson in the U.S. Circuit Court at Louisville early in April. The question to be decided was whether any law of the United States, any constitutional provision or any treaty stipulation had been violated.

On the evening train from Nashville the day before the case was called, arrived the judge. He was transported immediately to the Louisville Hotel, just opposite the Alexander Hotel, where had registered Governor Wilson, Eustace Gibson, Attorney General Hardin and ex-Governor Knott. The West Virginians were expected to make considerable change from the method in which they had presented their case before the District Court.

The *Courier-Journal* was none too happy over the news prospects. When the paper was put to bed that night, it carried this little item in its column of "News and Comment": "That rather tiresome affair known as the Hatfield habeas corpus case is again up in the Federal Court before Judge Howell E. Jackson on appeal. Meanwhile the Hatfields are fattening on Kentucky jowl and greens in the Pikeville jail."

Eustace Gibson was the first to speak when the case was called. He gave mainly a review of the evidence presented in the first trial, but he occasionally wandered away from his subject to talk of possible warfare between the two states and of the injustice brought upon the citizens of West Virginia. Ex-Governor Knott followed him to the floor and observed that the arguments of the opposing counsel seemed to be that "the Constitution of the United States was drawn expressly to give each state the power to harbor criminals." The Kentucky speaker admitted the petitioners were illegally taken from their home state, but maintained this in no way affected the legality of the arrest. The proper redress for the prisoners, in his opinion, would be in the civil courts where they might bring to account the man who had kidnapped them.

Governor Wilson next took his turn and his argument ran into the following day. At its conclusion, the case was submitted to the court, Attorney General Hardin indicating no desire to speak. Judge Jackson immediately delivered an oral opinion upholding the lower court. When he had finished, the West Virginians asked and were granted an appeal to the U.S. Supreme Court.

News stories with Washington date lines gave notice on April 12 that two former congressmen, who used to work together while members of the House of Representatives, would arrive the following day to oppose each other in the nation's highest court. They were identified as Eustace Gibson of West Virginia and J. Proctor Knott of Kentucky. Their business was to seek an early adjudication of the famous habeas corpus suit involving the two states.

In less than a week, these ex-solons filed a motion praying that the case, labeled *"Plyant Mahon, appellant,* vs. *Abner Justice, jailer of Pike County, Ky.,"* be advanced on the docket. Monday morning, the 23rd, arguments were begun. Gibson spoke for an hour and a half, Knott for twenty minutes.

During the argument, one member of the court, Justice Miller, frequently interrupted to ask questions, especially of Gibson. Near the end of his speech, Knott said he could not understand why West Virginia had turned to such a proceeding to secure redress when the better course of a direct suit against Kentucky was open to her. He added that the neighboring state's action reminded him of an incident in his own life. He was riding with a friend on a railroad train in Kentucky when a small yellow dog jumped out of the bushes and ran furiously after the chugging locomotive. As the dog rapidly was outpaced, the friend, a native of the soil, turned and observed: "Well, I wonder if that dog expected to catch the train and, if he had caught it, what he would have done with it." It is recorded that the customarily solemn-faced justices of the Supreme Court greeted this story with a smile.

The Supreme Court's opinion was handed down May 14. It upheld the judgment of the lower court and decreed that no legal way had been provided for compulsory restoration of parties wrongfully abducted from one state by parties of another state. Two justices, Bradley and Harlan, dissented. It was their belief that the court should have recognized the invasion of West Virginia by Kentucky, rather than the legality of the prisoners' detention, as one of the essential facts involved in the appeal.

Thus, to the highest court in the land, to the plush-seated and carpeted halls of justice in the Capital of the United States, had gone a case that had its beginning in one of the most remote sections of the East. The feud rifles that cracked along the Tug in a fight for family rights had echoed in that city of America most interested in state's rights. When access to the courts had been exhausted, the spotlight of attention shifted back to the mountains, to the cells of the Hatfields who had been arrested and to the cabins of the Hatfields who had not been arrested.

15

1888
Nancy Finds a New Lover

ONE OF THE GREATEST DETECTIVE PILGRIMAGES IN AMERican history followed the Supreme Court's ruling in the Hatfield-McCoy case. From all corners of the nation the hawkshaws came to share in the rewards offered by Kentucky for the Hatfields, by West Virginia for the McCoys. They descended upon the two states in a mad scramble and, in the ensuing months, learned that the mountains were not an unfertile field for detective agencies.

But their days in the hill country were stormy. Soon the mountain folk became extremely tired of their presence, and upon them were heaped blame and invective in generous degree. Some people saw the detectives as the root of all evil visited upon the mountains. One of these was the editor of the *East Kentucky Magnet* at Louisa.

"We propose a remedy," he wrote. "Put a sensible man in the place of Wilson and offer rewards for thieving adventurers, cowardly bullies and the curs (commonly called detectives). These men are after the rewards. They do not care whether they arrest a McCoy or a Hatfield just so they see a few dollars in the transaction. If everything is quiet, they will curry favors with the largest crowd, and while under the shelter of the longest, safest wing, hatch libelous statements in regard to the other party. Unfortunately, being believed, that party will arm themselves to be ready for an expected attack. The other side, hearing of these preparations, will oil the locks, load their guns, and a fight is the result. The detectives are always in the background until the reward is known. Fear and uneasiness are kept up by a constant stream of false reports. Hang the detectives, drive off all who are not residents, and those most concerned will soon find that it is safe and profitable to attend to crops and get their timber ready for the spring rains. Offer rewards for the detectives, and enough honest Hatfields and McCoys will unite to clear the country of them in less than two weeks. When the Hatfields and McCoys realize the injustice that is done them, and the opinions held in regard to them by the outside world, and all brought about by the workings of detectives, they will make it so hot that, if any of them (the detectives) escape, they will bury their bought badges and swear they had never heard of the Big Sandy country."

The bounties that attracted the detectives climbed to nearly $8,000, with both states equally anxious to pay off. Some of the sleuths had the glint of desperation in their eyes. All sorts of stories of the possible fate awaiting them were making the rounds. According to these rumors, there was no retaliation, no vindictiveness too severe to be employed by either clan. It was even said the two families had formed the pact mentioned by the *Magnet*'s editor, each agreeing to declare an open season on detectives on its side of the river.

Most of the hawkshaws had their eyes trained for Devil Anse Hatfield. The detective who captured this man would win great fame and an insured future. Strongest factor against success in this particular undertaking was the time-proved tenet that a general is the most difficult member of any army to capture. And the Hatfield leader, resorting to his experience of Civil War days, had organized himself an army.

Logan Court House, nearest center of population to his new home, heard all sorts of stories about what Devil Anse was doing up on Main Island Creek. The spot he had chosen on leaving the Tug was about midway between the county seat and his old home. Here, on several hundred wooded acres, the mineral rights of which already had been sold, he estimated he would be safest from the McCoys. Between him and his old enemies were miles of rough, hazardous travel, as well as the ridge of the highest mountain confronting those who crossed the border of Kentucky into West Virginia.

The cabin he built, a two-room house like the one he had deserted, was situated in a narrow valley between the ridges coursing down toward Logan from the backbone of the giant range. It was in a section so isolated that people with no business there knew instinctively that they should stay away, and those whose duties called them to the lonely valley went in trepidation. A few yards in front of the cabin ran a narrow steam with steep banks, and across this was placed a bridge that could be raised and lowered at will.

At a convenient distance from the cabin, Devil Anse and his followers erected a second building. It was a low, square, flat-topped structure six logs high, thrown up for protection—against that day when the McCoys should come in force to retaliate, or the law close in on them in such numbers that the Hatfields would not be able to hold their stand in the open. The walls were made of huge twenty-three-foot timbers nearly two feet in diameter. Entrance was by way of a single door of solid oak twelve inches thick, a portal that bullets from the most powerful Winchester failed to penetrate, and portholes were opened in all directions. Water and food were stocked in large quantities, for the Hatfields remained constantly alerted for the time when all of them, women and children included, would have to withdraw into this refuge. A fireplace was provided, and in one corner was tossed a feather bedtick.

Around him Devil Anse called his clansmen, both those with and those without families, and assigned them to guard duty. Among the group was Cap, home after a long flight through the West and down through Texas when things had become too hot for him after the battle of Grapevine Creek. Day and night watch was kept. No man ventured out without his guns.

Oldtimers at Logan still recall the wagon load of arms and ammunition that rolled through town from the direction of the railroad track early one morning. There was hushed talk all around the county seat that day. The law officers knew Devil Anse was setting up an arsenal, and they also knew they were not going to do anything about it. These guns had come from the factory, and the men in whose hands they were to be placed were well experienced in how to use them.

News of this shipment caused the jitters at Pikeville. C. M. Parsons, captain of the town's newly-organized militia, the Buckner Guards, wrote Adjutant General Hill a panicky letter telling him that attack on the Pike County jail might come at any minute. Hill replied by sending a generous supply of ammunition.

On June 1, less than a month after the Supreme Court decided the Hatfields should remain in prison, Captain Alf W. Burnett, venerable head of the Eureka Detective Agency, and two assistants set out from Charleston, West Virginia, in the direction of the Tug. They were in the employ of private citizens. Straight to the mouth of Pigeon Creek they went, then turned toward the mouth of Blackberry and the stronghold of the McCoys.

The detectives advanced cautiously. In time they got on the trail of Dave Stratton, the McCoyite who had been with Frank Phillips when the deputy sheriff killed Bill Dempsey. They learned he was down the river flatboating, and they began looking for him along both sides of the stream. At daybreak on the morning of June 22, they spied him, asleep on a sand bar. They approached quietly and, when near enough, Burnett leaped on him and put the muzzle of a revolver against his throat.

Beside the fugitive lay a Winchester rifle and a .45-caliber Colt navy revolver. Prisoner and guns were packed off to Charleston, where the captors collected their reward and told weird stories of the dangers through which they had passed. Nearly all of the Hatfield and McCoy men, they reported, were armed and out in the woods dodging the authorities, while the women remained at home and worked in the corn fields.

Before many weeks had passed, tales of wide variety were coming out of the mountains. There were accounts of breathless escapades and narrow escapes by the detectives, some of which obviously were imaginative and were placed in circulation in an effort to gain fame without the risk of earning it. A few of the tallest of these tales originated from a man who operated under the sobriquet of "Wild Bill" and dressed in the fashion of Buffalo Bill Cody. Some said his name was William L. Minyard and that he came from Indian-hunting territory in the West. His chief interest was in the fugitives on the Kentucky side and his favorite story was of the time he had hidden in a hollow log while Frank Phillips, spurring on the McCoys, searched futilely for him within hearing distance. It was the fortune of this sleuth finally to overdo his role and his make-up. Law officers brought him in on a charge of peddling moonshine up and down the Big Sandy, and they would pay no attention to his claim that this illicit business was part of the disguise he had rigged up to help catch the McCoys.

Late in July, a number of representatives of the Eureka Agency came into Charleston to claim rewards offered for some of the Kentucky fugitives. They had an exciting story to tell. At the mouth of Peter Creek a few days before, they had had a sharp fight with forty men, all of whom were armed with Winchesters. One of the McCoy band was reported to have been killed and the detectives themselves had some narrow escapes, as evidenced by the bullet holes they proudly displayed in their clothing.

Report of this violence made the public fear that the trouble would break out anew. If the McCoys had squared off against the detectives, it would be only a short while until the Hatfields came to the aid of the sleuths. Families in the counties nearest the border in both states realized this possibility and either armed themselves or moved away.

One piece of cheering news, no matter how inaccurate, began to circulate at this time. It was reported that some of the Hatfields were leaving the state to avoid arrest. Still later came word that the police at Roanoke, Virginia, had information that members of the clan were working their way through the mountains along the Norfolk & Western Railroad, with the intention of escaping northward. Newspapers gave this warning: "All are desperate men and will not be taken without trouble."

But stories of new violence along the Tug came too often for people to place much hope in a wholesale migration. Many of these obviously were fresh from some reporter's fertile mind. According to one report, Frank Phillips was said to have shot it out with three detectives, clipping the belt off one of the trio and making a prize of the revolvers hanging from it.

One Sunday, so went another of these tales, about sixty Hatfield adherents passed the mouth of Peter Creek and stopped long enough for Cap Hatfield to warn an old miner that he had better leave, because trouble was coming. Shortly afterward, a skirmish between the two clans began and continued for some time. When the smoke of battle cleared, three of the West Virginians were dead and two wounded, as against three slight wounds for the Kentuckians.

While energetic newspaper correspondents were thinking up engagements between the two clans, uninvolved citizens on both sides of the river were denying there were any new outbreaks. It was admitted that a Pike County sheriff's posse had fired at some West Virginia detectives and inflicted slight injury, but there was said to have been no resumption of hostilities since then.

One mid-August day, the Hatfields rode into Logan Court House and collected money for mineral rights they had sold to Eastern capitalists. Observers noticed that the visit was particularly peaceful. The feudists said several times before departing that they intended to remain at home, obey the law, and disturb no one unless they were attacked.

Judge W. H. Weddington, presiding over the Criminal Court at Pikeville, was among those who assured peace from the Kentucky side. He was most upset because newspapers said orders had been given for any stranger seen in the county to be shot. "Strangers are in no more danger here than they would be in Frankfort or Lexington," said the judge. "The McCoys are all pursuing the peaceable avocations of life, while the Hatfield party who are not in jail at Pikeville are fugitives in the mountains of West Virginia."

The judge also deplored the stories about Frank Phillips, explaining that the former deputy sheriff was living simply as a private citizen on a farm ten to fifteen miles from the courthouse.

Weddington made no mention of who was living with Phillips. The rumors of months past were not false. After the New York's night raid, when Johnse Hatfield and other members of his clan took to their heels to allow things to quiet down, Nancy McCoy had packed up and fled to the arms of her new lover, the doughty ex-deputy, Phillips, who still was the bane of the Hatfields. It was commonly rumored that Frank Phillips was agitating and leading the faction on the Kentucky side, and adultery and wife-stealing were in keeping with the reputation accorded him in some quarters, justly or unjustly.

16

1888
A Reporter Visits Devil Anse

THE NEW YORK WORLD, PROUD OF ITS WIDESPREAD NEWS coverage, waited for months to get to the bottom of the Hatfield-McCoy feud, the delay falling properly on the shoulders of its star reporter and world traveler, T. C. Crawford, off to Europe on a junket. The globe-trotting journalist returned in August, full of the beauty and historic background of the Continent, but this ardor was quickly dampened with word that he must go at once to the wilds of West Virginia.

When acquainted with general details of the feud, Crawford set his heart on interviewing Devil Anse. He learned that this probably could be most easily accomplished—and certainly with less chance of bodily harm—if John B. Floyd, mountain-born friend of the Hatfields and Logan County's representative at the state capital, could be persuaded to accompany him. So he put this down as his first objective on reaching his destination.

One of the persons from whom the reporter got his information concerning West Virginia was an officer of the Chesapeake & Ohio, a magnate distinguished for his candor. He told Crawford he would not go up through the feud country for a majority of the stock in his railroad. Strangers approaching Logan Court House, he said, were warned that they were going "straight into the devil's own particular country, where for nearly a hundred years the church and her agents have renounced all struggle with him." Mining engineers, he further related, had in any number of instances met with severe punishment for venturing into that region. Several of them had been murdered without attracting the slightest attention. People living in the neighborhood, whenever they heard shooting, merely went inside their houses and shut the door.

Crawford closed his ears to the warnings of the railroad man and headed for Charleston, West Virginia. There he found Floyd in receptive mood. The legislator was somewhat thrilled at the prospect of revisting the scenes of his childhood and coversing with the Hatfields. He even suggested they take along his friend Clarence Moore, of the United States Court, and the New York journalist was not, at the moment, one to object to reinforcements.

The reporter put Logan Court House down as "two days of the roughest riding from the railroad station," and it was riding he never forgot. The road wound along creek beds and occasionally through deep streams. During this perilous part of the journey, the writer remained constantly in dread of malaria and reptiles. Every curve had its dangers, every glen its denizens.

No European village, no matter how deeply buried in the mountains, stimulated in T. C. Crawford so spontaneous a reaction as he got from the settlement around Logan Court House. The first thing that caught his eye was its buildings, most of them low-roofed and unpainted. Many were situated along a narrow straggling street opening on the square and the brick courthouse, and some were clustered around the jail.

Crawford's stay in Logan was brief, but not so brief that he failed to get a lasting recollection of its people. He found them friendly in the morning and quarrelsome in the afternoon, and always suspicious of strangers. He noticed they would pass him on the street without even casting an eye in his direction; yet, when he looked back a few steps later, they would be faced about, standing stock still, staring after him. Fist fights were common in the heart of town, and always at night there were unexplained shots in the dark.

The visitor discovered also that men who had been friends all their lives would quarrel about such trivial matters as the height of a horse, the weight of a pig, or the best shot in the county. Once, near the courthouse square, he stood by to listen in one one of these arguments. It concerned the age of the horse belonging to a Bible salesman, who had just tied the animal to the fence around the square. Guesses among bystanders ranged from young to old—two years, five years, nine years, twelve, fifteen. At last someone thought of asking the salesman. "Well," he said, "the man I bought it from told me he wasn't but a year and a half old. That's all I know about it." This upset the arguers no end, and the discussion started anew, becoming hotter and hotter until one of them happened to turn again to the vendor of Bibles and asked how long since he had bought the horse. "Twenty years," he replied.

Crawford's impression of the mountain women was based largely on the few street-paraders who happened to cross his path. To him they were the most revolting-looking creatures he ever had seen. Nearly all appeared to be snuff-dippers. Two in particular stood out in his memory, one more than the other. This one he described as having sloe-black eyes, a small snub of a nose, a fat face, and a coarse mouth filled with stubs of black teeth. Paint liberally colored her face, and on top of her head perched a crazy straw hat loaded with artificial flowers the size of small cabbages. Her dress was a flaming blue calico that came only a little past her knees, allowing full view of a pair of coarse woolen stockings and man's shoes. The companion was of such the same type, except that she was blond and wore pink calico. Both were smoking long-stemmed pipes.

With all thought of romance driven from his mind by such women as these, Crawford looked toward Main Island Creek. Natives told him that Devil Anse lived fifteen miles up that way, over the roughest roads in the region.

The reporter had noticed from the start that Floyd, a veteran seeker of votes in the Logan hills, had the absolute confidence of the people. It was Floyd's suggestion that they go directly to see Devil Anse, instead of asking his permission. The only preparation he considered wise was to send word by one of Elias' sons that they were coming.

Next morning Crawford, Lloyd, and Moore set out. Their guide was a putty-faced mountaineer with "stupid blue eyes" and an "imbecile countenance set off by a short yellow beard and a long mustache." He had been recommended by the keeper of Bunce's Hotel, where they stopped. Crawford put the guide down as "the free and easiest specimen of American citizen" he had ever employed. On the start, the fellow walked up and chose the best of the four horses their landlord had supplied. When he was handed a valise, he refused to take it until his daily pay had been increased by fifty cents. He said he was willing to go along as company for $1 a day, but if the ignominy of carrying the bag were forced on him his charge would be higher. Crawford recorded that he was forced to yield to the demands of the "mountain scoundrel."

They began their journey in single file. Villagers standing by gave the reporter the impression that their mournful look was that of people watching a funeral march. On the edge of town, they descended the steep banks of the Guyandotte and forded the stream. While crossing, they met a number of mountaineers wading through the water, their shoes on their shoulders, and Floyd explained they were coming to the county seat because court was in session.

From the start, chiefly because of the joshings of Floyd, the guide looked on Moore as an object of derision. Every move the Charlestoner made brought loud guffaws from the man with the stupied blue eyes.

The reporter was soon disgusted. His horse, the guide's demeanor, and other factors combined to sicken him before they had gone a mile, and he suggested they return and start all over again. Floyd and Moore consented. Back at the courthouse, they dismissed the guide with $2.00, got a steady team of horses, and set out in the wagon in which they had ridden from the railroad.

Their second attempt was more successful. As they proceeded, the roads seemed to the reporter to wind in and out oftener. At each turn, without fail, they came upon a mountaineer who to all appearances was engaged in agricultural pursuits, but who invariably set off a series of signals—whistles, bird calls and wild animal cries—that swept like a fading wind through the hollow and on out of hearing ahead of the approaching vehicle.

"That," explained Moore at one point along their route, "is why we're unable to serve these mountaineers with court processes. They know we're coming long before we ever get there."

The wagon rolled on, over rocks, into deep gorges, along the beds of streams, constantly upward, through a sparsely-settled region where homes were so rare that Crawford stared at them as long as they remained in view. The day had cleared beautifully, and the sun now was shining hotly down upon them.

Later in the day, a man trudging along the road, a heavy bag of corn meal on his left shoulder and a Winchester swinging free in his right hand, gave them the first evidence that they were approaching the Hatfield stronghold. Behind him toddled a little girl, bare-footed, burdened also with a bag.

At the approach of the wagon, the man slowed up and slipped the rifle along the line of his hip. His face was dark, covered by a mustache and a short beard, and to the journalist he appeared as wild and ferocious as any game just started from the bush.

"Don't you know me?" called Floyd.

The man's face lighted up and he stopped, acknowledging the recognition with a brief greeting and a wave of the rifle. There was no evidence that he wanted to talk and Floyd made no effort to stop the wagon. It rolled on, lumbering over the rocks, and rounded a curve, the man still staring after it.

"That was Elias Hatfield, Devil Anse's brother," Floyd explained to Crawford.

After a time the road wound up beside a log mill on the bank of a noisy little stream. In the door of the structure sat a man whom the reporter described as "as unprepossessing, unhung a villain as I have ever had the misfortune to see. He had a small, bullet head, frosty complexion, washed-out eyes, little pug nose and great sandy mustache lining the cruel, tightly-lipped mouth. He balanced a Winchester across his lap. I learned afterward that this was French Ellis."

After brief conversation with Floyd, Ellis let them

pass. They rode on, a few hundred yards farther, and came to a field on the left, across which they could see a man Floyd identified as Devil Anse. The mountaineer straightened at Floyd's call and, without hesitancy, walked directly across the field toward them, shouting boisterous greetings.

Crawford was fascinated. He studied Devil Anse's powerful frame, broad shoulders, and deep chest, and noticed especially the stoop to his shoulders. The feud leader wore a brown coat, blue shirt, and blue jeans, the latter tucked into high boots. His coat swung free, baring a large colt revolver strapped to his hip, and in his right hand he carried a rifle. At closer range, the reporter could see he was a man of about fifty. No gray showed in his hair, mustache, beard, or bushy eyebrows. His nose was hooked like a Turkish scimitar, and well down over his deeply-lined forehead he had pulled a faded black hat.

Nothing but cordial hospitality was noticeable in the demeanor of this man whom hearsay had made into a ferocious clan chieftain. Crawford stared at him in amazement.

Without ceremony, Devil Anse led them toward his cabin, stopping the wagon within a few yards of its front door. On the far side, the newcomers could see several men with Winchesters patrolling back and forth, almost with military regularity.

In the room of the cabin they entered were several beds, and across them a formidable array of rifles. On the one farthest from the door lay a man who leaped to his feet and reached for a gun; then, recognizing a familiar face, settled back and said with a slow drawl, "John B. Floyd, you kinder ketched me off guard for onct, didn't you?"

Crawford could tell from Floyd's reply that this was the notorious Cap. He had heard earlier that Johnse was away somewhere hiding out.

As soon as the reporter's eyes became accustomed to the darkness of the cabin, he noticed that its floor was bare and that its most attractive feature was a huge blackened stone fireplace at the front of the room. He surveyed the furniture. On the right was a single bed and at the back another door. In line on the opposite side were three double beds and above them crude pegs on which hung various articles of clothing. A small table and a dilapidated old sewing machine were shoved together in the front corner on his left. Windows opened on each side of the fireplace, leaving the back of the room in deep shadow.

The visitors took seats in front of the hearth, and Devil Anse and Cap pulled up chairs on each side. As soon as they were settled, children edged into the room and stole up close to the mountaineers. One of them was a barefooted boy of six, dressed in gray trousers and ragged gray shirt, who listened intently to the words of the men while eyeing the guns on the beds.

During their conversation, much that the Hatfield men said was lost to the reporter because of their strange dialect. He listened especially to Anse, whom he sized up as a jovial old pirate, and with studied diplomacy led him into a discussion of the feud. The clan leader had no hesitancy about talking of the McCoys. He charged the killings to people of whom he knew nothing, said he was not present at the murder of the three brothers and had not the slightest idea who was responsible for burning the home.

"No man who were thar would tell anyone if he were," he said.

Frequently during the discussion, Cap interrupted to give his version. He was handy with names of people whom he said he believed to be guilty, but the visitors noticed that not one of them was a Hatfield.

When the conversation waned, the reporter spoke up.

"Mr. Hatfield, I want to ask you about your ideas about killing," he said to Devil Anse. "There is no one in this community who has ever charged you with having killed anyone for the pleasure of it, is there?"

"No," replied the leader. "I ain't that kind o' man."

"But if they were to kill any member of your family in a fair fight, what would you do?"

"Wall, I reckon I'd get 'way with 'em jist 'bout quick as I could."

"That is your idea, then?"

"Yes, sar. Any man what wants t' try it, he'll find out."

"Now, what would you do if any detective came here and tried to take you?"

"Wall, now, I ain't aimin' t' be bothered no mo'. I been hidin' out in th' brush an' kept 'way from my wife an' bebbies many an' many a time. I don't like t' be kept 'way from my bebbies."

Devil Anse spat toward the smouldering embers.

"I want this trouble settled," he said. "It's gone on long 'nuff. I aim t' stay at my home, whar I am, fur the present. If th' Guv'ner sends a paper hyar fur me in th' right form, why, I ain't a-gonna kill th' man whut brings it."

"What would you do?" asked the reporter. "Would you surrender?"

"Naw, I wouldn't. I mought go out in th' woods. I been out thar many a time, an' I reckon nobody kin ketch me in these hyar mountins. I jist ain't a-gonna be taken."

"How many men have you constantly on guard?"

Devil Anse looked at the journalist uncertainly before answering. Then he replied: "Nine."

At that moment, a stern-faced woman, with black eyes, black hair, and a stout, powerful figure, appeared in the doorway at the back of the room. At sight of her, the mountaineers pushed back their chairs and got up.

"Hit's time t' et," said Devil Anse.

He led the way outside, to the bank of a stream about twenty feet from the home. Here he pointed to a little tin basin and beside it a small towel. There was no soap. The guests took turns at the basin, while the Hatfields noisily sloshed in the brook.

Back at the cabin the visitors were escorted through a narrow passageway, lined with more beds, and to a second room in which there was another huge fireplace. In the center of this room stood a long table which was covered with steaming dishes.

At the rear was the stern-faced woman, surrounded by three younger women and two girls. Crawford noticed that the younger women were tall, broad-shouldered, and lithe, wore calico dresses and, without exception, were barefooted. One in particular caught his eye. She had regular features, sparkling black eyes, and rosy cheeks, but on her head was a shock of uncombed, dark brown hair that for him took away much of the beauty nature had given her.

After the men had been seated, Mrs. Hatfield stood beside the fireplace and, from time to time, passed out more hot dishes, handing them to her daughters who moved gracefully around the table. As she did this, the guests noticed that some of the sternness left her face and in its stead came a hospitable smile.

Included in the food on the table were corn pone, fried pork, butter, sweet potatoes, sliced tomatoes, and beans. Dishes were constantly circulated, and at intervals Devil Anse boomed out: "Let's see you men take holt an' eat somethin'."

At one time while they ate, Moore glanced casually about the room. In the range of his view were fifteen Winchesters, all within easy reach.

After dinner, a noticeable air of friendliness and informality crept into the cabin. Devil Anse was far more talkative. He sat in a relaxed pose near the fireplace and discussed any subject the visitors brought up. Children crept in close to him and also around Cap, seated across the hearth. Later the three grown daughters entered the room together from the kitchen and took seats in the background.

The clan leader spoke indulgently of the McCoys, expressed regret that the two families had quarreled, but added that he knew of no way to settle the feud. People had threatened his life and the lives of his children, he explained, and he had sworn over and over that he would kill those who bothered him.

"Are you a religious man?" asked the reporter.

"I ain't a church member," said Devil Anse, "lest you say I b'long to th' one great church o' th' world. If you like, you can say hit's the devil's church I b'long to."

"How is it," pursued Crawford, "that so many shots are fired in a mountain brawl and so few people are hit?"

"I'll tell ye," said Anse. "Th' human varmint is th' most corrious an' cunningist varmint thar is. When he goes into a fight, he turns his body sideways, so only 'bout four inches o' his life space is bar t' th' bullet, an' even that he don't hold up fa'r an' squar'. He jist keeps

addition to this, he has found and cut ten bee trees which have netted him nearly $50 in store truck."

By Christmas, there was other news concerning the Hatfields. During the holiday season, the *Big Sandy News,* published at Louisa, Kentucky, originated this story, which was widely copied by the press:

"There is no doubt that the notorious Johnson Hatfield, of the well-known Hatfield gang, died last week at Granville Thompson's a few miles from this place. Some time since, a party passing through the country in a wagon was compelled to leave the deceased, owing to his serious sickness, at Mr. Thompson's. The sick man's name was given as Vance. After a few days some of the party returned for their comrade, but found him too ill to be removed. He shortly afterward died, and, as there was a suspicion that it was Hatfield, an investigation was made. He was identified by one or two parties who knew him, and there is little doubt that it was Johnse Hatfield. The remains were cared for by the county."

This was a false report, but shortly afterward came one based more nearly on fact. It originated when two man-hunters appeared with an article wrapped in paper that they had brought all the way from Flat Top Mountain. It was their proof of claim for the reward offered for Tom Wallace—a scalp down the center of which ran a streak of prematurely gray hair. This repulsive evidence, first displayed at a corner saloon, was the detectives' idea of the easiest way to produce the corpus delicti.

Wallace's death added another link to the chain of successes registered by the detectives. But now, suddenly, came a surprise from the Hatfields. Dan Cunningham, Dick Evans, and another detective, parading under the glory of past performance, took Logan by storm. They flashed their badges from courthouse to blacksmith shop, and let it be known that they were planning an early raid on the Hatfield domain. It was their intention to shoot Devil Anse, Cap, and French Ellis, after which they were confident they would meet with little difficulty in capturing other members of the stronghold. U. B. Buskirk, prominent merchant, was the first to bring word of the outcome of their effort to Charleston.

It was his analysis that the detectives had done too much talking. Somewhere in the mountain forests between Logan and Main Island Creek, the Hatfields had surprised them, not just with loaded Winchesters, but with peace warrants sworn out against the trio before a justice on January 12. Laughter was long and loud the day the feudists marched the three hawkshaws into town and turned them over to the jailer.

The incident had an even more comical turn. The route into town had led across several streams. At each, the Hatfields, including Devil Anse, climbed on the backs of the detectives and rode piggy-back through the water.

The Hatfield leader must have taken special delight in embarrassing Detective Cunningham. A few nights earlier, Devil Anse's barn had gone up in smoke, at an estimated loss of $500, and the *Logan County Banner* reported:

"Some one, thought to be D. W. Cunningham, set on fire Anderson Hatfield's crib and stables, in which it burned a fine horse worth $150, about 150 bushels of corn and several other valuable things."

A neighbor wrote the paper indignantly:

"I think it is an outrage and disgrace to the public to let such go on. We want peace in our land and country, and not destruction of property by fire and trying to kill and destroy what the people have worked and made by the sweat of their brow. Anderson Hatfield is as peaceable a man as we have in Logan County, if he is let alone. . . . Now we ask the detectives to not interfere with our business and we will not interfere with them."

After the unfortunate fall season, winter advanced and the spring of '89 came; and a silence between the two clans that had begun in the autumn stretched into half a year. During all these months, the people wondered what was going on in the feud country. Newpapers, for the longest period since the McCoy home had been burned, were free from stories concerning new hostilities. But not for once had Attorney Lee Ferguson ceased his efforts to build an airtight case against the Hatfield prisoners in the hands of the law. Since Ellison Mounts had been jailed in October, he had been working on the weak-minded feudist in the hope of wringing from him an eyewitness account of some of the atrocities. By April he was rewarded. Mounts consented to talk, in front of half a dozen men including lawyers, and without promise of leniency. A part of what he said was translated into these words:

"I was present and participated in the murder of the three McCoy brothers, namely, Tolbert McCoy, Phamer McCoy and Randolph McCoy. It was on the night of the 9th of August, 1882, at the mouth of Blackberry Creek, Pike County, Ky. The three brothers were taken from a log school house in Logan County, W. Va., where they had been guarded for a day and night, and brought over the Tug River, which separates West Virginia from Kentucky. They were tied arm in arm with a plow line and led by one Charles Carpenter to the river and placed in a small boat, accompanied by Anse Hatfield, Bill Tom Hatfield, Tom Mitchell, Alex Messer, Dan Whitt, Mose Christian, Sam Mahon, Joe Murphy, Jeff Whitt, and myself. We brought them to the Kentucky side and led them by the rope up the bank fifty feet from the river. Carpenter tied them to a pawpaw bush and hung a lantern over their heads. Anse Hatfield then said to them: 'Boys, if you have any peace to make with your Maker, you had better make it now.'

"Tolbert and Randolph began praying, but Phamer (we called him Dick) did not. However, before the boys had time to finish their prayers, Johnse Hatfield shot Phamer. Anse then gave the order to fire, and shot as he gave the word, killing Tolbert and then emptying the contents of the revolver into the dead body. Alex Messer then fired and killed Randolph McCoy. As soon as the first shots were fired, the others followed suit, and all the bodies were riddled with bullets.

"The parties who were engaged in the shooting of the boys were Anse Hatfield, Johnse Hatfield, Cap Hatfield, Bill Tom Hatfield, Alex Messer, Charley Carpenter and Thomas Mitchell.

"After the boys were killed, we crossed the river back into Logan County, West Virginia, where we found Wall Hatfield and some others waiting for us. Wall then ordered us into line and administered an oath to all of us binding us to take the life of the first to divulge the name or names of any who were along, and to solemn secrecy, and wound up the oath by asking us if our feelings were not gratified. Anse, Cap and Johnse Hatfield and Tom Mitchell said 'yes.'"

Mounts gave equally detailed accounts of the shooting of Jeff McCoy, as related to him by Cap Hatfield, and of the New Year's night raid on the McCoy home. Attorney Ferguson, the prosecutor, was delighted with this windfall and readily released copies of the confession to the press.

Trial of the Hatfields began in Pike County Criminal Court late in August, after a summer of quietude. Ferguson had compiled sufficient evidence to make strong cases against only seven of the prisoners—Mounts, Wall Hatfield, Alex Messer, Charles Gillespie, and the three Mahon brothers. The first called was that of Wall, charged in the murder of the three McCoys in '82, and the first witness to take the stand was Randolph McCoy. Next came his wife and then his oldest son, Jim, followed by Joe Davis (the neighbor who had told of seeing young Randolph stab Ellison Hatfield), James M. McCoy, uncle of the victims, Daniel and Jeff Whitt and fifteen others. Their testimony was straightforward and simple, a large part of it repetitious.

Confusion centered around efforts to prove who was present when the McCoy brothers were killed. Jeff Whitt could name only twelve—Anse, Cap and Johnse Hatfield, Charley Carpenter, Alex Messer, Dock and Plyant Mahon, Dan Whitt, Ellison Mounts, Moses Christian, Bill Tom Hatfield, and himself. His brother Dan could list fourteen, including Joe Murphy, Tom Mitchell and Sam Mahon, but not including Plyant Mahon.

Still other discord cropped up in the testimony of the brothers. Dan gave this account of the murder of the McCoys:

"They were brought to the Kentucky side and taken up the river bank 150 to 200 yards to where there was a sink on the bank. Anse said we would rest there and the parties in answer all squatted around the McCoy boys and cocked their guns and pistols and said they were going to have some fun or a shooting match, I do not remember which. Myself, Jeff Whitt, Sam Mahon and

Mose Christian left before the shooting was done. We were fifteen or twenty steps from them when the guns were fired."

Jeff gave a similar story, except that he included Plyant instead of Sam Mahon among the four who ran. But Dan admitted in cross examination that, in conversation with the prisoners at the Pikeville jail, he had made the remark he would give $25 to know which of the Mahon boys had been among those who fled.

Wall Hatfield took the stand in his own defense at the height of the testimony. His words and demeanor were studiously pious. He told of repeated instances in which he had saved the McCoy brothers from being shot while they were held prisoners in the schoolhouse on Mate Creek and of pleading with his brother Anse for them to be turned over to the civil law for trial. When the evidence pinched him, he denied his guilt; when it pinched someone else, he was lavish with detail.

Some of this detail was so minute that it was convincing. For instance, the following from his testimony did as much as anything to establish that Wall was not on the Kentucky side at the time of the murders—and neither was his brother, Elias:

"David Wolford came to me asking that the boys be sent back for trial, and I urged him to go and see my brother Anse and beg to him for the boys. I then found out I could do nothing more for them and started up Mate Creek in the direction of where the corpse of my brother had been removed and in the direction of my own home, and after going a little distance out to the main road I met my brother, Elias, who asked me to go with him to Joe Davis' at the mouth of Blackberry. He asked Plyant Mahon and myself. Plyant Mahon and Elijah Mounts went with Elias Hatfield to opposite Joe Davis', and Elias sent Elijah Mounts across the river to tell Joe Davis to come across and to bring a pint of whisky Joe Davis came across with Elijah Mounts and, after he and Elias had talked a while, I asked Davis if he saw the little boy cut my brother. We then started back down the river and had gone one mile to the mouth of Sulphur and, just after we had passed the mouth of Sulphur, my brother, Elias, stopped to meet a call of nature, and while he was down the firing on the opposite side of the river began, about three hundred yards below us."

Judge John M. Rice was brief in his instructions to the jury. Wall Hatfield was to be found either guilty or not guilty and, if guilty, his punishment should be fixed at death or confinement in the penitentiary for life.

The jury was prompt in its decision. It found Wall guilty and sent him to the state prison for life.

Attorneys for the convicted man immediately filed a motion for a new trial, but this was overruled. They then entered and were granted a plea of appeal, and Rice suspended judgment for sixty days.

Trial of the other defendants followed in quick sucession. Dock and Plyant Mahon and Messer, their cases heard simultaneously, were given life, and Ellison Mounts, dispite his confession and his plea for lenience, was sentenced to hang. The jury trying Mounts deliberated only forty-one minutes. Charges against Sam Mahon, who had broken under the strict jail confinement and had been ill for the last six months, and those against Gillespie were continued.

The only one of the prisoners with anything to say at the time of the sentencing was Alex Messer. He listened to the judge's solemn words "confined to hard labor for the period of your natural life"; then he rose and addressed the bench.

"Hit's mighty little work I can do, Jedge. Hain't bin able to work none o' any 'count for several years."

Judge Rice had to rap hard to get silence in the court room.

Dock, Plyant, and Mounts joined Wall in appealing to a higher court. Mounts' petition was based on the grounds that his more severe penalty was influenced by the mournful testimony of Sarah McCoy and that the maximum retrubution imposed upon him should have been life imprisonment.

At 5:00 P.M. on Thursday, September 5, three carriages, surrounded by twenty-five mounted citizens as guards, rolled out of Pikeville. It was dark and raining hard; the roads were rough and dangerous. For miles, over mountains, across streams, through narrow defiles, to Prestonsburg, the vehicles moved with the guards spread out front and back, expecting an ambuscade at any moment. At Prestonsburg, the cavalcade got word that Cap Hatfield was headed for Knox County to raise a band to rescue the prisoners riding in the carriages. Sheriff W. H. Maynard, directing the caravan, gave orders to push on, without rest or sleep, toward Richardson, on the Chattaroi railroad, thirty miles away. There they arrived at six o'clock the following evening, tired, dusty, hungry, and sleepy.

When the vehicles rolled up to the tiny railroad station, the guards formed a phalanx around them until a train arrived. Then, out of the carriages, in close order, were led four of the newly-sentenced men and Mrs. Lizzie Cloud, the latter facing a year behind bars for grand larceny. Ellison Mounts had been left in the Pikeville jail, the date of his execution tentatively set for December 3.

Aboard the train with the prisoners went Sheriff Maynard and three of the guards, C. T. Yost, James McCoy, and Frank Phillips, the remainder turning about for the trip back to Pikeville. The destination of those who entrained was Ashland, and there they had to wait for a Chesapeake & Ohio train to take them on to Lexington. Among the bystanders on the C. & O. platform Phillips saw a familiar face and, in an expansive mood, went up with friendly intentions. But the man to whom he extended his hand flew into a rage and would have injured the smaller Phillips had not others interfered. The incensed individual was James Vance, son of the grizzled veteran who had gone down fighting on the mountain side.

Throughout the entire journey, the Hatfield followers had stared expectantly toward the hills, confident that rescuers would come. This hope stayed with them past Ashland and died out only when they arrived at the jail at Lexington. There Wall broke into tears and entered the prison in despondent mood, heavy with fear and dread of the years behind bars ahead of him.

"I've been euchred out of my life and liberty," he moaned.

Sheriff. Maynard heard the cell doors click behind his charges without complete relief. He was convinced the end had not been reached.

"In fact," he told newspaper reporters, "there is no doubt but that the thinking element of our community believe we are on the eve of a terrible uprising of the gang. Every man, officers as well as witnesses, in these late convictions, has taken his life in his hands and may expect to be called on at any moment to pay the forfeit. Indeed, you gentlemen down here little realize how difficult it is to be a true, good citizen in Pike County, ever ready to keep the peace as well as to assist in maintaining it. To do it requires unflinching nerve and backbone to stand the fire of midnight assassins at any moment. Our Pikeville military company, sirs, is a great blessing to us, and it is very probable we'll have frequent use for their protection within the next few months."

The sheriff and his assistants went on to Frankfort Monday, taking with them Alex Messer. The other three prisoners were left in jail at Lexington, where they were to await the outcome of their appeals.

Trial of the Hatfields at Pikefield again awakened the press to the news potentialities of the mountain country. The lethargy of past months was banished by rumors that the feud was breaking out anew, and editors cocked a wary ear in the direction of the Tug. At this period, any death by violence in the highlands was murder, and any murder was a part of the Hatfield-McCoy war.

In October, 1889, newspapers reported that the feud had stirred again, more recently at the farm house of Peter McCoy. This farmer had a daughter, Julia Ann, who, the press reported, was about to become the bride of John Hand, a relative of the Hatfields, and was standing before the minister, her hand in that of her fiancé, when a volley was poured through a window, killing the bridal couple and the clergyman.

The *Wheeling Intelligencer* was goaded to editorial comment: "The Hatfield-McCoy feud breaks out again with all the old time fury. The law has no terrors for these people. Perhaps it would be possible, by vigorous administration, to infuse into the law a little of the terror that peeps through the hangman's noose."

Suicide also was tied in with the factional troubles. About this time, it was announced that Joseph Unguart, a promiment citizen of Logan County, West Virginia, despondent over the loss of several relatives in the feud, had ended his life by hanging.

A reporter at this period gained entrance to the Pikeville jail and had a chance to interview Ellison Mounts. Through the bars the prisoner extended a limp hand to the visitor. Yes, he would talk, but only if the newsman would come inside his cell. He turned and lit a chimneyless lamp and motioned toward a narrow cot. At closer quarters, the reporter studied his subject between questions, and the impression of physical appearance he got was greatly influenced by the flickering yellow light. The condemned man seemed to him six feet tall, handsomely formed, "as becomes a Hatfield," bland, with dull gray eyes that alternately stared and blinked at vacancy. His face was smooth, his skin of ashen hue, and his countenance marked by the mental agony of one domed to die, although madly desirous of living.

Mounts was quoted, in the *Wheeling Intelligencer* of October 21, in a manner that in no way resembled his mountain dialect:

"I don't blame the McCoys," he said. "The Hatfields brought me to this. I was forced to do as I did. Twice they came after me with guns, telling me to come on and take the lives of those who had killed my father. I saw his murderers shot, and was at the burning of the cabin. I can't go into details. My guilt was not as great as Alex Messer's, or Wall Hatfield's, or the Whitts', who turned state's evidence. Yet my life pays forfeit, while they are permitted to live. No, I do not look for a commutation of sentence. Nobody seems to be doing anything for me. My lawyers come here and talk to me; then go away and forget that I am alive."

The reporter was tremendously sympathetic. He recorded that the doomed man's parents were both Hatfields—"cousins who loved not wisely, but too well."

While on his junket to Pikeville, the journalist did some other investigating. He interviewed several of the Hatfields, including Parson Anse, and found that the story about the shooting of Julia Ann McCoy and John Hand at their wedding was false. He also disproved a dispatch of recent date that a mob had organized to lynch Sam Mahon, whose trial had been postponed because of his illness.

"Mahon is dying, it is true," he reported, "but is generally believed to be innocent and, if he lives till court meets, the case will be nolle prossed."

On November 9, the Court of Appeals gave its decision in the feud trials. The opinion reviewed the details of the charges and then concluded:

"The history of crime, whether committed in this state or out of it, will present no state of facts more clearly establishing guilt than is found in this record, applied to either or all the parties convicted, and to find a cruel and more inhuman murder we must leave our civilization and resort to the annals of savage life. It is needless, however, to comment on the enormity of the crime or the helpless condition of the young victims of this murderous band. The law has been enforced in these cases, and in its administration the appellants can truly say the jury inflicting the punishment by imprisonment for life 'has tempered justice with mercy.' The judgment of conviction as to each one of the appellants is affirmed."

Newspapers made no comment.

18

1889 Devil Anse Goes to Court

RESIDENTS OF CHARLESTON WERE SHOCKED THE NIGHT of November 19, just ten days after the Court of Appeals ruled against the Hatfields, to hear that Devil Anse was in town—armed to the teeth and surrounded by a number of his feudists. A flutter went from one end of the state capital to the other.

Much secrecy seemed to surround the report, and few believed it true. The bravest followed a trail of rumors to the office of U.S. Marshal H. S. White. There, through a window, they could see proof that the clan leader was among them. A crowd soon gathered, jabbering so excitedly that newspapers concluded the occasion was "one of the greatest sensations Charleston has experienced for many years."

White had done a masterful job in persuading Devil Anse to come to town. For weeks he had been holding a summons for the clan leader to appear in Charleston to answer to an internal revenue charge that he was selling whiskey without paying the federal tax. The marshal knew there was no way to serve the summons. He had had previous experience with mountaineers. So in desperation he sent his chief deputy, William J. White, to confer with the feudist. This seemed on the surface a futile effort, but it was a last resort.

The deputy was a big, broad-shouldered, good-natured fellow, well acquainted with the mountains, and he made his way safely to the Hatfield cabin. There he was received with hospitality and good humor, not to mention a generous supply of armed guards In front of the huge blackened fireplace, he and Devil Anse talked at length, the marshal's assistant pouring out a proposition carefully pruned of threats. If the clan leader would come to Charleston and stand trial, the federal government would promise him protection against state authority and also against persistent requisitions from Kentucky.

Anse weighed the proposal in the coals of the fireplace, scratching his bewhiskered chin frequently Finally he straightened. He would go, but only with a bodyguard. White consented to the guard, and the feudist summoned five of his followers and told them to prepare for the trip.

At Charleston Marshal White greeted Devil Anse more as a visiting dignitary than as a person he was taking into custody. One of his first acts was to appoint twenty-five special deputies to see that no one disturbed the feudist and his bodyguard while they were in town.

These deputies went to work at once. They were stationed freely around the marshal's office as the crowd began to gather, and they enjoyed the advantages of their assignment. It gave them an opportunity to observe at close range the gaunt, bearded mountaineer whose name threw panic into people.

Devil Anse was dressed in a navy blue suit, his trousers stuffed in the top of rough, half-length boots. The condition of these boots caught the eye of the clan leader's good friend, Major Alderson, and the major at once rounded up a Ruffner Hotel porter who would undertake the task of giving the footwear a patent leather shine. A circle of deputies and gawking spectators watched the performance. For twenty-two minutes and ten seconds by the major's watch, the Negro labored with rag and brush before he finally stepped back to survey his finished handiwork. Then he pocketed his pay and hurried away, the envy of friends and the proudest of Negroes.

People wondered about the terrible reputation accorded Devil Anse. He appeared to be enjoying the show he was making and seemed glad to converse with those who got near him. Among these was a reporter from the *Wheeling Intelligencer.* For two hours they sat together, with the newsman asking questions and getting answers to all of them. The information that he obtained was compiled in a formal statement and submitted for the clansman's signature, which was given in the form of an X.

Some things that Devil Anse said were obviously confused or misunderstood by the reporter. He recorded that he "doctored" Devil Anse's grammar and read the statement to him before he got his X mark. If he did, the feudist overlooked some glaring errors. Devil Anse apparently felt that these inaccuracies made no difference, for details so jumbled were too recent for him to have forgotten their correct version. This was the way the statement appeared in the *Intelligencer* on November 22:

"My grandfather, Valentine Hatfield, was born in Russell County, Va. My grandmother, Elizabeth Vance, was a native of the same county. Eight boys and three girls were born to them. My father, Ephraim Hatfield, was born in Logan County, Va., in 1812. He married Nancy Vance of Russell County, Va., in 1837, and to them were born eighteen children, eight of whom died when young. Six boys and four girls lived to manhood and womanhood. These were Valentine, Anderson (they call me Anse), Ellison, Elias, Smith, Patterson, Martha, Elizabeth, Emma and Biddy.

"I was born September 9, 1838, and married Levicy Chafin April 18, 1861. Twelve children were born to us, viz: Johnson, William A., usually called 'Cap,' which nickname was given him when a small boy and has hung to him ever since, Robert E. Lee, Elliott, Elias, Detroit, Joseph, Willis Wilson.* The daughters are Nancy B., who was captured by John T. Vance May 16, 1889—the only one of my family ever captured by anybody dead or alive [he meant she married Vance], Mary Elizabeth and Rosada.

"I served in the militia in 1861, and regularly enlisted

* The name given this son indicates Devil Anse's admiration for his friend, Governor E. Willis Wilson.

in 1862 in the Confederate Army as first lieutenant in the Forty-fifth Virginia Infantry. I resigned in 1863 and then recruited a company which was kept in service in Wayne, Cabell and other border counties of West Virginia and Kentucky.

"Johnse, Marion and Tom McCoy (who are now trying to kill me) were members of my company during the war.

"When the war ended we all went home and were good friends, until in 1873 or '74, when a difficulty arose between my cousin, Floyd Hatfield, and Randolph McCoy, who had married sisters, over a sow and pigs. A law suit followed. McCoy was loser, and accused his brother-in-law of swearing falsely, for which he struck McCoy with a stone. Soon after, Staton was waylaid and killed by Paris and Sam McCoy. His brains were shot out. My brother Ellison prosecuted them for murder. He swore out a warrant for their arrest and asked me to execute it. I refused to do it because the McCoys and I had always been good friends.

"Some time subsequently my son Johnson and Rosanna McCoy, a daughter of Randolph McCoy, ran away from home to get married. The McCoys headed off the fleeing couple, and Rosanna, barefooted, bareheaded, riding a barebacked horse, made her way to the Hatfields under cover of darkness and informed them that Johnse Hatfield had been scooped in by the McCoys. The Hatfields formed an armed posse, headed by Anse, who went a near way through the woods, caught up with the McCoys, overpowered them without a fight and rescued Johnse, returning home with him. They were then happily married. In a few years, however, Rosanna deserted Johnse and is now living with Phillips, the leader of the McCoy outlaws, in Pike County, Ky.*

"Some twelve months after the above occurrence, Tolbert, Phamer, Randall and Floyd McCoy, who were still angered over the hog suit already described, and more so on account of the prosecution for the murder of Staton, went to the election precinct where my brother

* The part of the statement concerning Rose Anne McCoy was the worst confused in the interview. Here it is evident the reporter mistook Rose Anne for Nancy McCoy.

Ellison voted and murdered him by cutting and shooting him literally to pieces.

"For this offense they were arrested, and when they were taken to the mouth of Blackberry Creek for trial, by the Hatfields as guards for the officers, the McCoys gathered a posse to rescue them. They were taken across Tug River in a skiff to keep them from being rescued by the McCoy mob. Charles Carpenter, Alexander Messer, Daniel Whitt and some others were the guards. To get them in a still safer place, they were taken to a point up Mate's Creek in Logan County. They were ordered by the Hatfields to take the prioners to the Pike County jail in Kentucky. After they got them across Tug River, while Charley Carpenter was bossing the job, on the Kentucky side of the river, three of the men were killed. Floyd was the only one who made his escape.* Soon afterward, Alex Messer, Ellison Mounts, three of the Mahons and Valentine Hatfield were arrested for the murders.

"Mounts has been tried and sentenced to be hung, for the time has not been fixed as yet for the execution. Four others were sentenced in the penitentiary for life; among the number is Valentine Hatfield, who was absolutely not on the Kentucky side of the river when the murders were committed, but the McCoys swore him through.

"Seventeen other West Virginians have been indicted on the charge of being parties to the murder, myself and my sons, Johnse and Cap, being among the number, although as a matter of fact we knew nothing of the murders until several days after they had been committed.

"Nothing was done with these indictments for five years or more, until a lawyer named P. H. Cline, of Pike County, got up a petition, carried it to Governor Buckner and induced him to offer a reward of $1,500 for the arrest of the Hatfields. We know what the McCoys will swear to if they should ever get us. They will do anything to accomplish their purpose, and that is why we don't intend them to catch us. We never intend to be taken by such a crowd. You hear that!

* It is obvious here, too, that the reporter is confused. Floyd McCoy was at the election site at the time of the stabbling in '82, but he was not accused by the Hatfields of taking part in it.

"Frank Phillips gathered up a posse of upwards of twenty men, armed to the teeth. They came across into West Virginia and killed an old man by the name of Vance, whom they claimed had killed Harmon McCoy some time during the war. Deputy Sheriff Thompson summoned a posse and started in pursuit. They met on Grapevine Creek, near the state line. The Phillips men refused to surrender and opened fire on the officers. Little Bill Dempsey, one of the sheriff's guards, was shot in the leg. Bud McCoy was wounded in the shoulder. Dempsey crawled into a shuck pen with his broken limb, and was crying for water when Dave Stratton, James McCoy, Sam Miller, Frank Phillips and two other men came up. They began to abuse the wounded man. He told them he was summoned by the sheriff as a guard, and had to pursue them. Frank Phillips walked up close to where he was lying, drew his revolver and shot his brains out with one shot from his revolver.

"This is a straight statement of the feud up to this day. Every man in Logan County who knows me will tell you I am a peaceful, law-abiding man, and no man will say I ever told a falsehood. In this contest I have only defended myself, as any man would do under similar circumstances."

Before Devil Anse went on trial on the 20th, he summoned to his defense two able attorneys—G. W. Atkinson, in a few years to be governor of West Virginia, and General C. C. Watts.

"This is a trumped-up job," he told the attorneys. "I never sold no man a drop o' likker. I wantcha to git to the bottom of this charge an' you'll find it as I tell ye."

The trial lasted most of one day. It was held before Federal Judge John J. Jackson in a tiny little chamber much too small for the crowd that jammed rooms, halls, and steps of the courthouse.

Evidence brought out during the trial revealed that the charge against the clan leader had been engineered by some of the detectives who were trying to capture him. They had conspired with Dave Stratton, an enemy of Devil Anse, inducing him to go before the grand jury in May and give testimony which would bring an indictment. This was done in the hope that they could get the feudist to Charleston, where he could be nabbed and taken to Kentucky.

The jury gave particular attention to this phase of the testimony. At one point, the requisition for Devil Anse issued by the governor of Kentucky was introduced to aid in discounting the defense testimony, but this had no effect. When the evidence was concluded, the jurors deliberated only a few minutes before bringing in a verdict of acquittal.

For a few moments following announcement of the verdict, the trial chamber was enveloped in tense excitement. Most of the spectators knew that state officers and detectives were on hand to grab the bearded mountaineer the moment the federal authorities released him. But Judge Jackson, veteran of the bench since the time of Abraham Lincoln, put an end to this design. He decreed with dignity that no state officer was to lay hands upon the defendant. Then he turned and directed White to assign enough deputies to the task of guarding Devil Anse to guarantee his safety until he left the railroad.

Deputy Marshal White, Special Deputies Frank Stanhagon and Colonel John L. McDonald and several others, already selected for the assignment, gathered around the clansman and prepared to conduct him from the court room. As they moved out of the chamber, Judge Jackson turned again to the spectators and made an announcement that brought a roar of laughter:

"When Hatfield gets back to his home, I certainly have no objection to any of you arresting him who may want to try it."

19

1888-1889
Death by Hanging

MONTHS AHEAD PEOPLE BEGAN TO WONDER WHETHER Ellison Mounts ever would be hanged. As the day originally set for the excution neared, it was announced that delay in carrying out the sentence had automatically resulted from the law allowing a prisoner, after he had lost an appeal, thirty days in which to file a petition for a re-hearing. Time passed without the petition and, on the evening of December 17, Governor Buckner scheduled the hanging for February 18.

But the uncertainty over whether the trap ever would fall on Mounts stemmed from a more threatening source than a change of dates. The Hatfields were determined to release him before a rope could snap his neck or choke out his life. So mountain gossip advised, on the best authority at hand; and when rumors began circulating along the ridges of West Virginia and Kentucky, they usually had some degree of authenticity.

Fears of a Hatfield delivery grew strong in ensuing weeks. Newspapers were apprehensive and sent reporters into the mountains to watch. One of these arrived at Pikeville late in January. He found things peaceful but came upon information which frightened the public worse than ever. Twice since Mounts' conviction, a stranger had appeared in town and had presented at the local bank checks bearing a signature unknown to the tellers. Not long afterward, another stranger showed up, ostensibly tracing the checks. On Sunday, January 19, the Connolly House listed among its patrons a third unrecognized visitor who, in the afternoon, sauntered over to the jail and spent some time in the vicinity. Bystanders noticed that he inspected the building closely and that he made notes in a small book. Next day, two men rode up, on the excuse that they were following a horse thief. The description they gave of this elusive individual was identical with that of the strange man seen at the jail.

Residents of the town put these successive visitors down as spies from the Hatfield clan. They began to think oftener of the safety features of their jail, a brick structure equipped with a steel cage of the latest improvement, and they were reassured that everything was all right. Before reaching Mounts, the feudists from West Virginia would have to master three strong combination locks. But, just for precaution, the guard around the jail was strengthened, day and night.

By the end of January, plans were going forward for the erection of a gallows. This instrument of death was to be located in a field on the outskirts of town, in a valley overlooked by the graveyard.

Early February found the condemned man's friends alarmed over his sanity. For days he had refused to talk or eat, and this, his friends maintained, was evidence that he had lost his mind, which was weak to start with. They insisted that Sheriff Maynard summon a jury to decide on his sanity, but this the officer refused to do on the grounds that it was merely a ruse on the part of Mounts to postpone the hanging.

The sheriff's refusal gave rise to renewed rumors that an attempt would be made to rescue the prisoner. Additional pickets were placed around the town, and the sheriff, himself becoming alarmed, wrote Governor Buckner requesting assistance from the state guard.

Every afternoon, for more than a week in advance of the date of execution, services were held in the jail, These were conducted by the Reverend Doctor J. W. Glover, pastor of the M. E. Church, South, who mixed religion with medicine and supplemented his income further by serving as the jail physician. By this combination of occupations, he was able not only to test the piety of the prison inmates but their blood pressure as well.

Glover's prayers in behalf of Mounts drew much attention from everyone except the prisoner. The cotton-haired young man from the mountains took no particular interest in the fact that the hours remaining for him to get himself right with the Lord were fading away. He was even less concerned over the circumstance that he was to be the first person hanged in Pike County for what people remembered as forty years.

A crowd that by the time of hanging swelled into the thousands—estimates ran from four to eight—began to gather in town Sunday the 16th. Many of these could find no sleeping arrangements, and Pikeville suddenly became like a boom town of the gold rush days. Horses, vehicles, and people made noises in the streets all night long, and down around the jail, a stone's throw from the banks of the Big Sandy, such a hubbub was kept up that the sheriff and his specially-deputized guard detail suffered constant jitters.

On Monday, his last day, Mounts asked to see the scaffold. This was an odd request and it was refused. Officers interpreted it as another ruse connected in some way with the Hatfield plan to effect the prisoner's escape. The day passed quietly except for the noise attendant upon the arrival of spectators, who continued to come in droves, by water and by land.

Tuesday dawned clear, too warm for February. Excitement was at high pitch and the Pikeville militia was mustered on full duty, bayonets drawn. Before the morning was well advanced, a disturbance that for a time threatened to become serious took place in the heart of town. It began with the loud shouts of a man. People within hearing distance rushed to find the source and stopped suddenly when they recognized Frank Phillips.

The ex-deputy was in one of his rare states of intoxication and was, if anything, more vociferous than in the past. This was his day, the day the first of the feudists he had brought to justice was to be hanged, and he was making the most of it. Back and forth along the streets he stumbled, a revolver in each hand, announcing drunkenly that he had run the Hatfields and now, by God, he would do the same to Pikeville.

Sheriff Maynard was summoned and began to remonstrate with Phillips. It was a futile effort, but the law officer kept it up until several deputies edged in through the crowd, and then, at a signal from the sheriff, rushed the drunken man and overpowered him before he could shoot.

But now came another rush. Some of Phillips' friends were drinking too, and they suddenly closed in on the officers to rescue their intoxicated hero. Among the most rabid of these was Bud McCoy, Pike County's No. 2 bad man, who was coming to the aid of the No. 1 bad man. In the mad scramble that followed, Sheriff Maynard was kicked in the back and knocked to the ground. There, his face distorted with pain, he lay and yelled for the militia until about twenty-five of the bayonet-toters came running, dispersed the crowd, and finally restored order. Only a hanging could overshadow in importance such a wholesale disorder.

A few minutes after noon, the sheriff, occasionally grabbing his back and writhing with pain, appeared at the jail with the death warrant. Mounts still was indifferent to what was going on around him. He was pale and red-eyed, and his guards had noticed he had passed the night without a wink of sleep. While the warrant was read in a low, coarse voice, and even throughout the brief religious services that followed, he quietly puffed on a cigar, blowing out smoke rings that drifted serenely about his cell and sometimes completely enveloped his cotton-top head.

No other ceremony followed the reading of the warrant and the minister's prayers. Mounts, handcuffed, was led out, between lines formed by a guard of twenty-four well-armed men, and seated on a coffin box waiting in a wagon in front of the building. Beside him sat the Reverend Doctor Glover, strictly the mountain evangelist now, whispering to one of the Lord's children about to come home.

As the vehicle started moving, the guards spread out around it, guns in the crooks of their arms, ready to shoot at the slightest alarm. If the Hatfields were coming, they would have to come soon. Only minutes separated Mounts from his doom. Eyes of the guards—and of the prisoner—swung frequently to the mountains on the town's outskirts.

Slowly up through town the procession went, past the residential section, into the suburbs, and on toward the scaffold waiting at the base of a low hill. Kentucky law prescribed that no hanging should be public. But the law officers wanted this hanging to be public. They looked on Mounts' sentence as a sacrifice to bring a peaceful end to a bloody feud. If fear of the noose were implanted in the West Virginia mountaineers, it might weaken the trigger fingers so willing to commit murder. The law was circumscribed by erecting around the base of the gallows a board fence. Inside this arena were allowed only those with official part in the execution. Yet there was nothing to keep spectators from getting better than a bird's-eye view from the fields and hillsides beyond.

Over the crowd as the wagon rolled into view fell a silence so intense that the creak of the wheels sounded clear and nauseatingly real. Thousands of eyes watched the condemned man as he sat on the box in which he was to be buried and stared up at the instrument by which his life was to be snuffed out. They followed his glance as it dwelt first on the noose and the giant knot in its top perimeter, next on the open grave yawning a few yards away, and then was lifted, out over the crowd, to the mountains beyond. Mounts was helped up the scaffold, his light hair waving in the unseasonably warm breeze. The sun, shining almost directly overhead, brought out the sallowness of his face. Four months in prison had taken away much of the outdoor tan of the mountain man.

It was a few minutes before one o'clock when the rope was adjusted. The prisoner stood with his back to the scaffold, erect, facing out toward the valley and a major part of the crowd. His face was boyish and clean-shaven. The part in his hair was on the right side, and he wore a shirt with open collar and a line of embroidery down the front.

Deputy Sheriff Harry Weddington, presiding over the execution, asked him if he had anything to say. In a firm voice he replied that he had no speech to make, but that he was ready to die and hoped that all his friends would be good men and women so that they could meet him in heaven. From the minister standing at the foot of the scaffold came a reverent amen.

The effect on the crowd was electric. That vast throng of mountain people stood as still as the tombstones glistening in the graveyard on the hill. Not even the sun's rays flashing on the bayonets of the Pikeville militia broke the spell. Men and women stood motionless for seconds that stretched into minutes, and then heads were turned nervously toward the mountains. Behind them was a hollow running back into the ridges, and they realized that this was excellent cover from which the Hatfields could rush forth, rescue Mounts, and flee again to the hills.

Bosoms barely moved as the black cap was pulled down over the prisoner's face. While this was being done, he spoke aloud again.

"They made me do it! The Hatfields made me do it!"

His lips scarcely had ceased moving when the trap was sprung and there, between heaven and earth, dangled the body of a man. From the crowd arose a mighty shriek, and then a bedlam of excitement. Here and there throughout the throng, men and women toppled over in dead faint.

For ten minutes the body hung, turning slowly, back and forth, around and around, like the pendulum of a giant clock running down. Then the versatile Reverend Doctor Glover examined it and pronounced it dead. Men stepped forward to lower it. They took great care to preserve the rope. One piece of this, it was agreed, was to be sent Devil Anse as a warning.

Details of the hanging were slow reaching the outside world. The *Cincinnati Enquirer*, receiving its information via Catlettsburg, got a break on the story and scopped neighboring dailies. It told of the execution in two long paragraphs.

Even though it had a reporter on the scene, the *Courier-Journal* was forced to copy the *Enquirer*. Under the headline "Probably Hanged," it carried this item the day following the execution:

"A dispatch purporting to come from Pikeville announced that Ellison Mounts, the murderer of Allifair McCoy, was hanged at that place yesterday and that he met death coolly. Mounts was probably hanged according to program, but as Pikeville is over sixty miles from a telegraph station, and as the execution was not to take place until the middle of the day or later, nothing definite about the affair can be published this morning."

The trap scarcely had dropped on Mounts before all sorts of rumors began to make the rounds. One of the vilest charges made by friends of the victim was that the law had hanged a crazy man.

This and others like it dissipated the hope that the end of Mounts would mean the end of the feud. Out of the assortment came some tales coined in an effort to explain why the condemned man had not been rescued. One of these alleged that certain of the Hatfields had bribed the jail cook to poison the guards so their compatriot might be freed. The cook practiced on the jail cat until the feline died and then concluded she had gone far enough. A Kentucky correspondent reported that the sheriff was having the necessary papers prepared to bring the bribers of the cook to prison on a charge of conspiring to commit murder.

"Should they be brought back here during the present intense excitement," this correspondent added, "every mother's son of them would be instantly mobbed, as the people are crazed with indignation."

At this moment, the press revealed that a new drive was under way to have the Hatfields turned over to Kentucky authorities. West Virginia had installed another governor, Aretus B. Fleming, and newspapers reported that Prosecutor Lee Ferguson had just been to Charleston to lay Kentucky's complaint before the new administration.

It was said that Fleming had been highly sympathetic, had agreed to honor any requests presented by Governor Buckner, and had offered to call out the entire state guard if necessary to capture the Hatfields. The *Cincinnati Enquirer* doubted the need of the guard, explaining: "Bud McCoy, brother of the girl who was so foully murdered New Year's night,* for which Ellison Mounts was yesterday hanged, declares that he can raise 100 men at any moment to hunt for the Hatfield gang. So certain are the authorities that some of the outlaws will soon be in their power that they have left standing the scaffold used yesterday in the hope of further use of the instrument."

On the following day, Fleming gave a blanket denial of the statements attributed to him. He had not even seen the prosecuting attorney of Pike County, he said.

West Virginia's *Intelligencer*, remembering the correspondent's report that the Kentucky people were crazed with indignation, commented:

"It would not matter much whether the story is true or false, whether the men taken to Kentucky were guilty or innocent, so long as they happened to be Hatfields they would not live long enough in that atmosphere to be tried."

* The *Enquirer* is in error here. Bud McCoy was a first cousin of Allifair McCoy.

20

1890-1891
"The War Spirit in Me Has Abated"

FAILURE OF THE HATFIELDS TO ACCOMPLISH THE RELEASE of Ellison Mounts caused them to be blamed in ensuing weeks for several atrocities in which there was no definite proof they had had a part. The barrage of charges gave the appearance suddenly that no one in the region could commit violence except the West Virginians. Condemnation was general, as in this item out of the *Courier-Journal*:

"The news from West Virginia is that the Hatfields have sold some of their lands, have plenty of money and are likely to go on the warpath again. They seek revenge for the hanging of Ellison Mounts, at Pikeville, and will, it is said, make an attempt to slay or capture some of the Kentucky McCoys. It is also said that Governor Fleming will make a demand on Kentucky for the surrender of the McCoys, charged with murder in West Virginia."

Shortly afterward, when the rumor got around that Joe Johnson, considered an inoffensive old man, had been murdered near Pikeville, the blame immediately was fixed on the Hatfields. The preceding July 4, Joe had shot and killed Phil Tumbler, a notorious desperado, for insuling his wife while on a drunken spree. Johnson was released on bail, but shortly before Mounts' hanging his bondsmen surrendered him to the authorities, and it was another week before he could obtain other sureties. In the interval, he was locked up in the jail near Mounts and Charles Gillespie.

Joe was no snooper, and neither was he a confirmed enemy of the law. When the sewerage system of that part of the bastille in which he was confined became clogged, he had no hesitancy in revealing the cause. He pointed out to jailers that the trouble lay in the flush pipes, into which had been stuffed—he would not say by whom—pieces of blanket. The jail keepers caught the idea. It was another ruse to effect Mounts' release, to force his removal to another part of the prison where there was more likelihood of his escaping. They quickly set things in order again and laughed among themselves at the fancy calling-down the old man got from his fellow prisoners for turning stool-pigeon.

So, when Joe Johnson, according to report, was summoned from his home and slaughtered one night by a man who fired the fatal shot from horseback, the press and the public were quick to condemn.

"The law-abiding citizens of this community," commented one dispatch from Pikeville, "hoped that the death of the member of the Hatfield outlaw band on the scaffold would have the effect of preventing further outrages from this source, but it appears already to have lost its intimidating influence."

No one for the next eight months gave any attention publicly to the fact that the report about Joe Johnson was not true. He was alive and as safe as the day he walked out of prison.

At the opening of the spring term of Pike County Criminal Court, Judge Rice found 733 cases on the docket before him. But it was acknowledged that a great many of these might never be tried. The only reason some of them were kept before the court was in hopes that the people accused might sooner or later be caught napping. Among the most important were those against the Hatfields. So far, with the exception of Samuel Mahon, who was so afflicted with consumption that he was not expected to live until the next term of court, members of the clan already arrested had been disposed of and the only recourse seemed to be that of waiting until others were caught.

The *Courier-Journal*—almost alone, it would seem—kept alive hopes of capturing the Hatfields:

"Well, since 'Windy' Wilson has vacated the gubernatorial chair of West Virginia, we may have a few hangings here. The authorities want old Anse Hatfield and his sons, Johnse and Cap, as badly as the Texas man wanted the pistol. Governor Fleming of West Virginia thinks that a 'fair exchange is no robbery,' and will, it is said, 'swop' criminals with Kentucky to the extent of honoring requisitions for the three Hatfields if Governor Buckner will give up Frank Phillips and Bud McCoy. It would be 'devil eat devil' if such should take place. West Virginia would be better off without the Hatfields, and Pike County can well afford to relinquish all right and title to Phillips and McCoy. So, if this is done, there will in all probability be fine rope-stretchings."

Late in March a Hatfield went down under gunfire in a sudden outburst not even remotely connected with the feud. It was Jerry, ex-deputy sheriff of Pike County and more recently a prosperous young merchant of Logan Court House. He was shot by Mike Lee, and at least one reporter said the killing had followed a quarrel in a bawdy house at Logan. The gun used was one of the rifles furnished the local militia by the state.

Jerry was a cousin of Devil Anse and had been one of the clansmen who had accompanied the leader to Charleston at the time of his trial on internal revenue charges. Mike Lee lost no time in fleeting to a hideout among friends in the mountains, and the press warned him he had better stay there: "Since this shooting, the residents of the county are up in arms, and God only knows what may follow."

On April 21 a meeting with no immediate significance to either a Hatfield or a McCoy took place in the Knights of Labor Hall in the Cotton Block at Charleston. But the development if fomented had far greater potentialities than people at the time realized. It was a gathering of miners from all parts of the state, called to organize a district assembly of the United Mine Workers of America. The session was harmonious throughout, and the assembly formed was designated U.M.W. District No. 17.

Two days later, much more exciting news was sweeping up and down the Big Sandy River: "Frank Phillips has been killed!" A Colonel William O. Smith was reported to have been the slayer. It was said he held a warrant for the arrest of the ex-deputy and that, in trying to serve it, he had been forced to fire the fatal shot.

Mountain folks began to put together developments of the last few weeks and found that they jibed with the report. Smith had been a Confederate officer during the war and had gained such a reputation that he had earned the cognomen of "Rebel Bill." He had operated along the Big Sandy and was reputed to have held at bay a regiment of Federal soldiers, as well as to have captured a part of Garfield's regiment as it ascended the Sandy in pushboats. More recently he had been engaged in sawing lumber in the upper Tug country for the Norfolk & Western, and it was while busy at this occupation that he first had come in contact with Phillips. That was a few weeks before the rumored killing, and the ex-deputy at the time had threatened the ex-colonel with death, accusing him of capturing his father during the war and sending him to prison, where he died.

The night after this meeting, someone entered the bedroom of Colonel Smith and tried to assassinate him while he slept, but the attempt resulted in nothing more serious than a scalp wound. Smith accused Phillips. The latter offered as an alibi that he was at home fifteen miles away at the time of the shooting. But this did not satisfy the rabid Confederate colonel and he swore out the warrant.

People were much concerned over news of the tragedy. To most of them, Frank Phillips was a hero, the man who had followed the Hatfield crowd into their own lairs, in the face of all manner of danger, and had brought them back to the scenes of their crimes in Kentucky. They looked with tolerance upon his wildness of the last two years. It was blamed on the notoriety that had come with the capture of the West Virginians, and they conceded that it had seemed to turn his head in the wrong direction.

But there was something suspicious about the report of Phillips' tragic end. Certain details did not seem authentic. One account said he was killed on Peter Creek on Saturday, April 19; another, that his death occurred on John's Creek on Sunday, the 20th. Some confusion also surrounded the warrant Smith was supposed to have been trying to serve. It was said to have been issued after Governor Buckner had honored a requisition from Governor Fleming for the delivery of Phillips.

On the 23rd, Deputy U.S. Internal Revenue Collector Kendall arrived in Charleston from Logan County and put an end to some of the excitement. He said he had positive evidence Phillips was not killed. This turn of events was strengthened the following evening by the appearance at Catlettsburg of Colonel Wallace J. Williamson, who had been attending court at Logan. Like Kendall, he was certain Phillips was alive. If the former deputy had been killed, said Williamson, the killing was done by someone other than Smith, because the ex-Confederate had been at the courthouse during both of the days it was reported to have taken place.

The rumor concerning Phillips came at a time when the Kentucky legislature was in session. Even though the report in the end turned out to be false, it attracted attention to the eastern section of the state and especially to bills in the legislative hopper calling for improvement in mountain schools. The *Courier-Journal,* in an editorial, pointed out that lawlessness prevailed in the region because its people were not furnished necessary protection of life and property and therefore were forced to protect themselves. The newspaper added:

"Every plan of reform has failed. We have made no changes in the criminal procedure. We have not removed the difficulties that surround the courts. We have not upheld the hands of the judges. We have not in any way diminished the evils that have prevailed for the past ten years. Public attention has been directed to it. There has been some improvement undoubtedly, but this improvement has come from two sources; from the building of railroads and the building of churches.

"The state, having failed to improve its courts, should at least improve its schools, and in no way can this be done with such good effect as by establishing one or two normal schools in eastern Kentucky. People cannot be reformed from without; they must be reformed from within. The teachers that can do the most good are the educated men and women, familiar with this people and surroundings. It is well enough to send missionaries when teachers can not be supplied at home. But they can be supplied at home, and they will be supplied when the state does its full duty in this respect."

Hope at this time of diminishing the lawlessness of the mountains came from another source. It was recalled that in recent years newspapers had been started in such distant Eastern Kentucky counties as Pike, Breathitt, Lee, Wolfe, Bell, Harlan, Letcher, Martin, Johnson, Lawrence, and Carter.

"A steep and weary way," commented one observer, "lay before the printer who essayed to climb with his press to most of these points, but with a determination and perseverance worthy of the high calling pursued, a surpassingly large number of them have got there."

Another commentator thought he recognized what was happening. "One by one," he said, "the counties of the Cumberland region of Kentucky, where the darkness of ignorance a few years ago hung like a pall over the most outrageous crimes, are suffering an invasion from the prioneer torchbearers of the press. The brawlers who found opportunity and security in the hemmed-in lives of the people and the inaccessibility of the region are being compelled to retire from a business which ceases to be agreeable to them when their neighbors begin to measure them by a broader standard and to distinguish only ruffianism where they formerly imagined heroism."

But efforts to improve mountain communities vied for public attention with developments of a criminal nature which were far more interesting to most of the people. Early in May, at the very time when the newspapers were trying to center the minds of the Kentucky legislators on school appropriations, Mike Lee bobbed back into the headlines. He was captured and brought to jail at Logan to answer for the murder of Jerry Hatfield. A few days later, it was found necessary to transfer him to Charleston for safe keeping, because of Hatfield threats to come into Logan to get him. His trial followed a few weeks later. It was accompanied by a sentiment that his punishment should be made as light as possible, and this public attitude seemed to have effect. He was sent to the penitentiary for ten years.

In the midst of all this excitement, Charles Gillespie had been busy in the Pikeville jail. When the pieces of blankets in the flush pipes failed to change his position in the modern prison, he began to look about for other vehicles of escape. He was looking for them the day Mounts died and he kept on searching for them. One May morning the jail keepers found he was missing from his cell. So escape-proof was the jail supposed to be that they felt little alarm at first, confident as they were that he still was somewhere in the building. But Gillespie had found what he was looking for and had gone—back to West Virginia to stay.

Early on the morning of May 15, Mrs. David Stratton awoke to find that her husband had not come home during the night. She hastily dressed and went to look for him. A few rods from her dwelling, she found his mangled remains. His head was split and his breast was badly bruised. He was still alive, but died soon afterward without regaining consciousness.

The news highly excited the neighborhood, and did the same to other sections as it spread over West Virginia and Kentucky. Stratton was another man who had been a headache to the Hatfields. The public looked on him with awe. It was said he had shaken hands with Frank Phillips over the dead body of the veteran James Vance after they had slaughtered him up on the mountain side that day back in January, '88.

At Charleston, Detective J. W. (Kentucky Bill) Napier heard of the tragedy and hurried to Brownstown. There he swore out warrants before Justice Adkins for the arrest of Anse, Cap, Johnse, and Elliott Hatfield, as well as three other men, all of whom were charged with complicity in the murder of Stratton. Armed with these, he headed into the mountains to bring back the accused. He would have saved himself trouble had he waited to learn that Stratton had stumbled while coming home in an intoxicated state and had fallen under the wheels of a Chesapeake & Ohio train.

Weeks went by during which the detective, Napier, was missing. He was traced by the press to Racine in Boone County, on the way to Logan, and then was lost sight of again. He next showed up at Kanawha, where he promised to keep an acquaintance posted, by letter, on his progress, but days piled up without word from him. His friends feared the worst. Their fears were confused. On the one hand, they knew that the Hatfields had said more than once they would not be taken by Napier or anyone else; yet, on the other hand, they were supposed to have expressed willingness to come down to Logan and stand trial if they were served with warrants.

In July, press wires out of Charleston carried the story Napier's friends had been fearing. It said the detective's body had been found within half a mile of the Hatfield home with a bullet through the heart. He was reported to have been dead for some time.

Nearly two weeks went by with this story undisputed. Then the newspaper correspondent at Oceana in Wyoming County, West Virginia, came up with a report that "Kentucky Bill" Napier was at that place. He had seen the detective and had talked with him, had shown him the newspaper account of his death and had heard from his lips that he was the liveliest corpse to be found in those back woods. Napier was at Oceana to appear before a grand jury in connection with a moonshining case. Before he could get out of town, he was assaulted by two friends of the man against whom he was testifying, but the local police interfered and he was able to leave, supposedly as determined as ever to capture the Hatfields.

During the first week of September, an optimistic reporter for the *Huntington Times* wrote a story that was reproduced by papers chiefly because of the good news it implied. In days following, it was neither augmented, nor denied. Thus it stood:

"The famous Hatfield-McCoy feud is at an end. After partaking in the bloody butchery of all the men they could kill, after living as outlaws, with prices on their heads, defying arrest and courting meetings with their enemies, after seeing their young men shot down, their old ones murdered, with no good accomplished, they have at last agreed on either side to let the matter rest. Two men were seen on our streets yesterday, conversing together in a friendly manner and together taking in the sights of our city. One was a brother-in-law of the old man McCoy, the other a son-in-law of Anse Hatfield. They spoke freely of the famous feud, and said that by common consent it would be allowed to cease. Both the parties have gone back to work and are living honest lives without troubling about each other. A number of the members of both factions are still under indictment for murder and lesser crimes, but will probably now not be troubled by the authorities. West Virginia and Kentucky may both rejoice at the termination of the feud and may hope that their annals may never again be stained with a similar occurrence."

People read the article and laid it aside with a feeling that it had less chance of being denied if ignored. Both states were becoming too much interested in the wealth of their mineral and timber resources to tolerate such a war much longer, and they hoped the end was near. Governor Fleming had been giving the matter serious study since his inauguration and now decided on important and wise action. Fearing that the awards offered by his predecessor for the capture of the McCoys may have encouraged continuation of the trouble, he withdrew them and, to all intents and purposes, closed the state's interest in the affair.

The Pike County Criminal Court met for its fall term and, for once, the Hatfield cases were not of major interest. They still remained on the docket, but most people, including court officials, conceded they would probably stay there for years to come; there was little prospect the defendants ever would be brought to trial.

The focal point of interest, for a change, lay in the Pike Circuit Court. Several charges on its civil docket drew attention. J. Lee Ferguson, the county attorney, was accused by at least two Civil War veterans of stealing their pensions from the government, after instituting legal procedure to get them started. A slander suit was equally exciting. It involved Attorney A. J. Auxier, the county's constitutional delegate, Mrs. Frances Yost having "at divers times and to divers persons" passed the word that the barrister was the father of a child born to Barbara Marrs, wife of D. B. The press was not kind to Mr. Auxier. It recalled that, only the summer before, his brother's bride of three weeks had fled to her parents' home, from which she filed for divorce, alimony, and damages, charging her husband with "continued habitual drunkenness" and with "having communicated to her a venereal disease."

In the weeks immediately following, only one incident threatened to mar the calm. Bud McCoy, the bad man of the McCoy faction, was found dead near a lumber camp on Peter Creek with eighteen bullets in his body. The murder was blamed at first on the Hatfields, because no effort had been made to rob the victim. But it was discovered later that Bud had been slain by his own kinsman, Ples McCoy, a mere youth, and his pal, Bill Dyer, over a grudge of recent date.

Two more Hatfields came to Charleston to answer to the law in December. They were Elias and his son Greenway, both indicted in the United States Court for moonshining. There was much less publicity on the trial than when Anse had been arraigned and, as in the earlier case, the verdict was acquittal.

The calendar turned to another year. Hope that the feud was over grew stronger as January of '91 went by without the sound of a shot on either side. Late in February, a letter came to the editor of the *Wayne County News*. It displayed plainly that much labor had been devoted to its preparation.

"Logan County, W. Va.,
"February 24, 1891.

"Editor WAYNE NEWS:

"I ask space in your valuable paper for these few lines. A general amnesty had been declared in the famous Hatfield and McCoy feud, and I wish to say something of the old and the new. I do not wish to keep the old feud alive and I suppose that everybody, like myself, is tired of the names of Hatfield and McCoy, and the 'Border Warfare' in time of peace. The war spirit in me has abated and I sincerely rejoice at the prospect of peace. I have devoted my life to arms. We have undergone a fearful loss of noble lives and valuable property in the struggle. We being, like Adam, not the first transgressors. Now I propose to rest in a spirit of peace.

"Yours respectfully,
"CAP HATFIELD."

This letter obviously was written by Cap, but the words it contained sounded as though they came from the mouth of Devil Anse. Because of this, some people, including editors, attributed it to the father rather than to the son.

Regardless of its origin, the letter attracted considerable attention. "Cap has been using the paper twenty years for gun wadding in shooting McCoys, and no one should better know its value," observed the *New York Tribune*.

The *Tribune* had little faith in the promised cessation of hostilities. Its editors hurriedly wrote: "The rumor that the day Cap came to town with this letter he bought 200 long cartridges and took them home with him may have no foundation in fact, still it might be just as well for the McCoys to stay on their own side of the river for the present. 'I propose to rest in a spirit of peace,' continues the meek and lowly Cap, but our private and entirely disinterested advice to the white-winged dove of peace is for it to fly high in that neighborhood for a while yet, lest it be served up as the principal dish at a game dinner, while its downy covering is used to stuff a Hatfield or a McCoy feather bed."

The *Wheeling Intelligencer* recognized the Hatfield letter as an exoneration of West Virginia and reprinted it in an article on the feud that covered two and a half columns of the front page. Its treatment of the subject was concluded with these paragraphs of vindication:

"Many things that have been printed about the vendetta are pure fabrication, and in most of them the Hatfields had had great injustice done them. It has been many months since there has been any trouble on the border between the families in the feud.

"If Anse Hatfield and his friends had been left alone in peace by the Kentuckians, it is safe to say that the public would have heard the last of hostilities long ago.

"No more hospitable, honest or peacefully-disposed people live than the Hatfields. Their enemies were the aggressors, and the blows they have struck have been in revenge for the unprovoked butchery of their nearest and best loved relatives.

"Bad as the history of the feud is, it should be borne in mind that it was a family war and that the peace of no one else was disturbed. The quarrels and wholesale shedding of blood was solely in a revengeful warfare—no depredations were committed on the property of other people. They were at peace with all the world but themselves. Those who know them describe them as honest, thrifty, well-to-do citizens who would not harm a hair upon the head of anyone who had done them no injury."

Other papers, in discussing the matter, estimated that from 30 to 200 deaths had resulted from the war. While they were trying to estimate the toll, another development occurred that some of them pointed to as the influence behind the letter. It was announced that Aaron Hatfield, a nephew of Devil Anse, was to marry Miss Sophia McCoy. The ceremony, so the story went, was set for May and would take place at a monstrous barbecue in a grove near the Big Sandy. On hand would be large numbers from each family.

The *New York Tribune* handled the report with sarcasm. "Doubtless," it smirked, "Judge Lewis of Harlan County, one of the leaders in the Howard-Turner feud and who, instead of charging the jury, prefers to charge his double-barreled shotgun, will be engaged to unite the young people in the holy matrimonial bonds. The judge is able to repeat the marriage service without the aid of the book, so he can carry a pistol in each hand and 'cover' the bridegroom and the best man, thus probably preventing an outbreak before the completion of the short and impressive ceremony."

At Louisville, the *Courier-Journal,* in its treatment of the bethothal, turned to the classical example set by Montague and Capulet.

"Though one might fancy that Romeo in all the glory of slashed doubtlet, crimson hose, plumed cap and silver-hilted rapier, murmuring sweet nothings outside a marble palace in Verona to Juliet in the balcony, cut quite a different figure from young Mr. Hatfield, his legs dangling down the sides of a little gray mule, his new blue jeans suit donned for the occasion, his brogans given a fresh coating of tallow, and his flap-brimmed hat pulled down over his eyes to conceal his identity from a stray McCoy, plodding his way by the light of the moon over the mountain bridle path, and swimming his long-eared Rosinante across the flooded streams to keep his appointments with young Miss McCoy.

"If young Mr. Hatfield wooed his mountain bride with the witching strains of music, he never used a lute, as the gallants of Verona did in Romeo's day, but he probably played her 'Dixie' or 'Marching Through Georgia' on a new four-dollar accordion, painted in blue and gold, and instead of swearing eternal love by the summer moon, he promised her a pink calico dress and yards of ribbon every year if she would preside over his puncheon table and be mistress of his log cabin. But these things are neither here nor there, and if the mountaineers who used to plunk a ball into an enemy's eye at five hundred yards are to sing duets across a cradle whose inmate contains the mingled blood of Hatfield and McCoy, it is not for us to spoil poetry or to hunt flaws in the gilding."

The public read column after column on the forthcoming mountain wedding and waited. It sounded fantastic, but no more so than other developments in the Hatfield-McCoy feud.

21

1891-1896
Interlude of Peace

MAY CAME AND WENT, WITHOUT FURTHER NEWS OF THE scheduled Hatfield-McCoy wedding. In these weeks there was peace, with no disquieting developments from the mountains; so the public took it for granted that the marriage ceremony had been performed amid generous helpings of barbecue.

But in July, Elias Hatfield, serving as a deputy aiding in the delivery of a convicted murderer, came into Moundsville. A reporter saw his chance to be brought up to date on developments in Eastern Kentucky and rushed to interview the visitor.

Elias was in a mood to talk, to bare certain complaints that had been building up in his mind for some time. His first blast was at the newspapers. There was not a word of truth, he said, in the sensational articles about the feud printed in recent months. The Hatfield and McCoys had not seen each other in the last two years and, during that time, to his knowledge, had not been within twenty-five miles of each other. All that stuff about the two families intermarrying to patch up a peace, he was sure, was pure imagination.

He turned next upon T. C. Crawford. This reporter's visit to West Virginia, now nearly three years past, still irked Elias. He recalled that he had refused to talk to the newspaper man at first, but finally had succumbed to his insistence.

"I gave it to him straight, from beginning to end," he

said, "and stated that the trouble was all over. Well, when the paper came out, I found that he had misrepresented us and exaggerated the whole thing, and had us still killing each other."

When Elias went back into the mountains, they seemed to close behind him. For more weeks, there was silence, weeks during which the public still wondered what was going on between the feud families and held to the hope that peace actually had come.

The main point of interest and uncertainty was Devil Anse's cabin up on Main Island Creek. Few people went near it, chiefly because of the stories told of the dangers associated with it. One of these tales concerned a stranger who appeared at Logan Court House and asked for a guide to lead him to the Hatfield home. A Negro volunteered for the job. When necessary preparations for the trip had been completed and they were ready to leave, the guide held out his hand.

"What do you want?" asked the stranger.

"My money, boss."

"I'll pay you when we get back."

"Yassuh, boss," acknowledged the Negro, still holding out his hand, "but you ain't comin' back."

The few people who did have cause to stop at the Hatfield cabin returned with accounts of their visit which did not conform to reputation. They had been treated, they reported, with only the utmost hospitality and kindness. No lord was ever more gracious in his home than Devil Anse, according to them.

Two of these visitors were John Glenn and James O. Peyton, youngsters in their late teens. Glenn was working for H. S. White, the U.S. marshal who had deserted law enforcement for merchandising and milling in the mountain country. His job was at a sawmill on Beech Creek in Logan County, where ties were being cut for the railroad the Norfolk & Western was building from Kenova to Elkhorn. He had been sent to Milton after a string of mules, and Peyton, his cousin, accompanied him on the return in the hope of landing work at the mill.

White instructed Glenn to try to make it as far as Devil Anse's cabin the first day out of Milton, to spend the night there, and to cover the remainder of the distance the following day. The two youths reached the Hatfield cabin about dark. Anse greeted them cordially, helped them feed the mules and then led them in to the dinner table. There they sat down to a meal of vegetables and meats, including wild game.

After they had eaten, they sat with the family around the fireplace and listened to Devil Anse talk. An hour or so later, the feud leader arose and suggested they get some rest. He conducted them up a ladder, through a trapdoor into an upstairs chamber, where he pulled down the covers on a large feather bed. From a rack overhead he took a rifle and leaned it against the wall.

"Now, boys," he said, "if you hear any noise in th' night, don't worry none. Hit'll jist be us movin' 'round. But if anybody tries to come through that trapdoor, take that 'ar rifle an' shoot 'em. Hit won't be none o' us."

The boys slept little that night. They heard plenty of noise. It was in their minds that the Hatfields were making whiskey and they associated the disturbance during the hours of darkness with the nocturnal activities of moonshining.

Devil Anse knocked on the trapdoor before light next morning. Glenn and Peyton dressed hurriedly and went down to a breakfast of hot biscuits, ham, gravy, eggs, molasses and honey.

When breakfast was over and they had rounded up their mules, the two boys offered to pay for their lodging.

"Thar's no charge," said Devil Anse.

The boys explained they had expense money, that White had intended for them to pay.

"I told you no," the feud leader said, almost angrily, and walked away.

As they left the home, Devil Anse accompanied them, a rifle on his shoulder and two revolvers strapped around his waist. For half a mile or more he led the way, walking well in advance, up to the ridge of the mountains. There he stopped and waited for them to catch up.

"From here on," he said, "you won't have no trouble. You boys don't be afraid. Nobody'll bother you."

Some time later, White had occasion to send a little special correspondence to the *Wheeling Intelligencer* and in it doffed his cap to the Hatfields and McCoys. He told first of the railroad for which he was cutting ties.

"No road ever built in West Virginia," he stated, "will make such a change in the mode of doing business, of living and society, as this one will. The Hatfield and McCoy feuds will disappear; the illicit stills of the mountains of our state will be seen no more; the push-boat will go with the river rafts and flour will take the place of Indian meal. School houses and churches will take the place of the bear hunt and of the many hours idled away by both young and old during all seasons of the year."

Mr. White was perhaps over-optimistic in this part of his report. The remainder of his comment was more conservative.

"My mills are on Beech Creek, or near the mouth of the same, and fifty men and teams are employed, all within one to five miles of all of the Hatfield and McCoy strife, and no one would for a moment believe that the blood-curdling stories of murder and arson that fill the newspapers of the day have this community for the basis of all sensational news of this part of the state.

"It is true that a dozen men have been killed within six miles, but that is past, and the Hatfields have left Tug River and moved back in the country twenty miles, and the McCoys have moved back into Kentucky. Six of my men from Mannington, Dan Stevens and five others stopped at a man's house for dinner on the way here last week, and when they learned that their host was no other than Captain Hatfield, the short hair of their heads stood straight up. . . . But all the boys soon discovered that they were really among peaceable people, who would make no charge for their dinner and who are doing what they can to retrieve the bad name that was heretofore attached to them. The writer has purchased a good deal of poplar from Bad Anse's boys and relatives and feels perfectly secure in the enjoyment of the rights conveyed."

Another of the occasional visitors at the Hatfield cabin at this period was William G. Baldwin, head of the Baldwin-Felts Detective Agency. He had been employed to arrest one of the Hatfield boys on a moonshining charge and approached the home one night just after dark. Devil Anse confronted him and listened to his request for lodging, carefully worded to hide his identity.

"Well, stranger," said the feudist, "if you can put up with the fare, I guess you can stay all night."

Later in the evening, the host led the guest upstairs with an old brass lamp, prepared his bed, and wished him good night. The detective had never mentioned his name and there had been no questions concerning it.

About four o'clock next morning, the visitor heard someone coming up the ladder and reached under the pillow for his revolver. The trapdoor raised on Devil Anse, brass lamp in hand. He came no farther.

"Now, Mr. Baldwin," he said, "I think th' old woman's got brekfust ready. If you'll hurry down an' eat, I b'lieve I kin git you 'way from here without yo' gittin' hurt. You know, I've got some bad boys. If they find you're here, they may kill ye."

Baldwin left immediately after breakfast, with his host leading the way. On the ridge a short while later, they parted, the visitor without his quarry, but with a strong feeling that he was leaving the company of a man who would make a far better detective than he.

Devil Anse became a common figure around Logan Court House at this period. He had not appeared at the county seat often while he lived over in the Tug neighborhood, but, since moving, he frequently came into town, always with some of his clan, always armed. Many residents looked forward to his visits for the diversion he furnished. When they saw a crowd gathered on the streets, they rushed to it, knowing that it had formed around the feud leader, who would be telling some of his many entertaining mountain stories. These he told well, mixing them with as much play and clowning as his listeners would endure. Some people were genuinely fascinated by him; others were hypocritical, pushing in for the distinction of shaking his hand and then, behind his back, making fun of him.

But Devil Anse would not stay long in public places. Much of the time after he moved nearer the courthouse he spent in the woods, presumably hunting or making liquor. There was always a lot of wildcat whiskey in the Island Creek country. It had been a wilderness, an ideal spot in which to moonshine and still stay clear of the federal men, when he settled there. Some people were confident, whenever his long absences occurred, that he was hiding from the law.

Papers were issued against the feud leader many times, but no one would serve them, not even when he came to town. An ambush at the courthouse might easily have been staged, because he always could be counted on to show up at election time. On these visits, he and his followers continued to dominate, just as they had done when they crossed the Tug into Pike County in years past. They wanted it known they were taking orders from no one.

Elections in that day were held in a room of the old brick courthouse. Originally, voters were allowed to fill out their tickets anywhere they chose and to hand them in at a window of the building. But, in time, a new law was passed requiring a rope barrier to be erected, at least sixty feet from the balloting place, and specifying that voters were to enter the arena one at a time when they were ready to vote. At the first election after the law came into effect, one of the voting commissioners poked his head out of the window and announced the purpose of the rope. On the outside of the arena stood Devil Anse and his men. They listened quietly while the announcement was made; then walked in in a group, rifles in hand, and voted.

At the beginning of 1892, newspapers were confident the feud was a thing of the past. The *Courier-Journal*, before January had ended, was observing that "the old Kentucky feuds are dying out, and those who participated in them are finding their way to prison or the grave or to the oblivion of peaceful life."

The scaffold on which Mounts was hanged had been kept standing as a reminder that Kentucky had no scruples against judicial executions. It may have been perfect as a weapon to ward off factional disputes, but it seems to have had little influence on general misdemeanors. "The old scaffold," the press noted, "appears to be a favorite haunt for carousing parties. The bottle and the deck get in their work in its shadows, and recently a drunken card party at the gruesome resort broke up in a cutting affray. Like vice, the scaffold appears to lose its horrors on closer acquaintance."

One editorial writer noticed that the wild country along the borders of West Virginia and Kentucky was making strong effort to free itself from the various desperadoes "who have long given to those sections a character not in accordance with American civilization." For several generations, he recalled, it was impossible to secure the conviction of a murderer there. If the courts themselves were not influenced by partisanship, the witnesses were afraid to testify, and no man suffered for taking another's life unless the friends of the victim took the slayer's own in payment. "But, since the miners and the railroad builders and others have entered these regions," he added, "the population is being gradually reclaimed."

A major reason given for the disappearance of feuds was the removal, tragically or otherwise, of the leaders. In April rumor put an end to Cap Hatfield. It was said by raftsmen floating down the Big Sandy that he had been killed in a poker game by his brother. At the mushroom coal town of Williamson, the editor of the *New Era* was indignant. He most emphatically denied the report.

"We will state," he wrote editorially, "that Cap Hatfield has been an invalid for the past six months from the effects of a wound received when a boy. We understood that he had professed religion, and that no poker games have been played in his house for some time. It is unfair to even such men as he to circulate reports as the above without any foundation whatever."

A few days later the press observed that "it is still unsettled whether Cap Hatfield is dead or not, but his soul and his retainers are still marching on." The comment was based on a bit of news from the *Martin County Gazette:*

"It is reported here that old Anse Hatfield's gang pursued Wash Luster into this county from Logan and took him back to West Virginia, last Wednesday night, to kill him. He was accused by them of stealing."

Before another month passed, a new report that discounted all previous rumors was making the rounds. It said Cap had joined the Methodist church. One newspaper obligingly advised:

"The McCoy neighbors of the genial Cap will bear in mind the accommodating facilities of the Methodist faith, and will not tempt the saintly convert to fall from grace by presuming too much upon his Christian patience."

Much concern was felt at this period over the number of bodies found floating down the Big Sandy. One rafting crew, on a single run out, had noticed three, none indentifiable. People looked upstream and their thoughts turned to Pike County and to the Hatfields and McCoys.

In June the public learned that Pike's isolation had been somewhat reduced. The first telephone line had been extended to Pikeville. A railroad, meanwhile, had reached Williamson, twenty-three miles away, and there was a drive on to extend it the remaining distance.

Over the phone from Pikeville the following November came news the people had been expecting. It was word that Frank Phillips had been killed. In recent months, he had slain two men, and it was commonly accepted that a fatal bullet sooner or later would catch up with him. He was said to have died in West Virginia, true to expectations, yet not at the hands of the Hatfields. His assailant had been a Kentuckian with whom he had quarreled. But within a matter of a few days the rumor was denied. The extent of Phillips' injury was a wound from which he would recover.

More months passed without feud news from the mountains. Public confidence increased and it was announced in print that never in the history of the country had civilization made such strides as among the people of the hills. Before the year '93 was half over, it was recorded that a circus had visited a town in Eastern Kentucky without stimulating a shooting scrape or a drunk. The press took note of the changing times. "Three years ago," commented one newspaper, "the citizens dreaded the day that would induce mountaineers to come to town."

The big attraction of this circus, which circled through Eastern Kentucky, was Buffalo Bill Cody. He was at the peak of his fame and circus billings headed him in big letters. But at one point along the circuit through the mountains, an event that far outdid anything Cody could stage alone occurred without so much as a line of publicity. A gaunt, bearded man from the hills walked with a handful of companions through the crowd of gawking spectators and claimed the privilege of matching pistol shots with the famed Indian scout. The match was arranged at one side of the show grounds, and Cody and the gaunt individual banged away with unerring aim.

"Who is this fellow?" asked Cody when the shooting was over.

"Devil Anse Hatfield," he was told, "leader of the Hatfield faction that's been warring on the McCoys."

"I certainly would hate to engage in a pistol duel with him," Cody remarked seriously.

The months of '94 were not much more exciting than those of '93. An oil well was drilled in Pike County, six sets of twins were born in a single week in one mountain community, and W. E. McCoy got a license to marry M. V. Hatfield. Rumors that the Hatfield-McCoy feud had been revived were circulated twice during the year, but they were scouted by this bit of comment in the *Logan County Banner:*

"The Hatfield-McCoy war has broken out fresh in the newspapers. The Hatfields and McCoys, however, know nothing about it."

Only this item in the *Big Sandy News* concerned Cap and his strong-arm methods:

"For several years the natives in various localities in the mountains of Eastern Kentucky and West Virginia have forcibly prevented surveys of certain large tracts of lands, compelling the surveyors to get out of the country. Most of these natives have bought and paid for the land, but hold defective titles, while others are doubtless only 'squatters.' This condition has been the source of much annoyance and a serious impediment to development. Over in McDowell and Wyoming Counties, W. Va., a party of surveyors were chased away recently, and Cap Hatfield (who needs no introduction to our readers) telegraphed headquarters that for a reasonable amount he will see that the lines will be run."

The months stretched into '95, and in July of that year came further assurance that the feud bitterness was running out. Frank Phillips walked into Matewan, the little West Virginia town that had sprung up across the Tug from the sink where the three McCoys had died in '82. He was armed to the teeth and had several men with him. But his intentions were good.

For the best part of a day, he remained in the community, talking and spreading good will. He visited several of the Hatfields and, in their company, expressed a desire to cease hostilities and become a better man. The Hatfields were willing, recorded the press; so the ex-deputy departed for his home in Kentucky. He appeared to be serious in his declaration of peace, but there were many who were positive he was putting up a bluff.

22

1896-1897
The Second War

RESIDENTS OF MATEWAN WERE UNDECIDED WHAT TO EXpect when Cap Hatfield came down out of the mountains and stalked into town on November election day of '96. In the crook of his arm hung a shotgun and on his hip a revolver, while at his heels trotted his fourteen-year-old stepson, Joe Glenn, a Winchester thrown awkwardly across his shoulder. But fears subsided a few minutes later when the assortment of arms was stacked peacefully in the care of the venerable Dr. Jim Rutherford, mayor of the town and father-in-law of Floyd McCoy. That made sense. People knew of two factors that might cause Cap to start shooting—the McCoys and the doctor's son John. One was a sore now considered healed, but the other, the antagonism between Cap and John, had flared openly within the last two years. Under these circumstances, there seemed no better guarantee of peace than for the weapons of one adversary to be left for safe keeping among friends of the other.

The day passed in comparative quiet. Whiskey was plentiful, and there was some shooting and shouting, but no one was hurt. Rowdyism was in celebration rather than in anger.

Throughout the day, Cap and John Rutherford held their distance, avoiding each other whenever possible. This was mutually deliberate. Once before at an election their tempers had neared the shooting stage, and only a year past John had shot it out with a Hatfield sympathizer and had been wounded. But Cap had made his declaration of peace on reaching town this time, and that somewhat eased fears of an outburst.

Toward late afternoon, the crowd began to disappear, and among the last to leave were Cap and his stepson. On their way out of town, they came down past the polling place, the store of H. S. White, the ex-marshal.

Inside the store, officials were preparing to close up the ballot box, and Cap, once more in possession of his guns, stopped to get in a few parting words before trekking into the mountains. That was the mistake of the day. While he still stood in the street, out of the group of men gathered in front of the building lurched John Rutherford. He, like Cap, had been drinking heavily, and it was a dangerous time for their paths to cross.

The tempers that had been controlled all day ran wild under the stimulus of too much alcohol. Bystanders were not sure which antagonist fired first. Rutherford used a revolver, Cap his shotgun.

The outburst was as rapid as it was sudden. Both barrels of Cap's weapon were emptied almost simultaneously, and H. S. White, in line of fire through the open door of the store, grabbed his head and ducked, stung by two random buckshot.

Cap, with his shotgun useless, reached for the revolver at his side. In the barrage that followed, Rutherford fell. So did his brother-in-law, Henderson Chambers, who had run out the store door to see what was happening.

All at once the firing opened from a new quarter. Cap turned and saw young Elliot Rutherford, John's nephew, blazing revolver in hand. Others, too, had their guns out and there was nothing about their appearance, stand, or facial expression, to indicate which side they would take.

Cap's second gun was empty by this time and he waited no longer. Toward cover he rushed, dodging wildly over the few yards to a railroad bridge. Behind him came the stepson, frightened but game.

Sheltered by a stanchion of the bridge, Cap reloaded his guns and resumed firing. A little to one side, from the cover of a sycamore tree, young Joe Glenn opened up with his Winchester.

But only a few more shots were fired before Elliott Rutherford fell, and the battle was over. Cap called to his stepson. They ran out into the open on the far side of the railroad. It was a short distance from there to the covering of trees on a mountain side rising above the town, and they made it easily. To their ears as they went out of sight came the rising babble of a community as stunned as was the neighborhood the night the McCoy brothers were killed only a few yards across the river.

Matewan is in Mingo County, formed in 1894 from a part of Logan County. Into town early on the 4th came Mingo's sheriff, N. J. (Doc) Keadle, kindly, genial six-footer with an expanding reputation. People knew he was made of stout stuff, and it was said of him that he had a cool head and the nerve of a dozen ordinary men. Most of these things he had to be, for his job was stupendous. In the last thirty days, thirteen persons had been killed in his county, seven within the last forty-eight hours. Though he may not have been so recognized, this law officer was one of the primary reasons why feuds were dying out. He represented a revolution in administration, the advent of men entrusted with enforcement who could rub shoulders with outlaws and still make them live up to the law.

On reaching Matewan, Sheriff Keadle was met with a confused account of what had happened. The two Rutherfords were dead and Chambers was dying. It was rather definitely understood that Cap had killed John, but there was much doubt concerning responsibility for the death of the other two. Some of the bystanders maintained that little Joe Glenn had slain them.

The sheriff gathered a posse and headed into the mountains. The men who rode with him were much more apprehensive than he. Cap was his friend, and it was his feeling there would be little harm left in the mountaineer once his liquor died out.

For those left behind, the next few hours were excited and tense. Posses went in all directions, along railroads and highways, to search trains and vehicles for the fleeing pair. At Cincinnati, the *Enquirer,* trying to make the most of the reports which came in by wire, stirred the fever.

"The excitement," it reported, "has been intensified by wild rumors of an uprising of the whole Hatfield clan, numbering half a hundred men, to defend their leader and aid him in keeping out of the clutches of the law by evasion if may be, by force if necessary."

The newspaper covered its front page with columns of stories and artists' drawings, all about the recent shooting and the feud.

"The Hatfields," it warned, "have all been trained from infancy in the use of firearms, and their unerring aim with the deadly Winchester and their appreciation of the seriousness of the arrest of their leader at this time make the situation an extremely dangerous one to the officers. The feeling, however, is so high and the determination of the officers to bring Hatfield to justice is so strong that he will undoubtedly be forced to surrender, even though the state militia have to be called out. The whole country is aroused, and the interest manifested in the outcome of the bloody encounter which is almost sure to ensue within the next few hours is intense."

It was rumored on the 5th that Cap had been located in the Hatfield fort on Main Island Creek. Posses headed in that direction. Rewards posted by relatives and friends of the Rutherfords were trebled. An influx of detectives was anticipated.

Meanwhile, developments not yet reported were taking place. Among those on the trail of Cap were two experienced detectives thoroughly familiar with the country in which they were operating—J. H. Clark, known as one of the best shots in that section, and Dan Christian. A few hours after they started out, they were approached by a man who drew them aside to talk. He had information on good authority, he whispered, that the fugitives were following Tug Fork, purposely remaining where they could flee into Kentucky if necessary. The two sleuths changed their course immediately.

The public was surprised to hear on the 6th that Cap and his stepson were in jail at Huntington. They had been brought in quietly by rail the night before and were waiting there to be turned over to Sheriff Keadle. Clark and Christian, who made the arrest, had surprised them as they slept in a rocky crevice along Grapevine Creek.

To the detectives' surprise, Cap offered no resistance. He seemed only too willing to give himself up and even induced Christian to visit the near-by town of Thacker in the hope of telegraphing Keadle to come after him. Christian went to Thacker, but left without telegraphing or revealing the capture. The crowd he found walking the streets of that little mining town was in such an excited state he knew the two prisoners could never be delivered alive if brought there. When he returned, Clark flagged a train, and they made the distance to Huntington by baggage car.

Huntington was greatly excited over the arrival of the odd pair from the mountains. Cap, in prison for the first time in his thirty-odd years, assured his captors he would have surrendered anyway but for fear of mob violence at the hands of relatives of the dead men or the McCoys.

People looked at Cap with awe. They said among themselves he had a record probably unparalleled by any other living person, that he had killed at least eighteen men at one time or another. But Cap made no effort to enlarge upon his fierce reputation. He sat for a picture during the morning, with his homespnn-clad stepson standing beside him, and in the afternoon he talked quietly with a reporter for the *Cincinnati Enquirer*.

Visitors to his cell noticed that Cap was highly nervous, that the slamming of a door or the slightest noise caused him to whirl and tense himself. To some of these callers Cap proudly displayed the wounds of his recent battle. On his left hand was a scratch from a bullet. On the top of his left ear he pointed out another, and on the right side of his neck still another. The barrel of his shotgun, he said, bore a dent that explained why one of Rutherford's bullets had not entered his chest.

It was a great day for Cap, a chance for him to build up his reputation as a dangerous man, to strengthen further the rumor once persistent that he actually dodged bullets fired at him by the McCoys. But Joe Glenn spoiled his moment of triumph The boy boasted proudly that it was his Winchester and not Cap's shotgun and revolver that slew Chambers and Elliott Rutherford.

During the period in which the countryside had been searching for Cap, a posse of law officers went into the Main Island Creek section after Devil Anse. They found the feud leader in peaceful mood, surprised and disappointed to hear of the shootings at Matewan, and ready and willing to make the trip to Logan for questioning. They brought him and two of his younger sons down and lodged them in jail for a short while before releasing them. Anse had been found to hold no anger in his heart so long as the McCoys were not involved.

The public, on the other hand, was not so trusting. When it learned that Cap was to be brought to the Williamson jail and held there for trial, the clamor became loud that this was a dangerous thing to do. Devil Anse still was the recognized leader of his clan, it was recalled, and could easily enough raise a formidable force of mountaineers to rescue his son.

But all of this was false alarm. Sheriff Keadle had no trouble in transferring Cap from Huntington to Williamson, and there the prisoner stayed, in company with his stepson. Even then, the town and county took no chances. A special guard was kept around the jail at all hours.

Late in November, Sheriff Keadle came into Wheeling. When reporters cornered him, he gladly answered their questions. Things were quiet back in Mingo and the succession of killings apparently was at an end. One thing he wanted understood about these troubles, however: they were not a part of the old Hatfield-McCoy feud.

"There is no longer any Hatfield-McCoy trouble," he said. "The Hatfields stay on the West Virginia side and the McCoys on the Kentucky side. I think either would go ten miles out of the way to avoid the other."

He placed much emphasis on the point that the Hatfields were good citizens, and he was confident the younger men of the family—described by him as "good, sturdy stock and not the kind of men to seek trouble"—would make their mark. He reported that all were engaged in their usual occupations. Devil Anse was conducting a big timber operation on Beech Creek in Mingo and was employing a number of workers. Johnse was timbering on the upper end of Guyandotte River in

Mingo, and Cap had a farm on Mate Creek. Another son, Bob, was in the mercantile business at Wharncliffe, on the Norfolk & Western, and Elliott was practicing medicine at Delorum. Equally good things could be said about the family of Elias, now jailer at Logan Court House. One of his sons, Greenway, was deputy marshal. Henry D., who had studied medicine at the University of Louisville, had established residence at Thacker and was a surgeon for the Norfolk & Western, while still another son, fifteen-year-old Wayne, was a student at the University of West Virginia.

Sheriff Keadle went still further. He gave a detailed account of each of the thirteen recent killings in his county, and he made it plain that a Hatfield had been involved in only one of them.

A few weeks after the sheriff's visit to Wheeling, Wayne Hatfield broke into the headlines. He was at home from the university for the Christmas holidays and, to assist his father one morning, went into the jail to give the prisoners their breakfast. As he entered the prison, an inmate facing a federal charge struck him a terrific blow and made a break for liberty. The boy was stunned momentarily, but scrambled to his feet, ran to the door, and fired at the fleeing man, felling him with a wound in the side. Newspapers praised him for his quick action.

Cap came to trial early in April. The public noted with surprise that members of his family were on hand at each session of court. There had been rumors that the other Hatfields, including Devil Anse, were disgusted with him because he had stirred up new trouble at a time when they were trying to forget the feud and live in peace.

The trial was one of several docketed at a special session of the Mingo Circuit Court, sitting at Williamson. It was termed by the press "important because of the heinous crime with which the defendant is indicted and of the prominent part which the defendant has taken in all the trouble between the Hatfield and McCoy families." Some of those who heard the testimony thought it rather conclusive that the murder was premeditated and malicious, chiefly because Cap's cousin, G. W. Hatfield, a deputy marshal, said Cap had threatened to kill Rutherford or to have him killed. It was also accepted that Joe Glenn had slain the other two men, but the boy was not considered morally responsible.

Cap was not without his defense in the death of John Rutherford, the first indictment on which he was tried. He testified in detail that Rutherford had been the aggressor, and there were witnesses who bore him out.

The trial ran into the third day before the case was turned over to the jury. On the morning of the fourth, the jurors filed back into court with a verdict of involuntary manslaughter, bringing with it a penalty of confinement in the county jail for not longer than twelve months, a fine of not more than $500, or both. The judge decided a year's sentence would be enough in this conviction, for other counts against Cap remained to be tried at later sessions of court.

Joe Glenn's trial followed two days later. The boy, on advice of his counsel, pleaded guilty to involuntary manslaughter and was ordered to the State Reform School at Pruntytown. Newspapers reported that he was an unusually bright boy and that he would go to the reform school at his own request.

Cap's days in jail were not dull. Daily, friends and relatives came to visit him and were admitted to his cell. As time wore on, these gatherings grew in size, grew in noise, grew in privileges. The bottle was passed around and there was song. Cap was a hero in the eyes of many, including some of the county authorities. So trusting were the guards that days went by in which no one bothered to lock him in his cell, allowing him the run of the jail without interruption.

One night near the end of July, Cap held a special party, more noisy than the others. Next morning he was gone, leaving behind a hole in the wall and a hatchet with which it was supposed he had chopped his way to freedom. Some people, remembering the size of Cap, studied this opening and arched their eyebrows.

The jailbreak gave rise to numerous wild stories. Day by day, the press and the public enlarged upon them, tracing Cap first to the fort on Main Island Creek and then to the Devil's Backbone, the rocky precipice from which his father was said to have fought the Yankees during the war. To his support, it was rumored, had come three of his brothers and several other clansmen. A posse of several hundred men, led by Sheriff Keadle, was reported to be on his trail.

Two weeks went by and the stories continued to grow. In true fictional style, old Randolph McCoy, who for years had been running a ferry across the Big Sandy River at Pikeville, was brought into the picture. Reports said he had appeared at Williamson in homespun clothes and coonskin cap, a long squirrel rifle across his shoulder, ready to do battle against his old enemy, whom he described as "six foot of devil and 180 pounds of hell."

Five deputies were said to have been killed as they attempted to overtake the fugitive. This was reported to have aroused the public worse than ever, and judges and others chipped in to defray the expenses of the pursuit.

Devil Anse was brought to Williamson and questioned. The father disclaimed any connection with his son's delivery or any knowledge of his intentions.

By the middle of August, the many wild rumors treed Cap on the Devil's Backbone. There he held off the posse, it was related, until a heavy charge of dynamite was set off, blowing away a part of the precipice. But this was foolish strategy, so the story went. Under cover of the great cloud of smoke and dust that resulted from the blast, he and his followers fled and were still at large.

The public watched the newspapers for more news, but there the trail stopped. The rumors had worn themselves out.

Cap Hatfield remained at large. Residents of Mingo today believe that was the way it was intended. They recall hearing it said that Cap, if left alone, was a lot less trouble to the county at his own home than behind bars.

23

1897-1901
Strange Noises in Mountain Hollows

As the 1900's approached, the Hatfields and McCoys held tenaciously to a policy of peace, with Cap as the bellwether sworn to mend his ways so far as the McCoys were concerned. Each successive year served to dilute hatreds and to lessen grievances. It had been over a decade since the last violent outburst between the families. Many of the principals—both actors and causes—were gone, and the future appeared to lie indisputably in the hands of time and memories.

The McCoys, on the one hand, gave every indication that they wanted to forget. Randolph McCoy still operated the ferry at Pikeville and still ranted about the New Year burning of his home. But his words were confined to recollection rather than to revenge. So monotonous did his ravings become at times that his neighbors agreed among themselves it was a shame no bullet had taken him away that unforgettable night. In the same neighborhood, his son Jim was engaged in peaceful occupation, and the bullet of an enemy in no way connected with the feud finally had caught up with Frank Phillips. He was murdered up on Knox Creek.

With Cap on the right path, the Hatfields, too, posed as peace lovers and sought to live quiet lives. But this they were not permitted to do. Always in strong evidence were their beligerence and self-confidence, an air that created resentment in other people, both their neighbors and the newcomers who were flocking into the rich coal fields. No matter how much they wanted to change their ways, the public gave them no encouragement. Years more of turmoil—with outsiders rather than with the McCoys—lay ahead.

In 1898, some of the resentment they fomented caused Johnse to be seized and sent to prison. He was an easy pickup. Never a fighter like Cap, he had allowed the years to slow him down and to steal away the romance of his personal attraction. His wife Nancy long ago had faded from his life, and so had the girl people along the Tug thought he should have married. Rose Anne McCoy, the neighbors said, had died of measles during pregnancy, and they were confident she brooded over Johnse to the very end. Those who were with her in those closing hours noticed that she picked constantly at the bed covers, and this was interpreted by them as an omen that she had weighty things on her mind.

Johnse was turned over to the Kentucky authorities and tried at Prestonsburg. To the attention of the court were brought his many old offenses against citizens of the state, ranging from the murders in the sink-hole in '82 to the pillage of the McCoy home in '88. A jury found him guilty and the judge sentenced him to life.

This dose of Kentucky justice angered the Hatfields as they had not been angered for years. And it brought another murder. In July of '99, Devil Anse's eighteen-year-old son Elias slew Humphrey E. (Doc) Ellis, the citizen who had been most interested in seeing that Johnse was punished. Ellis had been standing on the rear platform of a train halted at Gray in Mingo County. Bystanders thought they heard the youth say, "There's the damned son of a bitch who had my brother arrested, but he can't arrest me." Ellis stepped inside the coach and returned with a revolver. But young Hatfield was waiting, gun in hand, and killed him with the first shot.

The public was indignant over what it considered such an inexcusable murder. Doc Ellis had been a popular man He had belonged to the Masons, the Eagles, the Odd Fellows Some people considered him one of the top citizens of that section.

His death brought an anonymous letter to the *Logan Banner*.

"I want to say why Doc Ellis arrested Johnse Hatfield and took him to Kentucky. Doc told me and others that Johnse was making threats and telling people that he would kill him and was acting in a way that he (Ellis) thought he would kill him, and rather than take the chance to kill or be killed he would arrest Johnse and take him to Kentucky. I think any good man would have done the same thing under the same circumstances."

The writer of this letter posed an accusing question. "Who has been killing men in this country for the last ten or fifteen years?"

In answer, he appealed for the "highwayman" who had killed Ellis to be brought to justice.

"If the officers of the law are afraid to do their duty," he suggested, "let us as a band of brothers do and act as we think proper in this matter. Most everyone you speak to about this matter will say that this gang ought to be taken out of here, but they will say to you: 'Don't say anything about me; I am afraid they will do me some harm in some way.' "

The jail sentence given the Hatfield youth was only partial satisfaction to the public. It wanted an eye for an eye. But the Hatfields usually managed to stay clear of such severe retribution.

Some of the feeling that the Hatfields should be made to pay in greater degree for their crime was shared by Governor J. C. W. Beckham of Kentucky. Periodically to his desk came a plea for clemency on behalf of Johnse Hatfield, but each time he refused it. Every six months this was repeated, with the same result, until Beckham finally left the state on a visit. In his absence, Lieutenant Governor Thorn granted a pardon.

Thorn's action brought a howl of indignation from the public. But the Lieutenant Governor was convinced the pardon was deserved, that it was the reward due a true hero. Sympathizing with Thorn in this conviction was the warden of the state penitentiary, who had a story he told with some embarrassment. A burly Negro inmate had leaped upon him with a sharpened table fork one day as he inspected the prison, and it was one man and one man alone who had saved the warden's life. The

Negro was jabbing the fork in his throat when Johnse Hatfield rushed up and intervened. The penitentiary official well remembered the fire in the eyes of the slim mountaineer as he slashed away with a tiny penknife until he severed the Negro's jugular vein.

Despite the manner in which the Hatfields domineered the country in which they lived, the population around them continued to grow. Efforts begun back in the '80's to develop the rich coal fields along the West Virginia-Kentucky border were bearing fruit. Strange noises were coming out of the mountain hollows. New industry was creeping in; and along the valleys, ravines, and mountain slopes tipples appeared in increasing numbers.

Natives watched the growth in puzzled wonder. The coal outcropping about their doorsteps had meant nothing like this to them. They stole down from their homes and looked on for hours at a time, generally along the railroad spurs jutting out of the most inaccessible spots. They were too fascinated to resent the hordes of small homes beginning to dot the area.

Such development led in time to word that this mountainous section, once shut off from the rest of the world and unappealing to newcomers, was the land of promise in the Eastern States. These tidings eventually reached a retentive ear, that of George L. Browning, young lawyer just out of Georgetown University. He had been expanding his education through summer courses at the University of Virginia and was eager for a place to hang his shingle.

One Saturday Browning set out on the train for Logan, West Virginia, following a course that was new and strange but mighty appealing to him in his youthful ambition. He rode the Norfolk & Western out by way of Bluefield and then on and on, more slowly, into the highest mountains he ever had seen.

It was two o'clock next morning when the train reached the little stop of Dingess. There he was told he must get off and spend the night and proceed next day by mountain trail to Logan.

The young lawyer stepped from the train, his heart in his mouth. Before him, everything was pitch blackness, and behind him the faint light from the train windows already was beginning to slide out of sight along the tracks.

But suddenly a lantern appeared, and in its glow two booted legs wigwagged toward the newcomer. When only a few feet away, the owner of the legs, looking swarthy in the yellow reflection, identified himself as a guide from the hotel. Browning almost swooned with relief, raised his voice in too friendly a greeting, and caught stride sociably as the man swung about to retrace his steps.

At one point along their path through the black stillness, the lantern light fell on a stack of bottles higher than a man's head. Browning stopped in amazement.

"What's that?" he asked.

"Whiskey bottles," said the guide. "Folks been pilin' 'em up thar fur a long time."

At the hotel, they found a night clerk sitting at a small table in the lobby, a revolver lying at each elbow.

Browning tried to be cheerful: "Well, I see you've got a couple of friends beside you."

The clerk snorted contemptuously. "Yeah, we find a use for them now an' then."

The young lawyer found the sleeping facilities of the hotel not too bad, but a poker game in the next room kept him awake most of the short period until dawn. He was up early inquiring about the way to Logan.

"You'll have to ride a mule over there," coldly announced the clerk. "We got six or eight here ready to go any time."

"But how'll I get it back?" asked Browning.

"The next person traveling this way'll bring it back."

Browning started riding as soon as he could get breakfast. The way was long and hazardous, but he made it without mishap, unaware that the greatest potential danger along the route was from rocks rolled down the slopes by resentful mountaineers.

The lawyer registered at the hotel in Logan from Eastern Virginia. Before he could leave the lobby, a man with a fox terrier at his heels approached.

"Howdy, stranger, you're from East Virginia, ain't you?"

"Yep," said Browning, puffed up with sudden importance.

"What's yo' business out here?" asked the man.

Browning opened up, not for once conscious of the man's nosiness. In elaborate detail he explained he was a young lawyer searching for a place to begin practice and, at the moment, was looking for the judge of the local court in the hope of getting some information concerning its dockets.

"The judge ain't here," said the man. "He's down at the ball game. Come on. I'll show you where he is."

As they started away, he announced gruffly, "I'm 'Lias Hatfield."

A tingly feeling came over the young lawyer. He looked at his companion cautiously as they walked toward the baseball diamond. There was no evidence of concealed weapons, but Browning was sure they were there.

Just before they reached the ball park, they met a man with a bulldog. Hatfield's terrier immediately got huffish and the other dog walked over him, knocking him to the ground. The blasphemy that followed was spontaneous and lavish. It rolled from Hatfield's tongue so rapidly that Browning tensed himself, ready to run at the slightest motion of his companion's hand, for the owner of the bull was told in violent language that the next time such a thing happened both he and his flea-bitten cur would die.

At the park, the lawyer was introduced to Judge Wilkinson. Browning was amazed to find his honor in shirt sleeves and open collar, looking like a farm hand rather than a jurist.

But the judge was cooperative. He gave Browning a note to the court clerk, and in a few minutes the young lawyer was examining the dockets for the next term of court.

He found the names of some 350 persons awaiting trial and noticed that many of them were Brownings. When he returned to Elias Hatfield, he questioned the accuracy of the predominance of defendants bearing his own surname.

"Yep, that's right," confirmed the mountaineer. "Thar's lots of em' here an' they ain't worth a damn. They're prolific as hell, too."

Next morning early, Browning, squirming under a

mental picture of himself trying to defend a person of the same name charged with any one of the numerous mountain murders listed on the court docket, rode the mule back to Dingess.

24

1901-1918
Time and Change

THE YEARS OF THE 1900's BROUGHT PEACE IN GREATER degree to the feudists. On both sides, a conscious effort to avoid bloodshed was having effect, no matter how much the newspapers and the public tried to revive the old trouble. New people—people who had no family ties with the first settlers in that part of the country—were taking a hand in governing the territory once conrolled by the Hatfields and McCoys, and police authority was increasing. Deeds once ignored as the business of the particular people involved now were bringing reprisals from the constabulary. West Virginia and Kentucky mountaineers still shot too fast for their own good, yet not so quickly as in the past.

A marked change was brought about by a filtering in of educational facilities. Children of feudists made their way in greater numbers to neighborhood classrooms—some in schools brought in by the madcap mining development. As they mingled with other youngsters of different heritage and different environment, their clannishness faded and their biased interest in their own households became more tolerant.

This metamorphosis took place early in the McCoys. Their removal from isolated mountain cabin into the life of a mountain town had broadened their interests. It was easier for them to forget. Jim McCoy in time got to be sheriff of Pike County and later policeman at Pikeville, and the responsibility of watching over the peace and safety of others created in him a strong desire to guard his children from the bitterness of the past. People knew him as a hard-working, industrious man, easy to get along with and a friendly neighbor.

Only in Randolph McCoy was the poison instilled by the feud years strong. In the waiting period between his trips with the ferry, the family war was his most common topic of conversation. He would talk about it at the slightest provocation, no matter whether the person who approached for comment was friend or stranger, and usually his thoughts led up to that terrible night in January, 1888. Whether he and Devil Anse ever met at any time in the years after the feud is not recorded, and their descendants have no recollection of such a meeting. Rather they are of the opinion the two old men purposely avoided each other, fearing that any encounter, no matter how casual or brief, might awaken old animosities.

Devil Anse, as his years advanced, took up the life of a moderately well-to-do farmer and conducted it with the ease of rural gentry. His crops and his livestock kept his larder well filled, and the added income from his lumbering activities put special comforts within his reach. The cabin on Main Island Creek underwent improvements. Weatherboarding covered its logs, and a front porch gave it a still more modern touch. This home was a common stopping place for travelers, from far and near, not one of whom was permitted to pay for his lodging. People who halted along the highway in that vicinity, as darkness approached, and inquired for the nearest place at which they might put up for the night were directed invariably to the renovated cabin. Some went in fear and trepidation, but all departed with praise for the hospitality they had encountered.

Neighbors found Devil Anse in all manner of occupations. One day Sheriff Keadle's son Emmett, passing the Hatfield home, saw the old man poking at a hole with a pointed stick. As the youth got down from his horse and approached, the feud leader made one last poke at the hole and remarked as he turned away, "Stay in thar 'til I want ye t' come out."

"What's in there?" asked Keadle.

"A pesterin' old ground hog."

Later, when the youth prepared to leave, Devil Anse handed him a dollar.

"Bring me some arsenic when ye come back this way."

"Will they sell it to me?" asked the youth.

"Jist tell 'em who hit's fer an' they'll sell it t' ye. Ground squirrels been a-eatin' my corn an' I'm a-gonna fix 'em."

Devil Anse's trips to town were widely separated. He usually rode in with a rifle thrown across the pommel of his saddle, or walked the highways with a Winchester swinging loosely in his hand. His manner was friendly, always, but he never allowed his guard to drop. When he drew up to talk on the streets of Logan, or Matewan, or Williamson, he was careful to place his back against wall or tree, and even then, consciously or unconsciously, his eyes played about the surroundings, as though scanning for hostile guns. On entering a courtroom or assembly hall, he sat at the back of the room, as near the wall as possible, and if available seats made it so that too many people were behind him, he refused to sit.

This habit of self-protection was strong in all his sons. It was least noticeable in Johnse, who since his release from prison had taken to drinking heavily. His manly beauty had faded, and a diffident manner that would have been dangerous for him during the feud days controlled him. Cap, on the other hand, was much more careful. While he loitered in jail, he had become interested in the study of law and after his release had pursued it until he was able to pass the bar. He hung out his shingle at Logan, but the public never became convinced that his intentions were downright serious. There were days in which he was missing from his office, and people got the idea he was off in the mountains making moonshine. They had heard he was selling a lot of liquor at the head of Island Creek, a report they accepted as the chief reason why he devoted no more time to law practice.

Self-protection was strongest in the younger Hatfield sons—particularly Elias and Detroit, commonly called Troy by his mountain buddies. The word was widely spread that these sons were best left alone. But their reputation for being able to take care of themselves eventually brought them employment. When the Virginia Railroad found it necessary to employ detectives to stop mountaineers from shooting at trains passing along Slab Fork between Princeton and Mullins, West Virginia, Elias and Troy got the job.

The man who hired them was John Kee, present representative in Congress from the Fifth West Virginia District. The railroad had engaged him as a lawyer to aid in buying up rights-of-way and later had assigned him the task of organizing a special agents department. After he managed to get the Hatfields on the payroll, the trouble along Slab Fork stopped.

Congressman Kee is a living witness to the ability of Elias and Troy to shoot. Once a special agent of the railroad came into his office and displayed a new revolver he had just bought.

"What'd you buy that for?" asked Kee. "You had a good gun."

"That gun wouldn't shoot straight."

"Why wouldn't it?"

"I don't know. I was out with 'Lias and Troy Hatfield and they were knocking the necks off beer bottles floating down the river every time, but I couldn't hit them with my gun at all."

"That," unkindly informed Mr. Kee, "was not the fault of your gun—it was your aim."

Later, Kee was transferred to the home office of the railroad at Norfolk, and some time afterward called Elias in on business. While he was at headquarters, Hatfield was entertained royally by the railroad counsel. A short while later, Elias was back in Norfolk. Kee first heard of his return through the clerk at the Virginia Club, where the lawyer was staying.

"I'm glad you've come," the clerk said with relief when Kee walked into the lobby of the club. "A fellow was here looking for you a while ago. I told him you'd be back soon and he sat there in a chair with his back against the wall. He looked like a preacher, with a black hat and a black string necktie. He stared at me several times and he had a look about his eyes as though he were planning to kill me. I noticed this same look when he stared at others who came in. He had a package under his arm and finally left, saying he would be back."

At that moment, in walked Elias. Under his arm he carried a quart of whiskey which he had brought to repay Kee for his kindness. That was the last time the two saw each other.

Elias and Troy left the railroad in 1910 and opened a saloon at Boomer. In a business agreement with a fellow saloon keeper, they divided the town and fixed the area in which each could sell. But their competitor afterward broke the pact by hiring an Italian to peddle liquor in Hatfield territory.

When the brothers learned of this trickery, they went to the mountain shack occupied by the Italian to warn him away from his practices. Elias approached from the front, Troy from the rear. When Elias opened the front door, a bullet struck him in the heart. He had no gun in his hand at the moment he swung back the portal, but, when he was picked up dead later, a revolver was clutched in his fingers.

After shooting Elias, the Italian whirled and fatally wounded Troy, pushing in from the rear. But before this brother died he fired three shots. One bullet struck the Italian between the eyes, another in the heart, and a third in the bowels. Doctors said any one of the three would have been fatal.

For the first time, a killing had taken away a member of Devil Anse's immediate family. Only once before, when the McCoys fatally stabbed his brother Ellison, had a slaying come so close to him. But now there was no one on whom to wreak vengeance. The sorrow of losing two sons at once was a terrific blow to the seventy-two-year-old feud leader who had fought a fierce and extended vendetta to protect his family. Along the slopes of Main Island Creek he sat in the gloaming and thought harsh thoughts that somehow seemed to soften with the futile realization that nothing could be done to avenge the deaths. It was at his period that an old friend saw his mood and recognized a long-awaited opportunity.

William Dyke Garrett, Hardshell Baptist who had fought beside Devil Anse in the war against the North, had waited for many years to convert the clan leader. Since 1867, the year he had married Sallie Smith from over on Crawley's Creek, this member of the Logan

Wildcats, known throughout the hills as "The Mountain Preacher" and "Uncle Dyke," had spread his divine message far and wide. He had pulled up often at the Hatfield cabin, talked of old times, and now and then had put in a word for the Lord. But Anse always held him off.

One day, after the death of Elias and Troy, Uncle Dyke sat on his porch, facing the mountain wall that blocked the view from that side of his cabin. Up the road came a weary traveler, plodding along, stick in hand. He turned in at the Garrett gate and the sight of him brought a gleam to the fading eyes of the old preacher. When the two veterans settled back a while later to match recollections, Devil Anse dominated the conversation. He seemed to have something on his mind. Slowly stroking his long beard, he in time turned the talk to religion, and before many minutes had passed, Dyke knew he had added another to his long list of converts.

The baptism took place on a Sunday, in the waters of Main Island Creek. When Devil Anse went down under the surface of the stream, his sons, including Johnse and Cap, went with him. The Hatfields had stacked their arms.

In the years immediately following, effort was made, more than ever, to blot out the past. Parents on both sides of Tug Fork tried consciously to separate their offspring from the idea that guns were weapons with which to kill their neighbors. This effort was not intended to make children allergic to firearms. Target practice was still a popular pastime, especially on Sunday afternoons, and women as well as man prided themselves in their ability to hit a bull's-eye.

H. W. Straley, III, now a valuation engineer with the World Bank at Washington, was one of the youngsters who came up during this period. An incident in his childhood stands out in his memory today. It was the time his mother, a descendant of the Drurys, a Hatfield connection, rescued him from a rattlesnake.

He had been playing in the yard of his home when he spied the reptile. A field hand working near by heard his excited cries and came to investigate, but the rattler had disappeared. He lifted the boy over the fence into the eld and returned to his work. A little later the lad tirred up the snake again. As he approached it, fasci-ated by its rattling noise, a shot suddenly rang out and bullet whistled past his ear. He whirled. There on the orch, framed by morning glories, stood his mother, miling reassuringly, a smoking .45 protruding from the olds of her apron. The boy looked back at the snake. It vas almost decapitated.

No one was more diligent in his effort to conceal the ast than Jim McCoy, son of old Randolph McCoy. He ad spent considerable money in an effort to prosecute he Hatfields, but his disappointments and failures in his respect were buried in his memories. He refused to alk about the feud with his children and strictly forbade heir discussing it themselves.

Jim sat in his home at Pikeville the evening his chil-ren came running in with word that a movie based on he feud was to be shown at the local theater. Out the oor, bareheaded, he rushed. His children knew he was reatly upset, for he never went outdoors without his at.

Down the street a few blocks to the Weddington Theater he hurried. There, amply repeated on posters in ront of the building, was an announcement—in the pi-neer movie days of the early teens—that a reel on the amous Hatfield-McCoy feud was to be shown that very ight.

The town policeman cornered the theater owner, Jas-er Saad.

"You can't do it, Jasper," he said. "I don't want to tart trouble."

Jasper Saad stared for a moment into the serious, hreatening eyes of Jim McCoy; then he promptly tore own the posters.

Children of the feudists were allowed to mingle with ach other as they desired. This, their parents felt, ould be further guarantee against instilling bygone atreds in a younger generation. Cap was as agreeable o this as anyone. He sat on a winter day in the large liv-ng room of his modern home on Main Island Creek, alking with H. I. Shott, news reporter at Williamson rom 1892 and today a leading newspaper proprietor of

Bluefield, West Virginia. Suddenly from an adjoining room sounded a piano, and mixed voices were raised in song.

"Who's that?" asked Shott.

"That's one of them damn McCoys and my daughters," replied Cap.

Devil Anse, as he mounted in years, fully converted to the ways of Dyke Garrett, maintained a desire to do more than wash his soul. He wanted to have the record cleared of the indictments against him and his sons at Pikeville, so that he could move about without the haunting recollection that the police might clamp down on him at any moment. This wish was the subject of many councils around his fireside before he and his sons agreed on the most promising strategy.

Cap's stepson, Joe Glenn, was singled out to go to Pikeville to lay a proposition before Jim McCoy. McCoy apparently liked the young man, who, like his stepfather, had settled on the practice of law, and it was thought highly probable the effort would be successful.

Joe went to Pikeville and met Jim in the office of the Commonwealth's attorney. The young lawyer went quickly into his proposition: he had been instructed by Devil Anse Hatfield to offer Jim $10,000 if he would have the indictments on the Pike County books nol-prossed.

McCoy shook his head.

"If you laid $200,000 down there," he said, motioning toward a desk, "I'd refuse it, because it's the price of my blood."

McCoy hastened to assure Glenn there were no hard feelings behind his words. Later he took the young visitor to his home and, when Joe prepared to leave, invited him to stop there whenever he came to Pikeville.

While the families were trying the erase the past, one Hatfield was making his way into *Who's Who.* It was Devil Anse's nephew, Henry Drury Hatfield, elected governor of West Virginia by the Republicans in 1912. He had risen rapidly, though not without diligent study and effort. He had obtained his bachelor's degree from Franklin College at New Athens, Ohio, and his doctorate in medicine from the University of Louisville. He had also done post-graduate work in New York. Hi practice, begun at Eckman, West Virginia, spread quickly. In a short while, he was employed as surgeon for the Norfolk & Western railway and for several large hospitals in his native state. His career in public life began when he was chosen for a seat on the county court of McDowell County in 1906. Two years later, he was elected to the state Senate and in 1911 served as its president.

Henry ran for governor on a program of progressive principles. One of his strongest supporters was Al J. McCoy, son of Selkirk.

The action of the state legislature during Henry Hatfield's administration showed the influence of his leadership. Some of the major laws it passed were designed to adjust the government to changing economic and social conditions. Workmen's compensation, regulation of public utilities, health, mine safety, and bucket shops were subjects of some of these.

But Henry Hatfield's greatest stroke was in his handling of a strike called in the Paint and Cabin Creek mines of the Kanawha coal field. The United Mine Workers of America, growing since it had got its start in that part of the country in the '80's and '90's, suddenly cracked its whip and made sweeping demands—better wages and hours, the right to belong to a union without discrimination, semi-monthly pay days, and better methods of weighing coal. Serious trouble, described as the worst in the history of West Virginia, flared up. State troops were sent to the scene to insure quiet—in the home and political stronghold of U.M.W. District 17—but several killings took place before this could be done.

Governor Hatfield stepped in and issued an ultimatum: this strife and dissension must cease within thirty-six hours. It stopped in twelve. But there were rumblings of future troubles from the labor people, who looked for direction to a leader named John L. Lewis.

The years slid by rapidly and peaceably. Talk turned to troubles overseas, and young people of West Virginia and Kentucky forgot the legends of the Hatfields and McCoys while their minds were centered on a war that was greater than any they had ever heard of before.

In the midst of all this war talk, Randolph McCoy, who had retired from his ferry boat service and was living with a nephew at Pikeville, fell into an open fire and was burned. The accident hastened the death of the ninety-year-old man. His mind was alert and his hearing was good to the last, but the worries of a troubled mind had weakened his body. He went to his grave still "a-cussin' " the Hatfields, still thinking of injustices he had never avenged. Behind him he left his wife—always kind old "A'nt Sallie" to the people of Pikeville. She would outlive him by several years.

Meanwhile, along the mountain roads continued to tramp McCoy's old enemy, Devil Anse. His sharp eyes never ceased to caress the slopes along which he had trailed the wild animals of the forest—and sometimes his not so wild neighbors. His manner was that of a kindly, courteous old gentleman. If prevailed upon, he would demonstrate his shooting ability, just as he had done as a young soldier with the Logan Wildcats. H. W. Straley, III, clearly recalls the last time he saw the old man shoot. A tin can was suspended from a string 100 to 120 feet out in the yard. Devil Anse sat at a small table, on the top of which lay his rifle. Without bending his head to sight, he moved the end back and forth to bring the barrel in line with the target. Four times he shot and four holes appeared in the can, which hobbed about crazily after the first bullet struck it.

But never in his late years would Devil Anse mention his family troubles. That was a chapter he had locked up the day Dyke Garrett plunged him under the waters of Main Island Creek.

1918-1921
A New Generation Takes Over

A YEAR AND A DAY AFTER THE SIGNING OF THE Armistice of World War I, West Virginia deputy sheriffs seized a quantity of arms and ammunition lying in the express office at the little mining village of Dawes, key point in the Cabin Creek coal district. They were acting on an executive warrant issued by Governor John Cornwell. When examined by federal troops stationed in the area, the shipment was found to contain rifles of the regulation army pattern, as well as soft-nosed and steel-jacketed bullets. W. L. Duff, a miner to whom it was consigned, was arrested on a charge of conspiring against the state.

Two days later, the Governor announced that Department of Justice agents were en route to the coal fields to clean out radical centers and round up International Workers of the World and Russian agitators.

More unrest, much of it stemming from the labor troubles back in 1913, came in rapid succession. Strikes were called in certain mines and were spread to others. Large areas of West Virginia and Kentucky were affected, but the worst disorders developed along the Tug, throughout the entire scene of the Hatfield-McCoy feud. Members of both families were involved, some as strikers, some as law officers.

But no longer was this a war of factions and clans.

Hordes of strangers from an industrial world had moved in to organize the mountainous area that settlers in the early days had avoided as country too wild to tame.

During the opening months of 1920, the U.M.W. centered attention on Logan and Mingo counties. If these hotbeds of coal digging could be organized, union leaders believed, others would fall in line.

By spring, the effect of the drive was widely felt, and mine operators were thoroughly alarmed. They sent out a warning: miners who joined the union would be evicted from company houses.

In May, the evictions started. By the middle of the month, the operators of the Stone Mountain Coal Company at Matewan prepared to clear mine homes in that community. Baldwin-Felts detectives from Bluefield, acting as mine guards, were brought in and on the 19th they began evicting families.

Shorty after sunrise that morning, they started on their rounds, stalking through the mining settlement like law officers closing in on fugitives. As they were dispossessed, families stood about helplessly in the street, awaiting guidance and thinking of nightfall. About them the green of spring had broken in full force—up along the steep mountain slopes on all sides of town, back in Warm Hollow where Ellison Hatfield died, a few yards across the Tug in the sink-hole where the McCoy boys met their fate. It was a setting for peace, but peace has no chance when labor and capital are at outs.

Before the day was far along, there were signs that trouble was brewing among the town authorities. Just as the evictions were getting fully under way, Albert C. Felts of the detective agency saw Matewan's mayor, C. C. Testerman, and Sid Hatfield, chief of police, approaching with a group of men. He anticipated trouble and told his companions to get their guns ready.

Testerman was in front as the group of townsmen came up. He was a typical mountain druggist, not too dangerous in appearance, businesslike in his actions. But a step behind him walked Hatfield, slim, solidly built, youngish at twenty-six. He had brown eyes, protruding ears, high cheek bones and sallow complexion. His relationship with the feuding Hatfields was distant. Even when angered he smiled, adding more force to a reputation that caused him justifiably to be known throughout the hills for his ability with a gun. He wore his vest open, the loose part flapping about the handles of two large revolvers protruding from his belt. But the handiness of these weapons was inconsequential. He shot from his pocket with deadly accuracy. So unerring was his aim that he was widely referred to as the "Terror of the Tug."

As the municipal delegation drew up in front of the detectives, the mayor protested to Felts about the evictions.

"I have ample authority for what I'm doing," Felts told him.

Mayor Testerman squared off before the detective. "Well, you don't pull anything like that and get away with it down here."

Sid Hatfield, the police chief, was more upset than the mayor after their talk with Felts. He wanted to swear out warrants for the arrest of the detectives and promptly phoned Tony Webb, deputy to Sheriff George T. Blankenship. May Chafin, seventeen-year-old operator on duty at the telephone exchange, plugged in on the conversation. She heard the chief of police ask where warrants could be obtained for the arrest of the detectives.

Sid Hatfield could not hold himself. "We'll kill the sons o' bitches before they get out of Matewan," he told Webb.

The morning advanced. Everywhere there was excitement, anticipation of trouble, impending danger. Mrs. Rhoda Compton, like almost everyone else in town, was watching for developments. From her window she saw a group of men chasing a detective down the railroad track and recognized Sid Hatfield as one of them.

Mrs. Compton was a motherly type, both at home and in the community, and her advanced years gave her certain privileges which she used whenever opportunity arose. She stepped to the door.

"For the Lord's sake go back and stop that trouble!" she yelled.

Someone answered, and Mrs. Compton was positive it was not Sid.

"Don't worry, Ma. No one'll bother you."

In the afternoon, Isaac Brewer, loafing about town, found the police chief, Sid Hatfield, and another man in conversation and joined them. Sid was sulking because the mayor had been reluctant to swear out the warrants. "We oughter get a bunch of men and go into the hills and kill these Baldwin men as they come out of the hollow," he suggested.

The other two agreed, and he added: "If the mayor messes around in my business, I'll cut him in two with a bullet, too."

Later, when the evictions were completed, Sid saw the detectives gathering on the streets. He walked up to Felts.

"You'll never get away from here," he said. "Warrants for your arrest have been sworn out at Williamson and will be here on the next train."

On toward the hotel at which they were stopping hurried the detectives. The next train was the one they were planning to take to Bluefield.

When they arrived at the hotel, they were highly excited. Miss Elizabeth Burgraff, one of the employees there, was among those who noticed it. She heard them talking as they packed their bags. The words of Albert Felts came to her plainly and stuck in her memory:

"I'm going to get Sid Hatfield, Testerman, and Blankenship before I leave town, and any others if they interfere."

She watched as they filed out of the hotel. They had their rifles in packages, but their revolvers were hanging at their sides.

On the way to the railway station, they passed Chambers' hardware store. In front of the building, a central gathering place, loitered about fifteen men, among them Sid Hatfield, chief of police. Albert Felts approached him.

"Sid, you're coming with us. I have a warrant for your arrest."

"Let's see it," said Sid.

While he studied the paper Felts handed him, a boy who had overheard the remarks ran to Testerman's drug store. In a few seconds, Mayor Testerman appeared, took a quick look at the warrant and charged that it was bogus.

Sid backed into the hardware store, leaving Testerman in the doorway arguing. Isaac Brewer was already on the inside, walking back and forth, steel-faced, waiting. The young police chief glanced at him and they understood each other.

Sid spoke through tight lips: "Let's kill every damned one o' them."

The shot that sounded a second later has been a subject of much argument. Eyewitnesses and others have never agreed from whose gun it came. But Brewer, who was standing beside Sid Hatfield, and Jeff Stafford, clerk in the hardware store, said it was fired by the police chief. At any rate, it started a fusillade that developed into a battle, and the first to fall were Mayor Testerman and Detective Felts.

After Sid fired from inside the store, Brewer was pushed forward, it seemed to him, and a bullet struck him. He attempted to draw his revolver, but a second bullet clipped him in the hand and he fell to the floor. From there he looked out and saw William Bowman and Sid standing over Felts, lying still on the pavement.

Bowman stuck his gun down at the detective and fired at close range. "Now, I guess you'll die," he said.

Brewer's eyes were putting in a full day. They saw things that were in strong conflict with what other eyewitnesses saw. Brewer was sure a bullet from the police chief's gun killed Testerman, making a widow of a woman Sid was known to admire.

Out in the street, the battle was in full force. Mrs. Stephen Porter, standing in front of her home near the railway station, saw three men fall. One she recognized as Robert Mullens, a miner, another as a Baldwin-Felts detective, but the third, who lurched from a doorway across the street, she did not know. Another Bluefield man, who appeared to be wounded, was standing at a corner diagonally opposite her home and was firing a revolver in two directions.

Mrs. Martha Hoskins, a school teacher, watched the battle from a window of her home. And she was getting a lusty eyeful until a bullet crashed through a pane near her elbow.

One detective, John McDowell, had reached the railway station ahead of the others. When the firing started, he dashed to the cover of a telephone pole and blazed away a few times himself; then ran toward the Tug and, like the other detectives who survived, waded across into Kentucky.

As the firing died down, John Akers took pity on a wounded detective, J. W. Ferguson, and helped him to a wicker chair on the porch of Mrs. Mary Duty's home. Leaving him there, he hurried back to the scene of battle, but had gone only a short distance before he heard shots behind him. He retraced his steps to find Ferguson lying in the roadway with several men standing near.

Akers glanced up at the porch. The bullet that killed the detective, he noticed, had plowed through the back of the wicker chair.

When the train for Bluefield arrived at Matewan a few minutes later, passengers got off to find eleven persons lying dead in the streets. Among the victims were the mayor, two miners, a boy bystander, and seven detectives, including Albert and Lee Felts. It was said that Sid Hatfield had killed the Felts brothers and at least one other of the Baldwin-Felts men.

From the shootings at Matewan, no matter how ominous, the union got only a temporary setback. During the following month, 6,000 miners in Mingo County were instructed not to report for work. Similar orders soon went out to mines across Tug Fork, in Pike County. As families were evicted from company houses, they settled in whatever temporary quarters they could find. Tent colonies sprang up along the valley of the Tug, with large settlements at Nolan, Rawl, Sprigg, and Matewan.

Clashes between mine officials and miners were frequent, and killings were almost a daily affair. Some days, for hours at a time, miners lay under cover on the mountain slopes along the Tug and fired back and forth at mine properties on each side of the stream. The governors of the two states involved were helpless. Cornwell gave notice he was sending fifty mounted men from the West Virginia state police to the area, and from Kentucky came word that the same number of picked men from the National Guard, most of them World War veterans, were headed in that direction.

Meanwhile a special grand jury had been convened to

investigate the Matewan killings. For weeks it remained in session, examining more than two hundred witnesses. One of the most important of these was Anderson C. Hatfield, hotel proprietor and son of "Preacher Anse." It was said that certain things he had heard around his hostelry while the detectives were quartered there would be particularly damaging to the miners. This word got around and it caused fears for Hatfield, especially after he received an anonymous letter telling him to prepare for death because he had only a few days to live.

In August, Hatfield sat on the porch of his hotel talking to Dr. Edward Simpkins, the town's dentist. Suddenly a bullet came from ambush, ripped through the hotel keeper and slashed into the dentist, taking away part of his jaw. Hatfield died in a Huntington hospital a few hours later.

The troubles between the mines and miners grew worse. Baldwin-Felts mine guards and strikers came together in a pitched battle in one area, and the detectives turned machine guns on the union men. In Mingo County, more anonymous letters threatening life and property were received and, in the resulting confusion, state police found they had more than they could handle. Governor Cornwell asked the commander of the Central Department of the United States Army at Chicago to send troops into West Virginia at once. Before August had passed, nearly 500 soldiers were on duty, taking a stand along Tug Fork opposite the camps of the Kentucky National Guardsmen.

Firing from the wooded heights overlooking the mines continued sporadically, and searching parties went out at all hours to break up these renegade marksmen. C. F. Keeney, president of District 17, announced that a general strike of 126,000 organized workers in West Virginia would be called if federal troops were used as strike-breakers instead of for the protection of the constitutional rights of citizens. State authorities replied that the soldiers would be removed from the strike zones of the Mingo coal fields as soon as Sheriff Blankenship could appoint 1,600 deputy sheriffs.

In Logan County, one deputy was killed and five men were wounded when a sheriff's force attempted to break up a mine local's meeting. Dynamiting began at strategic points, and tipples of some of the largest mines went down under the blasts.

Soldiers were withdrawn from the Mingo fields, but by November attacks on coal properties had become so frequent that Cornwell asked that the troops be returned. He also made plans to ask President Woodrow Wilson to declare martial law.

"The time of temporizing is past," the Governor declared.

Back to West Virginia came the troops and, with them, modified martial law. Public assembly was forbidden, unless the meetings were held in organized churches.

The press noted that West Virginia statute books bore a law under which anyone carrying concealed weapons could be fined $50 and sent to prison for six months; yet no enforcement was made. Men put on their pistols with their trousers in the morning and took them off to shove them back under their pillows at night. This was especially true in Mingo County, it was said.

One paper observed: "Mingo is directly on the Kentucky border across the river from Pike County, the scene of the famous Hatfield-McCoy feud, and a constant reminder to men on this side of the penalty unpreparedness carries with it in time of trouble."

On January 8, 1921, in the midst of all the confusion and bloodshed in the coal fields of West Virginia and Kentucky, the *New York Times* carried this news item, dated the day before:

"Anderson Hatfield, long ago nicknamed 'Devil Anse' for his exploits in the Hatfield-McCoy feud that brought violent deaths to so many members of both clans, died quietly in his bed last night of pneumonia at the family home at Island Creek, Logan County. The old mountaineer was in his 86th year."

Devil Anse's death had come late at night, on Thursday, and its cause had been as he often had predicted—natural. He died in good spirit, following weeks of failing health. To the last, he was silent about the feud.

Unlike that of his arch enemy, Randolph McCoy, his death was widely publicized. Newspapers recalled that, up to the time sickness had forced him to take to his bed, he had "worn" a rifle, but had worn it peaceably.

They also remembered that it was said he had fed and sheltered more people than anyone else in his county.

Logan got ready for the biggest funeral in its history. The day following the aged feud leader's death, word came from Omar, a community near the Hatfield home, that mourning friends from distant points in the mountains already were beginning to arrive.

Sunday was rainy, cold, dreary. Through the downpour in the early afternoon sloshed a throng of people, following the pathways up into the hollows of the Main Island Creek section. They came by foot, by horse, by mule, and by vehicle, some from Logan, some from communities much farther away. The special train from the county seat waited at Stirratt, nearest point along the main line.

At the home, mourners were directed to the back door. There they joined a line that passed slowly along the hallway extending through the home to the front porch, where lay the body of the veteran in a golden oak casket, his beard, tinged with gray, spread on his chest like the plumage of a large bird. From near by came the low, doleful singing of a mixed choir, led by Sim Thompson, famous mountain chorister.

Dyke Garrett was there, directing arrangements. He had decreed against a funeral sermon.

"I'll preach no man's funeral but my own," he said with solemn finality.

Once he turned aside from his duties to clasp the hands of two repentant men—Cap and Elliot Hatfield. The brothers had been estranged for years, and now they were back together, fulfilling a dying wish of their father.

At three o'clock, the procession started. As the lid of the casket was closed, ready for the journey around the slope of the mountain to the graveyard, Levicy Chafin took farewell of the man with whom she had lived for sixty-one years. At seventy-nine and in such weather, she agreed it was too much of an ordeal for her to attempt to go to the grave side.

At the burying ground near the graves of Elias and Troy waited the vault, closed to keep out the rain. When the flower-covered casket was put down beside it, the Reverend Green McNeely stepped forward and uttered a few words, simple expressions, not of the dead man, but of the lesson of death. Prayer was offered by W. A. Robinson, like the deceased a member of the Logan County Wildcats.

The crowd slowly closed in, shivering in the cold dampness, until it formed a great circle around the grave. Then, while someone held an umbrella against the rain, the casket was opened for the last time. The mourners pushed forward, some through curiosity, some in sad respect. McCoys as well as Hatfields were in the group.

26

1921
The Feud Guns Are Stacked

THE DEATH AND BURIAL OF DEVIL ANSE, WINDING UP another chapter in the nation's longest and most famous feud, brought no interruption to the labor hostilities of West Virginia and Kentucky. A new days after the funeral, more than a score of defendants, including Sid Hatfield, went on trial for the shooting at Matewan.

The trial was held in the new but small courthouse at Williamson. Judge R. D. Bailey, presiding, gave orders at the start for every person entering the building to be searched for weapons at the door.

Reporters jammed the little mountain town from many parts of the country. They were alert to what was happening and many were predicting things to come. Through their minds ran pithy thoughts concerning the troubles in the hills, including those of past years. Consequently, developments connected with the trial, whenever faintly plausible, were linked with the war between the Hatfields and McCoys. Such was the case when a fusillade of shots was fired from the slopes above Williamson and bullets rattled along the sidewalks just before dawn January 31.

"There is talk among the natives," wrote the correspondent for the *New York Times,* "that a resumption of the feud in the Hatfield clan as a result of the new trial now under way is likely. It may be that the proceedings will be the spark which will ignite the fire of the partly burned out feud which existed for years and was supposed to have been buried with the recent death of Devil Anse Hatfield.

"When the actual trial begins, members of the Hatfield clan will testify for the state, while still others will testify for the defendants. What the aftermath will be time alone will determine.

"Up to date the Hatfield clan is divided. While Sid Hatfield is being prosecuted, Greenway Hatfield, a wealthy coal operator and a brother of former Governor Hatfield of West Virginia, is assisting the state in the selection of the jury which will decide the guilt or innocence of the defendant and his associates."

From the start there was confusion over a similarity of names among the deceased, defendants, witnesses, and jurors. As court got under way one morning, the clerk called for Anse Hatfield. An attorney, jumping quickly to his feet, volunteered the information that Anse Hatfield was dead, but, almost before he could get the words out of his mouth, two talesmen stepped forward and identified themselves by that name. Proceedings were held in abeyance until it could be determined just which Anse Hatfield had been called.

The trial stretched out for nearly two months. During the closing arguments, prosecuting attorneys referred to the fact that Sid Hatfield had married the widow of Mayor Testerman within a few weeks after the shootings. She had been in constant attendance at court.

But no argument, no insinuation could alter the verdict the people had been expecting. Sid Hatfield was acquitted.

Meantime hostilities between the mine operators and miners continued, and grew worse. Deaths were common. By May there was open warfare throughout the mountains and valleys of Mingo and Pike. At night sporadic gun blasts flickered along the slopes like fireflies in the dark, and hoarse shouts from the vicinity of the mines came at all hours, mostly without explanation. New rifles and ammunition arrived daily, dropped in suitcases from Norfolk & Western trains passing through from Charleston. Rumor said the miners were planning to dynamite mine entrances to stop operations. The threat was grave. At Washington, President Warren G. Harding, newly inaugurated, signed proclamations declaring martial law in West Virginia and Kentucky, but withheld their issuance pending further advice from the governors of the two states.

On May 19, one year after the slaughter at Matewan, U. S. Secretary of Labor James J. Davis and John L. Lewis, U.M.W. president, sat down to talk possibilities of a peaceful settlement.

"Peace will not be attained in Mingo County," said Lewis, "until the operators recognize the fundamental and recognized right of the miner to belong to a union and to meet in peaceful assembly to discuss the problems and to bargain collectively."

He laid the trouble in West Virginia to private detectives. This was no new charge. Decades before, detectives had been blamed for continuation of the Hatfield-McCoy feud.

In June the Senate Labor Committee at Washington opened an investigation into the mine troubles. Witnesses were summoned from afar. One of those who appeared the following month was Sid Hatfield, and what he had to say highly excited the legislators.

Back at home after his testimony before Congress, Sid found a summons to appear at the courthouse at Welch, in McDowell County adjoining, to answer charges growing out of a shooting scrape he had been involved in after the troubles at Matewan. Friends advised him not to leave Mingo, but he brushed them off.

On August 1, he and his friend, Ed Chambers, also a defendant in the Matewan shootings, went to Welch, accompanied by their wives. As the four strolled up the steps into the courthouse yard, gunfire broke loose from above, and for a quarter of a minute it was furious. Sid and Chambers fell, drilled at close range. While the shots still echoed, Mrs. Chambers held off one of their assailants by beating him over the head with an umbrella. He had rushed down to make sure his victims were dead.

The affair was another brief outburst in a town accustomed to frequent killings. It caused unusual excitement only because one of the victims was Sid Hatfield, "Terror of the Tug." Police authorities held responsible several private detectives, one of whom had taken a particularly active part in the trials over the Matewan slaughter. All of them claimed self-defense, and self-defense is a safe and sound alibi in a neighborhood where no man goes without his gun.

The death of a Hatfield on the courthouse steps at Welch in 1921 had no connection with the feud of more than three decades back, but people the world over gave it that interpretation. Children and their children's children would think of it as one of the major killings of the Hatfield-McCoy war. And not infrequently, the Hatfield who crumpled up in death as he climbed the stairs with his wife would, in the language of the recollectors, be Devil Anse instead of Sid.

Before the month had passed in which Sid Hatfield was killed, thousands of armed miners and sympathizers gathered at Marmet near Charleston and prepared to march through Logan County into Mingo in protest against martial law. Others were assembled in Pike County, across the Tug, with the same purpose in mind.

The march got under way. Pilfering and murder were common along its route. President Harding at Washingon watched developments closely and on August 30 issued a proclamation commanding the marchers to disperse before noon of September 1. At Indianapolis, John L. Lewis, U.M.W. chief, announced that Philip Murray, vice-president of the union, was on his way to Charleston to urge the miners to return to work.

Noon of September 1 passed without evidence that the uprising had slackened. Federal troops from Ohio, New Jersey, and other points immediately started for the area. Soon the United States Army had taken over. Rifles and machine guns were spotted at strategic points, and airplanes circled overhead, searching for nests of hostile miners along the slopes of mountains where Hatfields and McCoys once had followed the trails of each other.

Gradually, singly and in groups up to as large as 400, the miners came out of the band of steel thrown around them and gave up. Within a few days after September 1, Army officers were able to report that not a shot had been fired in twenty-four hours.

The quiet continued. Troops, unit by unit, marched out of the coal fields, and civil authorities listed 375 names in a blanket indictment designed to fix the blame for the mine troubles. But the trial and convictions that followed were only another milestone in the union campaign to organize the coal miners. Years and years of struggles lay ahead; and, as the cause of organized labor rose in a cresendo of strikes and bickerings and unending strife, the taint of feuds in the hill country, chosen by the union for its first major pitched battle, receded into the background.

Within a short time after the death of Devil Anse, members of his family began to plan a suitable memorial to the veteran feudist. The idea grew and got much support; relatives and friends chipped in liberally. In time, sculptors at Carrara, Italy, went to work on a $3,000 life-size statue of the patriarch. When it arrived in the hill country, mules pulled it up the mountain side to the family burying ground, and there, with fitting ceremony, it was erected on a pedestal that raised the marble head thirteen feet above the graves over which it towered.

This memorial preserves for the ages the likeness of Devil Anse, in the fashion of the nation's greatest heroes and leaders. Ghostly and out of harmony with the life-inspiring green of the mountain slopes, it stands on a shelf in partial view from U.S. Highway 119. Chiseled in its cold stone is the likeness of the bearded veteran, bare-headed, solemn-faced, in frock coat and riding leggings, standing stiffly with hands at side and staring toward the hills he loved and over which he presided. On one side of the base was inscribed:

"Capt. Anderson Hatfield, 1839–1921. Levicy Chafin, His Wife, 1842—."

On the other side:

"Johnson, Wm. A., Robert L., Nancy, Elliot R., Mary, Elizabeth, Elias, Troy, Joseph D., Rose, Willis E., Tennis S., Their Children."

The years following added more peace to the record of a long-stilled feud. In late summer of 1928, Tennis Hatfield, sheriff of Logan County and youngest of "Their Children," sat on the porch of a home at Pikeville. He had just had his noonday meal and was enjoying the mountain air when his attention suddenly was drawn to a venerable pedestrian making his way slowly down the street.

"Who is that old man?" Tennis asked Joseph Stanley, Pike County jailer.

"That's old Uncle Jim McCoy."

The Logan sheriff got up from his chair and walked out into the street.

"I'm Tennis Hatfield, Uncle Jim," he said, extending his hand, and Jim McCoy grasped it.

Excitement ran through the bystanders. They gathered around the pair and took part in the spirit of the moment. This occasion must not be lost, they all agreed, so off they marched to the studios of Jasper Saad, who had deserted the movie business for what he considered the more peaceful occupation of photography. There, in a wall-papered room, Tennis and Jim had their pictures taken, seated with three friends.

That same year Henry D. Hatfield defeated the Democratic incumbent for one of the West Virginia seats in the United States Senate. It was the beginning of a six-year term of service for him at the nation's capital, more evidence that the stock running through the feud families was strong and ambitious. Washington would remember him for many years after he left the capital—for his fieriness and his domination.

On March 15, 1929, Devil Anse's widow, Levicy, died at her home at the age of eighty-seven. Like her mate, she succumbed to pneumonia. Newspapers the nation over took note of her death, and stone cutters made ready to climb the mountains toward Main Island Creek to chisel the year of her demise where it belonged after "1842" on the marble statue of her husband.

In August of the following year, death came to Cap, the trouble-maker of the family. This ardent feudist, who had spent his last years as a deputy to his younger brothers, Joe and Tennis, Logan sheriffs, died in Johns Hopkins Hospital at Baltimore of a brain tumor. He was sixty-seven, a blustering, heavy-drinking shell of the hardened young man who had taken over the leadership of a clan from his father back in the 80's.

The *New York Times* made record of the end of this last of the Hatfield clansmen with an editorial including this comment:

"When the death of someone like 'Cap' Hatfield comes, as it did in a Baltimore hospital the other day, there comes also the realization that the days of the American family feuds are past. American civilization has at least this much to its credit, for these feuds—mostly along the Southern border—were deadly, continuous wars with a tremendously high mortality rate."

The sands of time were running out for the feudists. Only one, Jim McCoy, most admired of his clan, especially among his old enemies, still remained, and he would go soon after, a greatly-mourned octogenarian.

When the dirt was heaped over his grave at Pikeville, it marked the final close of a stormy chapter of American history. Long forgotten were the four men who had been taken from Pikeville by carriage in the autumn of '89 to answer to the law for their part in the killings. Little interest was accorded them after the prison doors clicked at their backs. So far as the public was concerned, death alone could bring reprieve. This came first to Wall Hatfield, as he grieved himself away behind bars.

The feud had ended with the battle of Grapevine Creek in 1888, but not until the last survivor was in his grave could it be said positively there would be no revival. How many lives were taken by the guns of feudists will never be determined. Some chroniclers have placed the total at twenty-odd; others at fifty or sixty; still others at hundreds. Actually there is specific record of fewer than a score, but these, of course, do not include the "disappearances." No count ever was made of the men who went into the hills after their enemies and never came back.

No matter how willing have been the children of the feudists to let bygones by bygones and to relegate to the past the memories of what took place along the Tug in the bloody years of the last century, there was one contingent that even today is reluctant to consider the feud at an end. Just as the fathers squared off against each other along opposite banks of a stream, the children are squared off against each other in the realms of the public mind. Perhaps it is because the combination of names—Hatfield and McCoy—has become of household usage in America, symbolizing to the average person only one thing—a feud. Therein may have risen the plague that rests on the younger generations of the families who drew the attention of the world to the West Virginia-Kentucky border. They may walk arm in arm to war, to the altar, to the polls, and the public accepts them in these activities as peace-loving people. But the moment they are involved in any form of strife which possibly could pit one against the other, it is as if the spirit of the feud stirred again. So many times this has happened in the past; so many times it will happen in the future. The latest incident occurred in the spring of 1947, when a McCoy, interfering with the arrest of a friend at Matewan, grabbed the gun of a law officer and was killed by the chief of police, a Hatfield. This slaying took place nearly sixty years after the battle of Grapevine Creek, and yet headline writers eagerly announced the reopening of the feud. Over the nation, the idea was the same:

HATFIELD SHOOTS
MC COY AT SCENE
OF FAMOUS FEUD

MC COY IS SLAIN;
YES, BY HATFIELD

THE "RECKLESS MOUNTAIN BOYS"
AT IT AGAIN—DEAD, ONE MC COY

Perhaps that creator of great tragedies, Euripides, writing centuries before the birth of Christ, explained it in these words: "The gods visit the sins of the fathers upon the children."

But this visitation of the gods, so far as the Hatfields and McCoys are concerned, now occurs only in the public mind. For, while the press headlines a revival of the feud and raises again the old ghosts of buried tragedies, the children of the feudists go on their peaceful way, living together or in close proximity, marrying and intermarrying. Only the oldest of them—those whose memories reach back into the terrible years of the last century—have more than a fleeting notion that there ever was a time when the sight of a Hatfield by a McCoy, or a McCoy by a Hatfield, was an invitation to pull the trigger.

Hatfield and McCoy Family Trees

HATFIELD FAMILY TREE

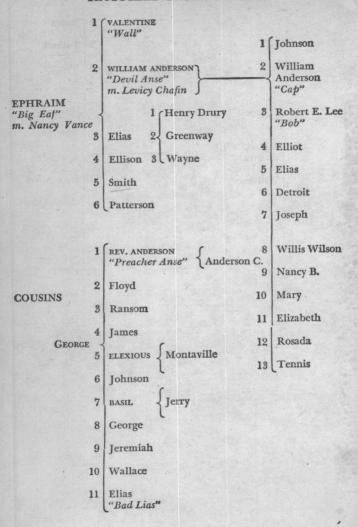

EPHRAIM *"Big Eaf"* *m. Nancy Vance*

1. VALENTINE *"Wall"*
2. WILLIAM ANDERSON *"Devil Anse"* *m. Levicy Chafin*
    1. Johnson
    2. William Anderson *"Cap"*
    3. Robert E. Lee *"Bob"*
    4. Elliot
    5. Elias
    6. Detroit
    7. Joseph
    8. Willis Wilson
    9. Nancy B.
    10. Mary
    11. Elizabeth
    12. Rosada
    13. Tennis
3. Elias
    1. Henry Drury
    2. Greenway
    3. Wayne
4. Ellison
5. Smith
6. Patterson

COUSINS

GEORGE

1. REV. ANDERSON *"Preacher Anse"*
    - Anderson C.
2. Floyd
3. Ransom
4. James
5. ELEXIOUS
    - Montaville
6. Johnson
7. BASIL
    - Jerry
8. George
9. Jeremiah
10. Wallace
11. Elias *"Bad Lias"*

McCOY FAMILY TREE

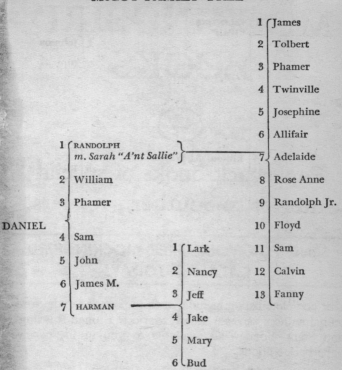

- DANIEL
  1. RANDOLPH *m. Sarah "A'nt Sallie"*
     1. James
     2. Tolbert
     3. Phamer
     4. Twinville
     5. Josephine
     6. Allifair
     7. Adelaide
     8. Rose Anne
     9. Randolph Jr.
     10. Floyd
     11. Sam
     12. Calvin
     13. Fanny
  2. William
  3. Phamer
  4. Sam
  5. John
  6. James M.
  7. HARMAN
     1. Lark
     2. Nancy
     3. Jeff
     4. Jake
     5. Mary
     6. Bud